#3734145Y

Library of Congress Cataloging-in-Publication Data

On file

ISBN 0-306-45628-1

© 1997 Victor Kamber
Insight Books is a Division of Plenum Publishing Corporation
233 Spring Street, New York, N.Y. 10013-1578
http://www.plenum.com

An Insight Book

10 9 8 7 6 5 4 3 2 1

Printed in the United States of America

This book is dedicated to my political heroes:

PAUL DOUGLAS, HUBERT HUMPHREY,
AND NELSON ROCKEFELLER

Leaders who believed that public service can make a
positive difference in people's lives, that politics is a noble
calling, and that campaigns can be fun, rewarding, and
conducted in a spirit of decency and civility. Their
examples shine more brightly today than ever.

Foreword

Vic Kamber knows politics.

Vic Kamber knows communications.

And Vic Kamber knows that something must happen to improve the quality of political dialogue in our nation. This book tells why and how it should happen.

In November of last year, we chose a president. "We" in that sentence means 49 percent of the eligible voters who went to the polls. *The New York Times* ran a story about an advisory referendum in Okinawa on whether United States troops should continue to be stationed there. The *Times* related that by a 10-to-1 majority, people voted that the troops should leave. But, the story noted, the decision was marred by a "turnout of only 59 percent of the voters."

How proud we in the United States would be if our last presidential race had a 59 percent voter turnout. Our low vote came after leaders tried a variety of things to stimulate the electorate, including motor voter laws that require states to register people for voting as they renew their driving permits or automobile licenses. While a few groups, such as African-American males, showed a slight increase in voting over the previous presidential contest, fundamentally an attitude of apathy prevailed among the voters.

Why?

There are at least five reasons:

First, leaders are not leading; they are following the polls. That results in pandering rather than leadership. In the last presidential race, both candidates promised tax cuts, while we have huge deficits. They were saying, in essence, that we should borrow from our grandchildren so that we can live in a little more comfort. It is but one of a host of examples of pandering.

The American people really do understand, in a vague way, that we cannot have health care for everyone without more taxes, that we will not move the nation ahead in education without more resources, and that pay-as-you-go government is needed and will require some sacrifice. But too many political candidates and office holders back away from even a hint at anything that might inflict a little pain on the public. When I was a child, I remember the big advertisements for "painless dentists." Few believed the ads, especially those who became patients. We are in an era in which people promote themselves as "painless politicians," and few believe them. For good reason.

If you will forgive an immodest reference, in my 1990 reelection campaign, early forecasts had me losing "because Paul Simon has taken so many unpopular stands." Such as opposing the death penalty and saying that there must be more federal revenue. And my well-financed opponent's ads hammered me hard on these things. But when the votes were counted, I had the biggest plurality in the nation of any seriously contested candidate of either party for governor or senator. Vivid in my memory is the street encounter with a man in Chicago who came up to me in the midst of my opponent's ads and said, "I think I disagree with you on every issue, but I trust you, and I'm going to vote for you." People want truth, not pandering. They recognize that to build a house requires sacrifice and that to build a nation requires sacrifice. Even Rush Limbaugh notes: "We were never required to make the kind of sacrifice that the World War II generation was asked to make.

Things came too easy for us. To put it bluntly, many of the baby-boom generation are spoiled brats" (*Washington Post*, February 20, 1994).

Real leadership demands sacrifice of people, not for the sake of sacrifice, but to attain concrete goals.

When Harry Truman and General George Marshall suggested the Marshall Plan, the first poll by Gallup showed only 14 percent of the American public supporting it. The proposal was overwhelmingly unpopular. And Truman had to deal with a Republican Congress. The Senate leader for the GOP on foreign affairs, Senator Arthur Vandenburg of Michigan, said he recognized its unpopularity but believed its message to be in the national interest and supported it.

I cannot imagine a scenario today where an administration of either party would even consider such a proposal without first taking a poll, and I also cannot conceive of an opposition party not taking advantage of an unpopular proposal.

Harry Truman, George Marshall, and Arthur Vandenburg were leaders. They did not take polls and pander.

A second reason for apathy is the preceding story. Truman was a solid Democrat and Vandenburg a solid Republican. But they worked together.

One of the things that has happened in my 22 years in Congress is increasing and excessive political partisanship. We have party-line admonitions and votes on the most petty things that have nothing to do with political philosophy. The result is a public perception that we are playing political games, rather than carrying on the public's business. Unfortunately, there is some truth to that perception.

Third, people sense that public office is for sale. It is not quite that bad, but access to public offices is for sale, and that means public policy often is for sale. When Alexander Hamilton and Thomas Jefferson had their historic struggle over whether people who owned property—those who were wealthier—should have a greater voice in our government, Jefferson prevailed. We decided that all citizens should have an equal voice. We have now reversed that through our system of financing campaigns. Those with money who are willing to spend it on political campaigns have a much greater voice in government that other citizens. Alexander Hamilton has finally won over Thomas Jefferson, at least temporarily.

Fourth, the media has added to the cynicism. When I started as a reporter, whiskey occupied center stage as the chief vice of journalists. My first boss had a fifth of whiskey in his top, right-hand drawer, and he opened that drawer frequently. Today the chief vice of journalists is cynicism. James Fallows comments in his book *Breaking the News*: "The view of public life that comes through today's press is less like the Super Bowl or the World Series or the Olympics, than another sporting enterprise: pro wrestling. To judge by the coverage, everything is a sham. Conflicts are built up and then they blow over, and no one is sincere. As onlookers, we can laugh at and look down at the participants, because everyone knows it's all for effect." The media reinforces the public expectation of the worst, and that makes it harder for real leaders to emerge.

But there is a serious fifth reason for the public's apathy. They watch the television commercials of the two sides attacking each other and the conclusion drawn by large numbers of people is that both sides are correct.

It is not candidates criticizing each other on the substance of the differing issues that I find objectionable. That is healthy. But commercials that attack the motivation, morality, patriotism, and competence of an opponent are not healthy. And they are too prevalent. In Vic Kamber's opinion, they are "poisoning politics." When excessive partisanship and incivility mark a campaign, it is difficult to move away from this overkill when Congress and state legislative bodies convene. And so civil society becomes less civil.

In Minnesota, a group of citizens attempted a partially successful experiment: getting candidates to agree that if an attack is made on an opponent, the candidate himself or herself has to read the script for the radio or television. That is a small step in the right direction. Candidates are unlikely to be as vicious as the surrogates they employ to say the nasty words.

I also favor public financing of campaigns, which would, for a variety of reasons, lift the level of campaign dialogue.

But there is no single answer.

However, Vic Kamber's thoughtful analysis should motivate us to improve the structure of our democracy. The roof is leaking, and the cloudburst of negative advertisements is compounding our problems.

PAUL SIMON
Southern Illinois University
Carbondale, Illinois

Preface

In the past few years, American politics has been poisoned by harsh personal attacks, primarily in short television spot advertisements. Political campaigns have become increasingly negative, and attack ads on television are more prevalent and shriller in tone. The arguments have often become ridiculous, irrelevant, and irresponsible. And democratic debate has been dragged down to the level of tabloid scandal.

The public has become justifiably disgusted with poison politics. Many voters are saying enough is enough, and pressure to tone down the negativism of political campaigns grows, even as television attack ads become even more venomous.

In a democracy, nothing is ever mere rhetoric. Any attempt to diagnose the ills of a democratic political system must focus first on what is said in the public arena. How we talk about our problems and choices determines how we are governed.

Unfortunately, like the dinner "conversations" of a married couple that has grown hostile and is on the verge of a divorce, our political talk has become increasingly bitter. But as a society, divorce is not an option. We have no choice but to figure out a way we can talk civilly and respectfully to one another. The alternative is nothing less than the demise of our democracy.

We need to do something about attack ads. But I disagree

with the purists, who are against all forms of negativism. Negative campaigning has been with us since the beginning of politics itself. The problem is not with negative campaigning as such, but negative campaigning absent of other substantive information, and negative campaigning that disregards any standards of fairness or accuracy.

The way to bring about real change in the way we conduct our democratic debate is not to talk in lofty abstractions, but to focus on specific examples and decide which forms of negative campaigning are fair, accurate, and relevant, and which are not. *Poison Politics* will examine historical and contemporary examples of negative campaigns and, by doing so, begin to start a much-needed discussion about what we can do to make our discourse civil again.

This is a subject I feel compelled to write about, because politics has been my lifelong obsession, and political dialogue is my chosen profession.

I grew up in Chicago, a city where politics is more deeply ingrained in every citizen's psyche than any place in America. For as long as I can remember, I wanted to run for office and serve the public. I was elected mayor of my eighth-grade class (remember, this is Chicago; mayor is a bigger deal than president and almost as important as pope). I then served as student body president and class president in my high school, and fraternity council president in college.

But between the time I graduated and today, something happened. As I got more involved in politics, I discovered that a politician's life is a lot less glamorous and a lot more burdensome than I had thought. In fact, elected officials have no life at all. It is one mindless political function after another, an endless stream of fund-raising calls (having to ask others for money reduces public servants to high-class beggars), and increasingly, being subjected to bitter and downright sleazy attacks in the media and on the airwaves.

So I shifted my focus from running for office to helping others get elected, first on behalf of the AFL–CIO, and for the last 16 years, on behalf of my public relations firm's clients.

As president of The Kamber Group, my role is mostly marketing and strategic planning. Actual campaign tactics and advertising are handled by a subsidiary, Politics Inc. So while I am involved in the strategies behind political advertising, my involvement is not direct. I do not create political ads myself.

However, as a political professional with more than 30 years of experience at all levels of campaigning and policy work; as an educator who has taught classes in campaign management, political communications, and rhetoric; and as a writer and media commentator on political issues, I have a great deal of experience and knowledge of political communications. Since I believe that the development of successful political messages is an art rather than a science, I am skeptical about calling myself an expert. But I do have a wide range of experience and knowledge to draw upon in observing our contemporary political debate.

In 1990, I was asked by The American University to write a monograph on negative advertising. I jumped at the opportunity, because it is something I had been thinking about for some time. I was growing disturbed at the tenor of many of the campaigns in which I was involved. The 1988 presidential campaign of George Bush, with its emphasis on Willie Horton, flag burning, and the American Civil Liberties Union, had taken politics to a new low, I believed, and something needed to be done about it. So I wrote a paper entitled "Trivial Pursuit: Negative Advertising and the Decay of Political Discourse."

Since then, things have gotten even worse in many respects. And while entire forests have been felled during this time for books about negative advertising, they have all been written by academics and journalists. Although many have been important and insightful, none has been written by a practitioner. I think such a perspective should be heard, and so I decided to take many of the ideas in the monograph and expand them into this book.

The rise of poison politics has spawned a new cottage industry of critics. More and more journalists, commentators, academics, and voters are publicly objecting to negative campaigns. Although these voices are being heard, action does not follow. If so many people agree that attack ads have gotten worse, why does it seem as if no one is doing anything about them?

That is the great irony. People say they hate poison politics, but then they go and elect many of the candidates with the harshest negative advertising. And then they attack campaign consultants for running the ads.

As a campaign consultant, I am aware of my profession's responsibility for the deterioration of political debate. I have advised several of my own clients to attack their opponents on many occasions. I have always tried to keep these attacks based on their opponents' records and statements on substantive issues that affect the quality of life of the voters. But I am not here to claim perfection or proclaim myself as a model. Far from it.

I approach this book neither as an apologist for my profession nor as a guilt-ridden confessor of my sins. Rather, I approach it as a realist who understands the many considerations that go into political decision making and the myriad incentives and disincentives that drive the choices candidates and their consultants make. When we change this mix is when we will change the nature of our political and campaign dialogue.

Similarly, I am not a purist who believes that going negative is inherently bad. I believe that comparative and negative politics have an important place in our democracy, so long as they are policy- and values-based, so long as they are accurate, and so long as their purpose is not to reduce voter turnout but involve citizens in elections and motivate them to go to the polls.

The purpose of this book is to provide the type of analysis readers may find useful in forming their own opinions about what is fair and what is foul in the campaign debate, and to stimulate a healthy debate about how we want to conduct our elections.

I believe in partisanship. You should fight hard, believing your side to be right. However, there is a difference between attacking your opponents and demonizing them. In democratic politics, it is possible to fight hard and still fight fair. Democracy is the peaceful struggle between conflicting ideas. You cannot always be genteel in political debate. But the meanspiritedness that has taken over this country is beyond partisanship and peaceful struggle. Too often, ideas have been lost in the rancor.

The challenge before us is to define what is fair and proper negative campaigning, and what is not. I believe that decency, integrity, and ethics are ideals to which most political professionals aspire. Unfortunately, it is not always easy to agree on what these lofty words mean. And in between an advertisement that tells the world a candidate is the second coming of Jesus Christ and one that charges a candidate's opponent slept with farm animals lies a massive gray area.

Poison Politics is meant to bring the gray area into sharper focus and stimulate a nationwide debate on the ethics of negative campaigning. This book is not the last word on negative politics. Instead, I hope it will begin an important discussion on how we should conduct our public discourse. In a way, this book is an argument about how we should argue. I know that not everyone will agree with me. In fact, I hope that people will disagree, because argument is what democracy is all about.

Although I have found life just outside the glare of the spotlight to be professionally invigorating and personally rewarding, I am not sure that is the best thing for democracy. If serving the public in elected office is so unpleasant, so burdensome, so bitter, then who will heed the call? If campaigns are so ugly, who will turn out to vote? If we neither attract the best and brightest candidates nor exercise the highest responsibility of citizenship, then how can we expect government to address the problems we face individually and collectively as a society?

I have traveled a long journey from mayor of my eighth-grade class in Chicago to political and public relations consultant in Washington, D.C. It is my hope that *Poison Politics* will help readers and society start their own journey toward the type of democracy the greatest nation on Earth deserves. Then, maybe a 13-year-old who thinks like I did will actually decide to run for office in the year 2016, and choose politics as a fulfilling and honorable career.

Acknowledgments

I have a deep debt of gratitude to many people whose insights, comments, and hard work made *Poison Politics* the book that it is. This was a collaborative process, and *Poison Politics* is all the stronger for it.

First and foremost, I want to thank Steve Weeks, an exceptionally gifted writer, deep thinker, superb listener, and all-around good guy, whose imprint is on this work and whose contributions were, quite simply, invaluable.

I also want to thank Bruce Kozarsky, senior vice-president and director of editorial services at The Kamber Group (TKG). Bruce is a brilliant writer whose intellect and knowledge of issues helped shape this work into a manageable and readable book. Without his leadership, the editing and coordination of this book would never have happened; without his talent, TKG would not be a success today.

And I want to thank Dennis Walston, TKG senior vice-president and director of the Art Department, who has been with the firm almost since the day it was founded. Besides being one of the most creative and innovative art directors in the country, Dennis manages the equally impressive achievement of making TKG a fun place to work and keeps us all laughing—usually at ourselves. The jacket cover is reflective of

Dennis's vision, as well as the outstanding work of designer Karen Thompson and production manager Rita Facchina.

Poison Politics evolved, in part, from a 1990 monograph I wrote for The American University, entitled "Trivial Pursuit: Negative Advertising and the Decay of Political Discourse." Three former TKG staffers, Chris Runge, Ferne Carpousis, and Rory Davenport, played key roles in this paper's production. A second white paper that was a follow-up to "Trivial Pursuit," entitled "Throwing Out the Rulebook: Changes in Negative Advertising and Campaign Strategies in the 1992 Elections," could not have happened without the considerable editorial talents of Art Levine.

There are many other current and former TKG staff deserving of my thanks. Julie Speece, my longtime executive assistant, is like my right arm, and words can never express my gratitude for everything she does. Torie Keller, Mark Marrow, Ellen Conte, and many others provided essential research. Baxter Peffer, Jim Monroe, and Enid Doggett worked aggressively to publicize my work on this issue.

Alan Kellock, my literary agent and a good friend, was very helpful in focusing and shaping *Poison Politics*, and worked tirelessly on my behalf. I am deeply indebted to him.

Two individuals at Oklahoma University (OU) were enormously helpful in researching this book: Dr. Lynda Lee Kaid, director of OU's Political Communications Center, and Chuck Rand, who directs the University's political commercial archives—the most comprehensive in the country.

I want to pay particular thanks to Frank Darmstadt and Charlie Cates of Insight Books for their belief in this project, their editing and advice, and their strong support.

Finally, former Senator Paul Simon is deserving not only of my thanks for his thoughtful and outstanding foreword to *Poison Politics*; he is deserving of America's thanks for a legacy of public service that is a model of principle and civility. If more candidates and elected officials were like Paul Simon, I would not have had to write this book.

Contents

Chapter 1

The Power of Negative Thinking

Imagine a young man who comes from an aristocratic family, a clan with a long and great history, but one that also has some dark secrets. There is madness, alcoholism, and scandal in the family past, but the young man is charming, self-confident, visibly ambitious. He was a lackluster student in college who, after a brief fling with the law, went into politics. In politics he is sometimes manipulative, always forceful, often successful. His position on the issues is usually vague or unformulated, at least until he can gauge public opinion, and he repeatedly changes his stance on several of the crucial issues of his time. His wife and he are so estranged that she built a completely separate estate to live in, a few miles from the family manor they inhabit. There are rumors that she is a lesbian. The politician has had a long-standing affair with a young lady and other dalliances as well. He is physically disabled, unable to walk on his own power; his frail legs are shriveled almost to bone, and a fall could result in incapacitating trauma, even death. He smokes, he drinks, and when he still could, he often walked in his sleep. Sometimes he tells off-color jokes.

This same man, Franklin Delano Roosevelt, was the greatest president of our century. Whether one agrees with him on all the issues, or on his handling of certain problems—he was

1

involved in so many that it is impossible for all but the most slavish devotees to believe he did the right thing in every instance—Roosevelt was an immensely successful national leader, the very model of a modern president. He left a legacy of strong and charismatic leadership, against which all subsequent presidents have been measured and found wanting. Both Democrats and Republicans are eager to claim him for their own.

Yet, as this century draws to a close, its greatest president would today be utterly unelectable. Faced with questions about his personal life, battered by speculation about his physical condition, exposed as the manipulative and often tyrannical politician he certainly was, Roosevelt would not fare too well in today's free-for-all climate of media scrutiny. And that's unfortunate, because a leader like FDR is precisely who we need right now.

THE LANGUAGE OF DEMOCRACY

Roosevelt was a genius of democratic rhetoric. The man who studied classical rhetoric at Harvard and absorbed the sermons of Endicott Peabody at Groton was able to explain complex issues in plain language that everyone could understand. He was capable of describing the great threats facing the country and then delineating his often-radical approaches to them in a way that was comprehensive and comprehensible, interesting, yet inspiring. His Fireside Chats did more than simply assuage the troubled soul of America. They outlined his policy proposals and argued for his programs. They informed, enlightened, even entertained. They brought a troubled nation together through seemingly unendurable crises, creating a coalition that looked beyond individual differences to work for the greater common good.

FDR spoke a language of inclusion and inspiration. Phrases like "A day that will live in infamy," "We have nothing to fear but fear itself," and "The arsenal of democracy," have entered our common language, and their potency, both in memory and in lasting power, keeps them from becoming empty clichés. In some ways, his words were as important as his policies. But while his political legacy endures in such vital programs as Social Security and the minimum wage laws, his rhetorical legacy inexorably fades away. And if we lose even the memory of his words, then we have lost one of the greatest exemplars of democratic speech. Right now there are no signs of FDR's mantle being assumed, or even aspired to, by any contemporary politician. And the mood of the public, the media, and political professionals is such that anyone who tried would be answered with ridicule.

In a democracy, politics is dialogue. The way we talk to each other determines the way in which we are governed. If we cannot discuss issues of substance, we cannot resolve the problems facing us. If we cannot use rhetoric to unite and inspire us, we will remain divided and dispirited. If we cannot talk to each other in a responsible manner—if we cannot simply get along—we will be unable to create the necessary comity in order to sustain a functioning democracy.

These days, we talk to each other through the media, particularly television. If we are going to improve our democratic rhetoric, we have to change the way we talk to each other on television. Right now, it is the pits. Too many political campaigns are endless barrages of bizarre accusations, silly name-calling, ridiculous charges, even more ridiculous counter-charges, scandal, sleaze, smears, and outright lies. The media report it all with a sneering cynicism. And the voters stand on the sidelines, watching the whole ugly spectacle as if it were just another tabloid television show.

In the last 40 years, American politics has undergone an almost revolutionary transformation. The change has occurred so rapidly that we have never had the chance to think out how it has affected not just the form of our politics, but also its content. The rise of television, the increasing power and independence of the press, the diminishing power of political parties and the ascendance of "entrepreneurial" politicians, the increasing cost and sophistication of political communication, and the escalating tone of negativity in our campaigns are all recent and related developments.

But the rise in negativity is not simply driven by technology. Negative politics has always been with us, sometimes more venomous and irresponsible than it is now. Our current problem is not just the level of aggression and irresponsibility in our political dialogue, but also its predominance in the absence of anything else. Previous eras saw severe personal attacks on political candidates, but they also saw detailed and sometimes inspiring deliberation over the issues. Our present political discourse is nothing but spleen.

PURISTS AND PARANOIDS

For all the books, studies, papers, op-ed pieces, and appearances on talk shows bemoaning the increasing vitriol and vapidity of our political debate, we have not gotten any closer to a solution. That is because the problem has been stated in erroneous terms. This book is an attempt to redefine the problem, so we can approach it in a more realistic and, I hope, more effective manner.

There is no shortage of critics of negative advertising. Unfortunately, most of them come from one of two schools (or some admixture of both), oversimplifying the debate and ultimately missing the whole point. These two schools are the purists and the paranoids.

The purists believe that negative ads are debasing democracy, and they are half-right. Unfortunately, they also think that democracy has degenerated from some golden age of enlightened rhetoric (which even a cursory look at the history of campaigning will prove is a sentimental exaggeration) into a morass of negativity and scandal-mongering. The 1988 presidential campaign was called "the sleaziest in history," which shows a woeful ignorance of the knockdown, drag-out campaigns of the 19th century. And the purists fail to recognize the legitimate use of negative messages in political debate.

If the purists are half-right, the paranoids are all wrong. They believe that slick campaign operatives are using sophisticated techniques of mass persuasion to trick voters into voting against their own best interests. Whole forests have been denuded in order to print the countless books and articles attempting to prove that, somehow, American elections are just a sham, that political consultants are evil geniuses who, through their understanding and manipulation of the media of mass communication, sell candidates the same way the evil geniuses of Madison Avenue sell us soap.

There are several problems with this argument. First, it vastly overestimates the intelligence of political consultants. I like to think we are smart, but we are not geniuses, and most of us are not evil, either. Half of all political campaigns are failures (even more in the primaries) and no one, not even maestros such as Roger Ailes or James Carville (who have since left the "biz"), wins all the time. Voters are more informed and autonomous than the paranoids ever give them credit for, and more often than not, their electoral decisions are based not on smoke and mirrors of political spectacle, but on the issues. Anyone who has ever worked on a campaign knows that, far from being easily manipulated, the American voter is politically skeptical and sometimes maddeningly independent.

At the same time the paranoids underestimate the American voter, they also consistently overestimate the power of television. They see the medium as a malign technology, by nature manipulative and dishonest, when, in fact, television is simply a tool, a powerful and possibly transformative tool, but one that is inherently neutral. Television can be a positive or a negative force, depending on how it is used. The medium is *not* the message—the message is the message. Unfortunately, the great promise of television remains unfulfilled, and what could be a powerful engine for democratic deliberation has become increasingly trivial and sleazy. Too often these days, television blurs the distinctions between fact and fantasy, information and entertainment, news and scandal, public interest and public salaciousness; however, the fault lies not in the technology, but in those who operate it.

The problem with both the paranoid and the purist arguments is not just that they are mistaken, but also that they are profoundly elitist. Somehow, the American voters have no control over what they do; they are involved in politics only "symbolically" or as "dupes" in some grand conspiracy, and the choices they make in the voting booth are either coerced or irrelevant. In short, the paranoids and the purists have little faith in those who actually make the decisions in this democracy.

THE ARGUMENT FOR NEGATIVE ADS

Some defenders of negative ads argue that winning is all that matters in electoral politics, that strategy and tactics can only be judged by their effectiveness, not their ethics, and everything is permitted, so long as it gets a candidate elected.

"We had only one goal, to help elect George Bush. That's the purpose of any political campaign. What other function should a campaign have?" said the late Lee Atwater, who ran the notorious 1988 campaign.[1]

Unfortunately, that attitude is not restricted to cynical political consultants. The bottom-line, win-at-any-cost competitiveness that pervades our society has made us a cruel and divided nation. It has turned us into creatures of the marketplace, judged only by what we make and what we buy. Greed and ambition, unrestrained by civic virtue or personal responsibility, have resulted in a diminished public realm and a harsh and selfish politics. Now that capitalism has proved itself to be the most efficient means of economic organization, its values are left unquestioned, and its chaotic and even violent disruptions of common life are being left alone to wreak havoc among us. Do we have to learn all over again the lessons of the last century and a half, that the market, while a useful mechanism for economic growth, will create great inequalities, dislocation, and suffering if it is not meliorated politically? In the same way that the economic market, left to its own devices, can be a destructive force, so, too, the political market, if not guided by higher principles, will cause irreparable harm. If campaigns are ruled by no other standards than victory, then we will end up with political leaders who are cynical, opportunistic, dishonest, and shortsighted. And in a democracy, you get the leaders you deserve.

But there is an argument to be made in defense of responsible negative advertisements. The voters need to know the whole story, and solely positive arguments do not provide it. A campaign is not going to willingly offer negative information about its own candidate, and yet that is essential information for the voters to make an informed decision. So it is up to candidates to point out their opponents' shortcomings.

Negative messages are not only an essential aspect of political argument, but they can also be a public service. This applies not just to comparative discussion of the issues, but also to the broader and more amorphous questions of character. Issues of character are often of more lasting importance than positions on ephemeral issues.

For some candidates, negative campaigns are the only option. How can a political neophyte challenge a long-term incumbent without running against the incumbent's character and/or record? Democracy is supposed to hold politicians accountable for their actions, and the mechanism for this accountability is the ballot box. If negative information about them is withheld or suppressed, how would the voters ever be able to make an informed decision and give corrupt or incompetent candidates their comeuppance?

But negative arguments are only one part of political rhetoric, and negative ads should only be one component of an integrated campaign. The problem today is that too many candidates are eschewing traditional means of campaigning, direct contact with voters and opponents such as speeches, rallies, and debates, and instead opting for a vegetable-garden strategy, throwing rotten tomatoes at their adversaries from the safe confines of a television studio. The tenor of campaigning becomes ever more shrill and negative as opponents hide behind technology instead of engaging each other directly.

We cannot, indeed we should not, get rid of negative ads. They are an essential part of political argument. But we cannot allow our political debate to grow harsher and more trivial.

There are two standards to which we can hold political messages, both positive and negative, and these are truth and relevance. Without a standard of truth, political discourse becomes mere verbal hostility, and then we might as well go back to beating each other with clubs. After a fact can be proven true or an argument made defensible, there remains the question of whether it is relevant and belongs in the debate.

There is a big difference between making a responsible negative argument, based on the facts, and slandering an opponent. One is a viable form of political argument, and the other is simply trash talk, or poison politics. Poison politics is irresponsible, unsubstantiated, erroneous, misleading, unfair, irrelevant, divisive, hateful, spiteful, crude, and degenerate. Poison politics appeals to the baser emotions of fear, hate, and prejudice. Poison politics divides rather than uniting us. Poison politics includes not only slander and abuse, but also the more subtler forms of negativity, such as the use of racial, ethnic, and cultural polarization; the demagoguery of hatred and greed; and the increasing cynicism with which our system is viewed. It creates an ugly cycle of anger, distrust, and cynicism. Poison politics is the political equivalent of violence. And like violence, it has been around as long as humankind.

Chapter 2

Mudslinging through the Ages

Successful politicians throughout the ages have been able to exploit the fears and prejudices of their constituencies and fellow leaders in order to promote their own policies and advance their own careers. In other words, poison politics is as old as politics itself.

THE ROMAN REPUBLIC AND CICERO

Although Cicero is remembered as a great orator, it is often forgotten that he was a negative campaigner of the first rank. The first century B.C. was a time of almost perpetual civil war, and the violence was not just physical, but also rhetorical. Cicero was the master of invective. His speech accusing Cataline of conspiracy is one long tirade.

> Cicero urged his rival: Just get out. Every decent, law abiding citizen fears and hates you. You are blackened by every kind of family scandal; your personal reputation is in shreds. Your eyes are glutted with lust, your hands are stained with blood, your body is corrupted by debauchery. Every youngster whom you have ensnared with the delights of your own low life you have equipped with weapons of murder and shown the way to seductions.[1]

9

Cicero went on to claim that, among other things, Cataline killed his first wife to make room for another. The verbal onslaught was too much for Cataline to withstand. Demoralized by Cicero's speech, Cataline left Rome in disgrace and was killed in battle soon after.

Cicero sailed the shifting winds of Roman political intrigue, meeting with both success and failure, yet able to survive to see old age, a feat not many of his colleagues were able to accomplish; however, he soon began to alienate even his allies, for his sharp invective and biting wit found too many victims. Plutarch was forced to concede, after recounting some of Cicero's harsher jibes:

> No doubt it is part of the business of a lawyer to employ these rather cruel jokes at the expense of his enemies and his legal opponents. But Cicero's propensity to attack anyone for the sake of raising a laugh aroused a good deal of ill-feeling against him.[2]

After the assassination of Caesar, Cicero attacked Mark Antony in a series of speeches called the Philippics. He castigated Antony for his alliance with Cleopatra, blaming him for bringing feminizing, Egyptian, Asiatic influences into Rome.

But the Philippics brought on Cicero's doom. On Antony's orders, Cicero's head and right hand were chopped off and displayed on the speaker's rostrum at the Roman Forum, the sight of so many of his rhetorical triumphs.

THE GOLDEN AGE OF POLITICAL PAMPHLETEERING

Political invective reached its artistic heights in 18th-century England, a society profoundly influenced by Roman classicism in general and Ciceronian rhetoric in particular. The writers and speakers of that time not only imitated Cicero's sonorous cadences and generous use of subordinate clauses, but also his taste for personal attacks envenomed with sardonic wit. The result was a remarkably literate form of trash talk, a stately vocabulary used to express aggressive, even violent attitudes. Political battles were frequently hostile, conducted with rancorous humor and spiteful satire. "Every crisis," one historian writes, "produced heated journalistic exchanges intended to bolster partisan support, sway adversarial opinion, or nurture opposition."[3] These exchanges were usually anonymous—it was considered libelous even to use someone's name—and, therefore, often harshly personal. The pejorative term for such verbal abuse was "billingsgate," describing the vulgar language of the Billingsgate fish market stalls.

In 18th-century England, the distinction between high art and low politics was blurred, if not ignored altogether, as struggling talents with literary ambitions put bread on the table by writing spirited political hackwork, and prominent men of letters engaged in satire and scurrility. The predominant media were the pamphlet and partisan newspaper, as the print revolution was just beginning to take off. And the sheer talent involved in political propagandizing was extraordinary. Just about every major literary figure and a whole host of lesser lights were involved in political argument and intrigue. John Dryden wrote "Absalom and Achitophel," one of his greatest poems, as a political allegory. Alexander Pope wrote scalding political and social satire. Before he wrote *Robinson Crusoe*, Daniel Defoe had a long, and often hazardous, career in political satire and espionage. John Gay, Joseph Addison, Richard Steele, David Hume, and Samuel Johnson all contributed to the political debate, either in caustic attacks or high-toned argument. Later on, Henry Fielding edited several political newspapers; in his *Champion*, he used the literary persona of Captain Hercules Vinegar to lambaste his opponents. Jonathan Swift, author of *Gulliver's Travels*, was one of the most talented political satirists of his time.

Swift started out as a Whig, then became a Tory and stayed one. He wrote for an audience of country gentlemen and, therefore, at least tried to maintain a sense of dignity, if not decorum.

His political diatribes are loaded with classical allusions and allegories, oblique topical references, appeals to his readers' sense of style and wit, and scathing, often obscene abuse of his opponents.

When the Whigs complained about Tory attacks, Swift responded with this anecdote:

> It is, I think, a known Story of a Gentleman who fought another for calling him *Son of a Whore*; but his Mother desired her Son to make no more Quarrels upon that subject, *because it was true*.[4]

Swift seemed to appreciate the political use of the issue of motherhood, for he paraphrased the sermon of a bishop in the following manner:

> The Bulk of the Clergy, and one Third of the Bishops are stupid Sons of Whores, who think nothing but getting Money as soon as they can: If they may but procure enough to supply them in Gluttony, Drunkenness, and Whoring, they are ready to turn Traytors to GOD and their Country, and make their Fellow Subjects Slaves.[5]

Swift then went on to say that there was no need for the bishop to hide his charges in pretty speech:

> For my own Part, I much prefer the plain Billingsgate Way of calling Names, because it expresseth our Meaning full as well, and would save abundance of Time which is lost by circumlocution.[6]

INCONTINENT POLEMICS
AND THE REIGN OF TERROR

Across the Channel, France was another matter entirely. There, the Age of Reason gave way to the Age of Revolution, and poison politics became a Reign of Terror.

Although the French Republic had immense ideological

divisions, there were no real political parties, at least not in the modern sense. To a certain degree, the press acted in that role, educating citizens in the often-confusing world of revolutionary politics, applying its own opinions and knowledge to public events, acting as a mediator between the people and their representatives, reinforcing loyalties, and generally acting as political organizers rather than simply conduits of information. As would be expected, this led to an often shrilly partisan press. As Simon Schama writes:

> The liberties enshrined in the Declaration of the Rights of Man for the protection of free speech, publication and assembly had brought forth a political culture in which the liberation of disrespect literally knew no bounds.

The result was, in Schama's words "a polemical incontinence that washed over the whole country."[7]

Few journalists were more incontinent in their polemics than Jean-Paul Marat, who started a revolutionary newspaper called *L'Ami du Peuple* (The Friend of the People). The general tone of Marat's journal was one of vituperative hysteria, described by Simon Schama as "apocalyptic," "verbally violent," and "hectoring messianism."[8] Jeremy Popkin writes that

> Marat's journalistic strategy was based on the assumption that the *peuple* did not know and could not articulate their own interests and that shock tactics were necessary to enlighten them.[9]

Like his message, Marat's style was also violent and excessive. He raised rudeness to the status of political virtue, believing, after Rousseau, that polite manners were only practiced by "charlatans." His declamations were turgid and seemingly endless, with sentences running on for a full page of denunciation and abuse, attacking

> the instruments of chicanery, ... the valets of runaway princes, ... the skinflints, the royal pensionaries, the arrant aristocrats, the magistrates, the valets of the court, the

> public spies, … the men ennobled for money, and sold out
> to the ministry, creatures of the prince, instruments of
> despotism, cowardly workers of iniquity.[10]

He not only made arguments against his opponents but
also stirred his supporters into combustive fear, warning them
what would happen if they failed to heed him:

> Torn from your homes, you will fall under the swords of
> the executioners, after having seen your wives and your
> children disemboweled, your houses and your daughters
> will be the prey of a brutal soldiery, all those among you
> who took up arms for the country will have your throats
> slit, your faithful defenders will perish in the cruellest
> torments, and all those not put to death will be led away in
> chains.[11]

Careful to remind his readers that not even the esteemed editor
of *L'Ami* was safe, Marat claimed that he himself would be "the
first victim slaughtered if you weaken."[12]

Of course, Marat was stabbed while sitting in his bath by a
woman from the provinces who justified the murder by saying,
"I know that he was perverting France."[13]

Following Marat's assassination came the Terror, a period
of violence that "the friend of the people" anticipated with his
bloodthirsty words.

THE FIRST CAMPAIGNS

Mudslinging has a long, if not especially noble, tradition in
America. In fact, it dates back to our very earliest elections.
Since George Washington never had to run for office, the first
presidential campaign did not occur until 1796. And it was a
regular street brawl.

The Federalists wanted a strong central government,
whereas the Democratic-Republicans (precursor to today's
Democratic Party) sought regional autonomy with the states
allied in a loose confederation.

In the 1796 election, John Adams represented the Federalist faction, while Jefferson stood for the Democratic-Republicans. Both candidates stayed above the fray while their underlings bloodied each other.

The Democratic-Republicans called Adams "an avowed friend of monarchy," and the Federalists countered by claiming that Jefferson was "an atheist, anarchist, demagogue, coward, mountebank, trickster, and Franco-maniac, and said his followers were 'cut throats who walk in rags and sleep amidst filth and vermin.' "[14]

Adams won by a narrow margin, and because of the peculiarities of the electoral system at the time, Jefferson assumed the vice-presidency. In accepting the office, Jefferson remarked that the office was "honorable and easy," while the presidency "is but splendid misery." But that didn't stop him from running again the next time around.

The campaign of 1800 was even more vituperative than its predecessor. Jefferson was called

> a mean-spirited, low-lived fellow, the son of a half-breed Indian squaw, sired by a Virginia mulatto father ... raised wholly on hoe-cake made of coarse-ground Southern corn, bacon and hominy, with an occasional change of fricasseed bullfrog.[15]

(This makes today's Republican attacks on President Clinton and Democratic attacks on Speaker Newt Gingrich seem positively tame by comparison.)

The *Connecticut Courant* warned that if Jefferson were elected,

> Murder, robbery, rape, adultery, and incest will all be openly taught and practiced, the air will be rent with the cries of the distressed, the soil will be soaked with blood, and the nation black with crimes.[16]

Despite all the inflammatory rhetoric, Jefferson was elected president, and for the first time, control of the American government changed from one group to another.

JACKSONIAN DEMOCRACY

As states began loosening property restrictions for voting rights, and the franchise was gradually, though far from completely, extended, the working class got more involved in politics. This added to the rather boisterous nature of campaigning, although in 1828, it was the gentleman's party (called "Friends of Adams," or National Republicans) who resorted to the lowest and loudest personal attacks against the Democratic candidate for president, Andrew Jackson.

The attacks on Jackson focused on both his personal life and military career. Old Hickory had fallen in love with Rachel Donelson Robards, a young woman whose previous husband had beaten and then abandoned her. When news came that her husband had been granted a divorce, the two were married. However, two years later the young couple discovered that, in fact, the divorce had not been granted, and the husband was now suing for divorce on grounds of adultery. The divorce was granted. Jackson and Rachel remarried, but the taint of scandal remained. Jackson's loss to John Quincy Adams in the 1824 election could well be attributed to the mudslinging over his private life.

In the next election, it only got worse. One anti-Jackson newspaper asked: "Ought a convicted adulteress and her paramour husband to be placed in the highest office of this free and Christian land?"[17] Opponents of Jackson campaigned outside his Nashville hotel, carrying banners that read: "THE ABC OF DEMOCRACY: THE ADULTERESS, THE BULLY AND THE CUCKOLD"[18] And they sang, "Oh, Andy! Oh, Andy! How many men have you hanged in your life? How many weddings make a wife?"[19]

Rachel was not the only Jackson family member whose name was dragged through the mud. One newspaper printed the following charge:

> General Jackson's mother was a COMMON PROSTI-
> TUTE, brought to this country by the British soldiers. She
> afterward married a MULATTO MAN, with whom she

had several children, of which number General JACKSON
IS ONE!!!

Jackson and his supporters responded in kind. When
Adams bought a billiards table, the Jacksonians "accused him
of installing 'gaming tables and gambling furniture' in the
White House at public expense." They also denounced Adams
for a variety of sins, from breaking the Sabbath by traveling on
a Sunday, to pimping for the Russian Tsar.

Old Hickory was elected, but Rachel died soon after the
campaign ended. Jackson blamed the slander campaign for her
death. "May God Almighty forgive her murderers, as I know
she forgave them." The General said, "I never can."[20]

THE INFAMOUS ELECTION OF 1884

The presidential campaign of 1884, pitting Grover Cleveland, father of an illegitimate child, against James G. Blaine, an
unscrupulous political profiteer, even by the lax standards of
the time, is significant not only because of the accuracy of the
personal attacks (most of them were true), but also because
both candidates were equally tainted by scandal, and the electorate had to decide which was worse—sexual or financial
impropriety.

Cleveland, a reform governor from New York, was re-
nowned for his honesty and diligence in fighting the corruption
of Tammany Hall. When a story broke during the campaign
that Cleveland had fathered an illegitimate child, the candidate
simply told the truth. Back when he was sheriff of Buffalo,
Cleveland had an affair with Mrs. Maria Halpin. Although
Halpin admitted to having several other boyfriends, when she
gave birth in 1874 and claimed the child was Cleveland's, he
took responsibility, supporting the boy financially, and eventually getting him adopted by a wealthy New York family.

Blaine himself had a sexual peccadillo (his first child was

born only three months after his wedding), but that was soon overshadowed by charges of his profiteering from railroad legislation while presiding as Speaker of the House. Throughout the campaign, Blaine either protested his innocence or came up with various excuses for his wealth, whereas Cleveland dealt with his one scandal with characteristic candor.

The campaign was ferocious, with Democrats chanting, "Blaine, Blaine, James G. Blaine, the Continental liar from the state of Maine." The Republicans countered with a chant of their own: "Ma! Ma! Where's my pa?" To which the Democrats responded, once Cleveland was elected, "Gone to the White House, ha, ha, ha."

One Chicago reformer stated the case for Cleveland this way:

> We are told that Mr. Blaine has been delinquent in office but blameless in private life, while Mr. Cleveland has been a model of official integrity, but culpable in his personal relations. We should therefore elect Mr. Cleveland to the public office which he is so well qualified to fill and remand Mr. Blaine to the private station which he is admirably fitted to adorn.[21]

THE ROARING TWENTIES

With the increasingly sophisticated use of radio and the application of modern sales techniques to political competition, the presidential races of the 1920s were in many ways the first mass-media campaigns.

Ohio Senator Warren G. Harding, the Republican presidential candidate in 1920, was nominated through a last-minute compromise among Republican power brokers—a meeting that begot the cliché of a "smoke-filled room." During the subsequent campaign, Harding stayed close to his home in Marion, Ohio, and let voters and journalists come to him.

The Republican candidate had good reason to avoid the close scrutiny of an active campaign. Though Harding often claimed to be happily married, in fact he had two mistresses. Nan Britton was a young lady in Chicago, with whom Harding had fathered a child. Carrie Phillips was his close friend's wife. Just after Harding's nomination, a journalist asked him:

> Senator Harding, I wish you to assure these gentlemen and myself, upon your sacred honor and before God, that you know of no reason, arising out of anything in your past life, why you should not stand with confidence before the American people as a candidate for the highest office within their gift.

Harding walked out of the room for 10 minutes, during which time he called Miss Britton in Chicago to guarantee her silence, and also made arrangements for Mrs. Phillips and her husband to go on a long cruise to the Orient. When he returned, he answered the question: "No, Gentlemen, there is no such reason."[22]

Almost from the start, critics complained about the lack of substantial debate in the campaign. *The New Republic* said that even a candidate stumping from his front porch had "to spend a lot of time standing upon his legs and talking about four or five things called issues."[23] New techniques of salesmanship and publicity created a mediated distance between the candidate and voters, causing that journal to argue:

> The final vote is not the result of direct acquaintance; it is the result of news reports, the advertising, the oratory, the elusive rumors which are the modern substitute for direct acquaintance.[24]

Publicity wizards on both sides believed that "The Man with the Best Story Wins."[25]

The candidates' stories were scripted for the newspapers, magazines, and newsreels. Publicity stunts engineered by advertising genius Albert Lasker included his bringing the Chicago Cubs (a baseball team Lasker conveniently owned) to play the local Marion club. At another event, Al Jolson led 70 movie stars in a rally that featured the performer singing "Harding, You're the Man for Us."

The Democratic candidate, James M. Cox, was a newspaper publisher from Ohio, just like his opponent. However, his campaign could not have been more different. He went out on the hustings, traveling 22,000 miles and addressing more than two million people. An intense, even pugnacious speaker, Cox called Harding a "Happy Hooligan," leading the staunchly Republican *Chicago Tribune* to comment that "the barroom flavor of his campaign" showed "a mind and character which do not belong in the White House."[26] Cox complained of the sophisticated sales techniques used by the Republicans and their advertisers. "I do not subscribe to the idea of 'selling a candidate,'" Cox said, in words that are eerily similar to many of today's criticisms of media campaigning. "I believe in converting voters to the principles and policies enunciated by the platform and the candidates." His running mate, Franklin Delano Roosevelt, echoed the sentiment, saying, "Photographs and carefully rehearsed moving picture films do not necessarily convey the truth."[27]

Harding went on to win by a landslide, proving that sales techniques and controlled campaigns could in fact be successful. However, he died in office in 1923, and the administration subsequently fell apart among various scandals, including the infamous Teapot Dome scandal.

After Harding's successor, Calvin Coolidge, made one of his more verbose public announcements, "I choose not to run for President in 1928," the Republicans nominated Secretary of Commerce Herbert Hoover. The Democrats countered with New York Governor Al Smith. Hoover was rural, conservative, Midwestern, Quaker, and "dry." Smith was urban, small-p progressive, Eastern, Catholic, and "wet." The no-nonsense technocrat Hoover was diffident, even aloof, whereas his challenger came from the crowded yet affable confines of a Bowery tenement, the Fulton Fish Market, and the backslappy Tammany machine. Evangelist Billy Sunday described Smith's crowd as "damnable whiskey politicians, bootleggers, crooks, pimps and businessmen."[28] Anti-Catholic sentiment was fanned in the heartland by revered Kansas newspaper editor William Allen White's claim that "the whole Puritan civilization which has built a sturdy, orderly nation is threatened by Smith."[29]

Smith tried to defuse the issue of religion by stating, well before the campaign, that there was no "conflict between religious loyalty to the Catholic faith and patriotic loyalty to the United States."[30] After that statement, Smith considered the issue closed. He was unaware, however, of the extent to which anti-Catholic prejudice still prevailed.

In Birmingham, Alabama, an effigy of Smith was shot at, spit upon, stabbed, beaten, and finally hung. One preacher told his congregation: "If you vote for Al Smith, you're voting against Christ and you'll be damned."[31] While Smith made his way through Oklahoma, the KKK burned crosses along his train route and shouted, "A vote for Smith is a vote for the Pope."[32] The night after Smith gave a speech on religious intolerance in Oklahoma City, thousands flocked to the same arena to hear a popular evangelist sermonize on "Al Smith and the Forces of Hell." Anti-Catholics reprinted the 1836 book *The Awful Disclosures of Marian Monk*, an odious libel about orgies and murder in a nunnery. Leaflets in upstate New York attacked their own governor in vile doggerel.

> When the Catholics rule the United States
> And the Jew grows a Christian nose on his face,
> When Pope Pius is head of the Ku-Klux-Klan
> In the land of Uncle Sam
> Then Al Smith will be our president
> And the country not worth a damn.[33]

Hoover won the election. And a year later, the stock market crashed and the country sank into the Great Depression.

ROLLING WITH THE PUNCHES

Politics has always been a rough business. Democracy has both ameliorated its harsher aspects (e.g., we do not decapitate the losers and parade their heads around on poles) and brought the masses into full and enthusiastic—sometimes too enthusiastic—participation. The assumption that American politics was once a pristine undertaking, animated by articulate rhetoric and executed in flawless high manners, is not just fanciful, it is delusionary.

But that does not excuse the loathsome standards (or lack of them) to which our contemporary political campaigns have descended. To look back on the past is helpful, even essential, in understanding where we come from and who, in a larger sense, we are; however, we should never sacrifice the ideal of progress. Just because the campaigns in our history had their moments of ignominy does not mean that it is all right if our present electoral contests do the same. In fact, we should hold ourselves to higher standards, because one of the things that democracy requires is continual striving to improve, not just the results of our politics, but also the manner by which we transact it. Previous campaigns in our history were nasty and brutish. Ours should not be.

The next several chapters explore the reasons why poison politics is on the rise in late-1990s America: the growth of the political mass media, the rise of "the spot" as the primary form of campaign communication, the explosive and execrable phenomenon I call "antipolitics," the news media's changing roles, and the dominance of the video culture. I then analyze what I consider the most grotesque forms poison politics takes: exploitation of fears of crime; myths and stereotypes about race, gender, religion, and sexual orientation. We move from there to more of a microanalysis of the ingredients that go into poison politics: selling candidates like soap and the rise of the political consulting industry. Finally, we discuss the ideals of political rhetoric and some of the antidotes to poison politics, including legislative reform and citizen action.

Chapter 3

The Rise of Political Mass Media

Almost from the beginning, the electronic media were used to attack political opponents. These attacks have ranged from the crude and rude to the sophisticated and sublime. Some have proved effective; others have created a backlash against their own candidate.

Before television, of course, there were radio and film, two powerful media whose roles in the development of political advertising were quickly overshadowed by the emergence of the tube. In the early days, political parties sponsored whole entertainment shows on radio, much like *Texaco Theater* or the *King Biscuit Flour Hour*. Songs and comedy would be interspersed with political messages, and the general tone was light and frothy, with few direct attacks. The 1924 campaign was the first year political parties bought airtime for speeches. The Republicans outspent the Democrats three to one, and Calvin the Taciturn was elected.

With the stock market crash and the emergence of a new radio network, full sponsorship of radio shows declined, and airtime became divided into spots. The presidential campaign of 1928 saw the first short-format political broadcast, in which thousands of "Minute Men" read scripts prepared by the Republican party.

But it was Franklin Roosevelt who harnessed the immense potential of radio communication and brought democratic rhetoric into American living rooms.

FDR TURNS ON THE RADIO

Franklin Delano Roosevelt was the greatest president of this century, and his vast talents were not only political and personal, but also rhetorical. He understood that in the age of mass communication and electronic media, words had the power of shaping reality; sometimes they were as important as deeds. He crafted a democratic rhetoric that was both motivational and informative, entertaining and inspiring, and led our country through the challenges of the Depression and World War II.

FDR's rhetorical skills on the radio were partly honed by his love of reading out loud. He preferred reading to an audience to reading alone, and every Christmas would perform Dickens's *A Christmas Carol* for assembled family and friends. And he always had a knack for the memorable turn of phrase. In his speech nominating Al Smith at the 1924 Democratic Convention, he called the Governor of New York—whom he would succeed in Albany in 1928 and later defeat for the 1932 presidential nomination—"the happy warrior of the political battlefield."[1] Not only did the nickname stick to Smith, but it has since been applied to many other politicians whose cheerfulness is undaunted by political struggle and even defeat.

Roosevelt's bout with polio left him with a profound sympathy for the disadvantaged and victims of catastrophe or circumstance. It also changed his sense of humor from a clubman's ready wit to the deeper irony of one who refuses to be demoralized by suffering. "Really, it's funny as a crutch," FDR would say, or "Sorry, but I have to run now." Those jokes would both blunt his own pain and deflect the self-conscious discomfort of those around him. While his physical handicap was scrupulously hidden from public sight by a protective family and staff, and a respectful press, FDR's compassion and humor often shone through in his speeches and radio addresses.

In accepting the Democratic nomination, FDR ended his speech with the following peroration:

> I pledge you, I pledge myself, to a new deal for the American people. Let us all here assembled constitute ourselves prophets of a new order of competence and of courage. This is more than a political campaign; it is a call to arms. Give me your help, not to win votes alone, but to win in this crusade to restore America to its own people.[2]

Even within the partisan context of a convention, FDR spoke in broadly inclusive, explicitly nonpartisan terms. Later he delivered his first campaign addresses over the radio from the comfortable confines of his Hyde Park estate, sketching out his policies in "this quiet of common sense and friendliness."[3] Using the medium to create an intimacy that previous radio campaigners had been unable to master, Roosevelt was able to make his well rehearsed speeches sound ad-libbed and his well planned program seem spontaneously generated.

FDR's first Fireside Chat, explaining the economic crisis and the need to have a "bank holiday," covered a complex subject in simple, even familiar terms, leading Will Rogers to note: "He made everybody understand it, even the bankers!"[4] That first address provoked half a million letters, many of them addressed to "Dear Frank," a familiarity that not even his wife Eleanor allowed herself. Instead of creating a distance between the people and their leader, FDR used the electronic medium to bring them closer together.

Of course, FDR was a great politician as well as a great performer. As we will see throughout this book, rhetoric and policy are profoundly interrelated, and it is often difficult to separate the two. Not only did FDR's rhetoric join together a fractured nation, but his policies used the federal government as a force for unity, strength, and positive change.

Faced with the prospect of world war and seeking to assist

the Allies without getting the United States involved in an unpopular foreign engagement, FDR proposed the Lend Lease Act, by which America would help its European friends and challenge Nazi aggression through what he called the "Arsenal of Democracy." FDR explained how our country's technological and business strength could be used to lend the instruments of war to the battle-weary British, directly appealing to both workers and factory owners to step up production and support his proposal. In a press conference announcing the Lend Lease, he made the following analogy:

> Suppose my neighbor's home catches fire, and I have a length of garden hose four or five hundred feet away. If he can take my garden hose and connect it up with his hydrant I may help him put out the fire. Now what do I do? I don't say to him before that operation, "Neighbor, my garden hose cost me $15; you have to pay me $15 for it."[5]

During the war itself, FDR assuaged the nation's fears and strengthened its resolve. His Fireside Chats were so effective in rallying morale—not only at home, but also abroad—that the Nazis regularly scheduled massive bombing attacks on the nights of his radio addresses in the hope that the bombings would crowd FDR's speeches out of the news and act to demoralize the Allies. As Robert Sherwood, one of FDR's speechwriters later wrote, "But they needed far more bombs and bombers than they possessed to nullify the lasting effects of those words."[6]

Although FDR had a phalanx of talented speechwriters such as Sherwood and surrounded himself with brain-trusters for facts and ideas on the issues, much of the rhetoric was his own. One of his speechwriters remarked, "Franklin Roosevelt is a better phrase maker than anybody he ever had around him."[7] And he didn't just communicate with the voters through the radio. In his first term alone, FDR held 337 press conferences. And he virtually created other important functions of the modern presidency: the official visit, the executive order, and the formal policy speech. He brought the office of the presidency into the modern age, consolidating executive power and focusing attention on the president himself as national leader, rather than just leader of the party. He also helped arrest the steady erosion of party cohesiveness, by creating a loyal Democratic coalition that dominated American politics for more than 30 years and still leaves its imprint on the party of today.

POLITICS GOES HOLLYWOOD

Film was often used in political campaigns during the days before television. Candidates would pose for photo-ops at work, in leisure, and out on the campaign trail. The only similarity among all these appearances is that they were contrived solely for exposure on the newsreels that played every week in movie theatres across the country. Newsreels provided many Americans with their first glimpses of national politicians and helped promote individual candidates over the party. In many ways, they were the precursor of television news, and some of the same problems that plague video journalism today were evident in the newsreels: an emphasis of entertainment value over political content; a cautious avoidance of the issues, particularly controversial ones; and a struggle between the media and the candidates over control of the message.

In the 1924 presidential campaign, all three major candidates—Coolidge, Davis, and LaFollette—appeared in short films that were shown in movie theatres. Al Smith and his running mate, Joseph T. Robinson, showed their own films along the campaign trail, setting up screens and projectors from specially equipped trucks. In 1936, Alf Landon made the first biographical candidate film, now a mainstay of modern presidential campaigns.

Theatrical films had a brief yet interesting history in political advertising. They were used extensively in the 1934 California gubernatorial campaign, where conservative business interests, including the movie studios, were vehemently opposed to the candidacy of socialist muckraker Upton Sinclair. MGM and the other studies even threatened to move back East if he was elected. The anti-Sinclair coalition hired an advertising agency and consulting firm to attack the Democratic nominee. MGM produced short films that were shrilly partisan: Trainloads of hobos arriving in California as a result of Sinclair's election, with Bolshevik agitators explaining their support for Sinclair, "His system vorked vell in Russia, so vy can't it vork here?" The films, entitled *California Election News* and designed to look like newsreels, were shown between features in movie theaters.

Initially, the MGM strategy backfired. Movie patrons protested the propaganda shorts, demanding their money back or threatening to lay waste to the theaters. Jewish leaders protested the portrayal of Bolsheviks with Semitic accents. Finally, Fox and Warner Bros. pulled the shorts from their theaters. But MGM remained unapologetic. Shortly after the election—incumbent governor Frank Merriman was reelected—Irving Thalberg defended the films, saying, "Nothing is unfair in politics. We could sit down here and figure dirty things all night, and every one of them would be all right in a political campaign."[8]

Audience revulsion to the anti-Sinclair shorts showed that Thalberg perhaps did not understand politics as well as he thought. People go to the movies to escape, not be preached to.

It was television that proved to be the ideal medium for political messages. However, television was slow to develop, and politicians were slow to catch on. In 1948, Harry Truman ran a traditional whistle-stop campaign, traveling tens of thousands of miles, making hundreds of speeches, and personally addressing millions of people. The campaign made one spot that was never aired. Meanwhile the Republican nominee, Thomas Dewey, refused to use television at all, saying it was not "dignified." When Truman won, a reporter asked him if television had helped his candidacy. The assembled journalists and politicos simply laughed at the question.

THE FIRST SPOTS

The first campaign to use the televised spot advertisement was William Benton's run for Senate in 1950. The former adman had cofounded the Benton–Bowles agency and was so successful that he retired at the age of 36. His partner, Chester Bowles, who also retired and became successful in Connecticut politics, convinced Benton to run for the Senate from that state. With the help of Encyclopedia Britannica Films' producer Frank Cellier, Benton produced a series of 60-second spots for television.

The ads had a homey touch. One showed Benton and his wife going over the scrapbook he kept "ever since he was able to give up his business career and go into public service."[9] In another, his next-door neighbors, who just happened to be cochairs of Independent Voters for Benton, invited viewers to meet the senator and his family. And the televised appeal seems to have worked, for Benton narrowly defeated Prescott Bush (George's father) by a little over 1,000 votes, whereas his partner Bowles, who eschewed the use of television advertisements, lost his reelection bid for governor.

That same year, Dewey decided that perhaps he needed to be a little less "dignified," and he appeared on an 18-hour television "talkathon" during his campaign for reelection as New York governor. He won by more than a half million votes.

PRESIDENTIAL POLITICS GOES VIDEO

By 1952, 40 percent of American households had televisions, and politicians realized that they could no longer ignore the medium. Dwight Eisenhower hired the advertising agency BBD&O (Batten, Barton, Durstine & Osborne), and the campaign produced several spots entitled "Eisenhower Answers America," in which Ike's canned responses were edited in between voter queries to give the illusion that he was actually addressing a live audience and answering spontaneously, when, in fact, he was sitting in a studio, reading from a script, his only audience the technicians and advertising gurus of his campaign.

But the Republican video campaign was not above slinging a little mud. One of the most powerful, even brutal, attack ads ever produced was aired in that first year of televised presidential campaigning. In the spot, two soldiers are seen on a battlefield, discussing the uselessness of the war in Korea. Suddenly, one of the soldiers is killed; the other goes off, charging the enemy. The tag-line said simply, "Vote Republican."

The Republican Congressional Committee produced and aired a program entitled *The Case for a Republican Congress*, in which real Republican congressional leaders interrogated actors posing as Democrats in a mock trial. The campaign also used anti-Asian racism in an advertisement called "Korea—the Price of Appeasement." This cartoon spot "featured a satanic Asian brandishing a blood-covered sword."[10] A positive spot also used animation, this time from the Disney studio, along with the jingle "You like Ike! I like Ike! Everybody likes Ike!"

The Eisenhower ads prominently featured Ike's wife Mamie in an indirect attack against the divorced Stevenson. And the red-baiting demagogue Joe McCarthy even got into the act. In a televised speech, McCarthy said that Stevenson would have to answer for his "aid to the communist cause" and twice referred to the Democratic candidate as "Alger" instead of Adlai. Nixon also raised the issue of the accused Communist spy by saying in a televised address: "If Stevenson were to be taken in by Stalin as he was by Alger Hiss, the Yalta sellout would look like a great American diplomatic triumph by comparison."[11]

The Democrats attacked Eisenhower's advertising strategy, calling his campaign advisers "high-powered hucksters of Madison Avenue." But their complaints might have been born of jealousy, for the Stevenson campaign also used television spots, though much less capably. They put 95 percent of their entire television budget into a series of 30-minute speeches by their candidate. The speeches attracted large audiences, but as Stephen Bates and Edwin Diamond point out in their history of political spots, it was "in all probability an audience of people already committed or leaning to Stevenson."[12] The candidate, while possessed of a razor-sharp wit and gift at turning a phrase, was not especially telegenic (his balding pate and intellectual seriousness inspired the term "egghead"). He often disregarded his cues and ran out of time before his speech came to its intended climax.

Some shorter spots were cut from these long speeches, but there was little left in the Democrats' budget to buy airtime. On the eve of the election, they aired one last appeal (sandwiched between two Republican broadcasts) in which President Truman said that the election "may decide whether we will find lasting peace, or be led into a third World War."

In the end, how important were televised spots in the first video campaign? Rosser Reeves, the advertising maven of the Eisenhower campaign, later said, "It was such a landslide that it didn't make a goddamn bit of difference whether we ran the spots or not."[13]

Even so, televised spots were here to stay.

EISENHOWER–STEVENSON REDUX

Determined not to be defeated once again by the Republicans, or by television, the Democrats went on the offensive in 1956. Again, it was Eisenhower versus Stevenson, and the Democrats tried to use Ike's record against him. In a series of spots entitled "How's That Again, General?" the Democrats used footage from Eisenhower's previous campaign promises compared to facts about the president's performance.

The Democrats also went after Nixon, hoping to take advantage of Eisenhower's questionable health, and the possibility that the vice-president could assume the highest office in the land.

Video

Still photo of Nixon in profile, shifty-looking, narrowed eyes;
   small on screen. Super over photo in large white letters,
   filling screen: "NIXON?"

Audio

ANNOUNCER [voice-over]: "Nervous about Nixon? *President*
   Nixon?"

Eisenhower ran a traditional Rose Garden strategy, aug-
mented heavily with televised spots. The production value was
vastly improved over the 1952 spots, and very few of them had
simple, talking head shots of the president. The Republicans
produced a mix of different spots, including a half-hour film
and a 15-minute short entitled "These Peaceful and Prosperous
Years." Eisenhower also appeared in several staged "question
and answer" spots. On the whole, the Republican campaign
was remarkably positive and issue-oriented, but alas, pretty
boring.

Eisenhower was reelected, and, again, it is difficult to
gauge the effectiveness of each side's television campaigns. Ike
remained popular in office, and two events that occurred right
before the election, the Soviet invasion of Hungary and the
Suez Crisis, may have solidified voters' inclination to support
an incumbent president with expertise in military and foreign
affairs. Or perhaps voters agreed that these were indeed,
"peaceful and prosperous times."

KENNEDY – NIXON

The 1960 election pitted Vice-President Richard Nixon
against the young senator from Massachusetts, John F. Kennedy. Although historians have focused primarily on the first
televised presidential debates, the television-spot strategies
of both candidates have not received similar attention.

Kennedy's aggressive (and expensive) television campaign began in the primaries, where he pursued two tactics: to defuse suspicions about his religion (the Al Smith experience still weighed heavily, and conventional wisdom was that a Catholic couldn't get enough Protestant votes to win), and to attack his opponent Hubert Humphrey. Heavily Protestant West Virginia was the pivotal primary, and it was there that Kennedy directly answered the questions about his Catholicism in a paid television appearance. He followed up with a series of spots on the same issue, in which he told the voters of West Virginia, "There is no article of my faith that would in any way inhibit—I think it encourages—the meeting of my oath of office." The whispering about "dual loyalties" was quickly put to rest. America had grown since 1928.

Kennedy's second tactic in West Virginia was to attack Humphrey as a tool of the machine politicians. "Are you going to let yourselves be used by the forces who, in their smoke-filled rooms in Los Angeles, expect to handpick the next president of the United States?" the spot asked West Virginia voters. Kennedy outspent Humphrey by four to one in the primary and won by 20 points. Humphrey dropped out of the race.

In the general election, Kennedy turned his sights on Nixon. One of his negative spots attacked Nixon on the issue where the vice-president was supposed to have the advantage: experience. The spot called into question how qualified, and how competent, Nixon actually was, by using the words of his own boss, President Eisenhower.

Video

President Eisenhower addressing a news conference.

Audio

REPORTER: "I just wondered if you could give us an example of a major idea of his that you have adopted in that role as the decider and final ..."

EISENHOWER: "If you give me a week, I might think of one. I don't remember."

Background noise: Laughter.

While Kennedy attacked Nixon, the vice-president ran against the communists. Then, Nixon dropped out of the televised campaign entirely, making no paid television appearances for three months, while he fulfilled his campaign pledge of visiting all 50 states. Finally, two weeks before the election, the Nixon campaign came out with a media blitz, which included spot ads, "fireside chats," appearances by Eisenhower, and a four-hour telethon, "Dial Dick Nixon," the high point of which was the vice-president discussing the rising cost of living with Ginger Rogers, who told Nixon that she was on a salary, too, and often found it hard to make ends meet.

Nixon was certainly untelegenic and uncongenial to the advice of his image makers, at least, this time around. But also, voters were ready for a change. Kennedy was a dynamic and charismatic leader who seemed capable of leading the country into a new era. He certainly looked better on television than Nixon, but perhaps the voters made their decision based on something more substantial, such as the fact that he was the better candidate.

THE ATOMIC AGE

From almost its first incarnations, the televised political advertisement lent itself to both forms of political argument: positive claims and negative attacks. And some of the uglier forms of attack, such as racism, red-baiting, and waving the bloody shirt, were evident even in the beginning. But in some ways, they only hinted at television's potential as a powerful medium for poisonous trash talk.

Chapter 4

Putting the Spot
in Focus

Television's impact on the electoral process has been a much-discussed, even overly discussed topic. Unfortunately, this has given birth to a host of misperceptions about political mass media and their role in poison politics. These misperceptions are especially powerful concerning the short television advertisement or "spot," particularly when it is negative. Given the subjective and amorphous nature of the spot and its effects on voting behavior, it is not surprising that much of the debate over negative ads is either confused or stated in erroneous terms. We need to clarify the role of spots and reframe the debate, so we can address the problem effectively, instead of simply beating each other over the head with clichés. Here follow the five biggest assumptions about political spots—some are mistaken, some are largely accurate, though often used out of context, but all of them need to be reexamined.

SPOTS ARE MANIPULATIVE

It is funny how the critics of television spots always talk about manipulation, but they never point to a single person who has actually been manipulated. Of course, *we* are all too sophisticated to be taken in by even the slickest political packaging. So who are the dupes? Do the journalists, academics, and political operatives (always on the losing side) who complain about manipulative ads really think they are that much smarter than the American voter?

In the first study to measure the actual impact of political advertisements, Thomas Patterson and Robert McClure of Syracuse University found that "spot commercials do much more to educate the public about the issues than they do to manipulate the public about the candidates."[1] They argue that "voters are not easily misled."[2] Voters are, first of all, politically sophisticated. Most of them already have fairly developed political belief systems or party loyalties. The rest are skeptical enough, after years of exposure to Madison Avenue humbug, to discount phony claims and view manipulative attempts with suspicion and, often, derision. Especially in political advertising, voters have erected defense mechanisms to protect themselves from manipulation. The American voter is smarter than most of the pundits think.

The problem with negative ads is not that they are manipulative, but that they often appeal to emotion instead of reason, and those emotions appealed to are often our darker ones. Attack ads that seek to persuade voters from the baser motives of fear, hatred, greed, and prejudice are what is wrong with our political discourse. Television is what gives those appeals emotional power, but the fault lies not with the medium, but with the message.

NEGATIVE SPOTS DO NOT ADDRESS THE ISSUES

Many negative spots are packed with information, and much of it is important. Darrell West, a professor at Brown University, who has studied negative ads produced from 1952 to 1992, found that "the most substantive appeals actually came in negative ads."[3] He reports that "attack ads are more likely to occur on substantive issues than on personality aspects of presidential campaigns."[4] And they contain "a considerable amount of policy-oriented information."[5] Of course, they are sometimes inaccurate or unfair, which West is quick to point out. But when they are fair and accurate, negative ads are an indispensable source of political information.

In their study, Patterson and McClure found that *spots contained more issue content than news broadcasts*! Indeed, they cover important topics such as the budget, healthcare, and economic policy, which are often ignored by the media in their focus on the horse race or the inside story of the campaign.

That is not to say the spot is the ideal form of political communication. There is only so much that can be said in 30 seconds. They often do reduce issues to soundbites or slogans, but at least those issues are addressed. According to Patterson and McClure, "Although the issue material contained in spots is incomplete and oversimplified, it also is abundant. So abundant in fact, that presidential advertising contributes to an informed electorate."[6]

Not only do negative ads address issues, but also they are often the only medium to do so. In his study, West found that in the presidential campaigns of 1984 and 1988, a full 100 percent of all "ads dealing with specific policy proposals were negative."[7] This is especially troubling, for if negative ads are the only source of information about the issues, then voters are bound to find that all policy options are objectionable, instead of learning which ones are favored by candidates. This no doubt contributes greatly to policy gridlock. Negative ads play an integral role in political debate, but they cannot be the only messages of substance. (The media certainly are not going to make up for this deficit of positive discussion of the issues.) It is difficult, perhaps even impossible, to come to an informed decision based only on negative information.

And when negative ads do address the issues, they often

are couched as matters of character in ways that are often sleazy and dishonest cheap shots that do not belong in political debate. Our campaigns have become increasingly ugly and trivial; issues have taken a backseat to scandal and smears. Instead of entering a meaningful dialogue, candidates reduce issues to fighting words. When negative ads and their campaign corollaries of sound-bite attacks and countercharges are used in the absence of other information, the issues simply become clubs with which the candidates beat each other up, and deliberative democracy turns into a gladiatorial sport. What results is a diminished debate, and we come to our decisions uninformed and unwilling to explore issues any further than the aggressive use of harsh rhetorical points. Instead of a debate, we merely get dueling sound bites. And instead of deliberative democracy, we get fast-food-quality decisions.

NEGATIVE SPOTS TURN OFF VOTERS

Political campaigns have two major strategies toward voters: Affirm support and turn out the loyal, and persuade the undecided. In any given year, the Democrats and Republicans each hold 40 percent of voters, with the remaining 20 percent being undecided. Every campaign is a fight for that 20 percent. It would be ironic if negative ads had a backlash effect and actually kept those voters away from the polls.

The data on voter turnout are mixed and often contradictory. That is due, in part, to the complex dynamic between voters and campaign messages. In many polls and surveys, voters complain about the rancorous tone of political debate. But then other polls and surveys show that they also respond to negative messages. If negative ads did not create a noticeable, and sometimes instant, effect in poll numbers, campaigns would not use them. "When we ask people about negative ads," pollster Mark Mellman concluded, "they'll say they don't like them. But that's not the point. The point is they absorb the information."[8] That may be true, but the focus on the short-term gains of negative spots has created an atmosphere in which cynicism and disgust ultimately prevail.

However, it is not so simple as some critics think. The voters most disturbed by negative advertising are those who are already politically active and most likely to vote—committed partisans do not like seeing their candidates attacked. In other words, the undecideds, those least likely to vote anyway, are also least affected by negative ads. In many hotly contested elections with vicious negative campaigns, voter turnout has been extremely high. To take just two examples, the 1991 Louisiana gubernatorial race between Edwin Edwards and David Duke, and the 1990 race between Jesse Helms and Harvey Gantt both had record turnouts. But other mudslinging races show contrary evidence. For example, in the 1996 Helms–Gantt rematch, turnout was actually lower than in 1990—the opposite of what it should have been since 15–20 percent more voters typically show up for presidential elections than for midterm elections. And in the 1996 New Jersey Senate contest between Robert Torricelli (D) and Dick Zimmer (R), turnout was more than 10 percent lower than in 1992. Some of that may have been attributable to the lackluster 1996 presidential race, but I suspect that Senate campaign—a classic in poison politics (see the Epilogue)—was the biggest factor.

There has been a general, though not uniform, decline in voter turnout since around 1960, and several studies and countless pundits have tried to link lower turnout to negative advertising. But these arguments suffer from the classic *post hoc* fallacy. Just because negative content in political advertising has increased, and voter turnout has declined, does not prove a direct causal relationship. The two are connected but in a much more complex and insidious way. Instead, lower voter turnout and trash talk in television ads are the symptoms of a wider and more dangerous problem: the increasingly cynical attitude toward government that is poisoning our politics and causing many voters to give up and stay home.

SPOTS ARE TOO SHORT
TO GET A MESSAGE ACROSS

In the 1994 Republican primary for senator in California, candidates Tom Campbell and Bruce Herschensohn denounced each other in 10-second ads. Herschensohn, a former television commentator, said, "I'm Bruce Herschensohn. My opponent, Tom Campbell, was the only Republican Congressman opposing the 1990 anticrime bill. He's liberal and wrong."

Campbell responded: "Bruce Herschensohn is lying. Tom Campbell voted to extend the death penalty to 27 crimes, and was named 'Legislator of the Year' by the California Fraternal Order of Police."

There's a lot wrong with these spots—they're typical of the trivial and mean-spirited campaigns of 1994. But they are chock-full of information that is relevant to the voters. However, critics of the spots focused on their length, not their content. Somehow a 10-second spot is far too short for anything of substance to be discussed, and the emergence of these "sound bits" were further evidence of how short, negative spots had gotten out of hand.

Actually, 10-second spots have always been with us. In 1954, Minnesota gubernatorial candidate Orville Freeman used a 10-second spot that said, between rings of an alarm clock: "Minnesota needs a wide-awake governor! Vote for Orville Freeman and bring wide-awake action to Minnesota's problems."

You can say a lot in 10 seconds, even if Orville Freeman did not. Jimmy Carter's campaign oath, "I will not lie to you," did not take half that long. One of his slogans, "Leaders, for a Change," was a pithy conflation of two major themes, and when he failed to deliver on those promises, the Republicans turned the slogan against him in their generic campaigns of 1980: "Vote Republican, for a Change." Walter Mondale effectively—and legitimately—derailed Gary Hart's primary campaign in less than three seconds with "Where's the beef?" In the general election, Mondale's defense of his tax plan may not have been a good tactical move, but it certainly was clear: "Whoever gets elected is going to raise your taxes. My opponent won't tell you. I just did." George Bush probably gave Bill Clinton his most effective slogan when he broke his famous tax pledge, "Read my lips, no new taxes."

Political slogans have always been with us, many of them quite informative. Woodrow Wilson's supporters said, "He kept us out of war." Eisenhower promised, "If elected I will go to Korea." Often, slogans are resonant; sometimes, they can move a nation. It only took John F. Kennedy five seconds to say, "Ask not what your country can do for you, but what you can do for your country."

Yes, on average, spots have gotten shorter. But this is part of a larger trend—perhaps best personified by the Internet, where one "surfs" rather than stops to actually read or digest something—in most forms of communication (except, alas, for books and President Clinton's speeches, which just keep getting longer). Our attention spans are shorter, and the information we receive is increasingly being packaged into smaller and smaller bits. That is not a healthy development. Issues need more time to be fully discussed, and shorter soundbites and spots simply cannot convey much essential information. But, as in many things, size is less important than what you do with what you have got.

The problem with spots is not that they are just getting shorter, but that they are becoming more nasty and meaningless, and they are supplanting the other traditional forms of campaign communication and political rhetoric. There is a place for 30-second, and even 10-second, spots, but if they become the only message that voters get to hear, then our debate has been diminished to the point of obscurity.

TELEVISION ADVERTISING HAS MADE
CAMPAIGNS TOO EXPENSIVE

Campaigns are too expensive, with 1996 taking things completely over the edge, and in most campaigns—whether direct, independent expenditure, or "issue"-related—a significant portion of the money spent goes to televised advertising. But two things must be considered when we examine money and the televised campaign. First of all, the cost of campaigning has to be put in perspective. Second, we have to look at where the money comes from and how it affects elections.

Television advertisements have had a significant impact on the cost of campaigning. Yet they are the most effective means of conveying information to the voter, especially those who are relatively uninvolved, those who do not follow politics and are unlikely to seek out candidate information on their own. The ubiquity of television and radio advertisements in campaign season may seem redundant to those of us who follow politics, but there are many who do not, and those messages are all they will have to help them make an informed decision. And as newspaper readership continues to decline, even among the well educated and well informed, spot ads become the most viable way of reaching active voters as well.

According to Bates and Diamond, "A dollar spent on TV advertising may reach as many voters as $3 worth of newspaper ads or $50 worth of direct mail."[9] They also point out that spots are usually not targeted and reach all television viewers. However, television images require repetition in order to have effect, so that dollars spent on television advertising have to be spent again, and again, and again. And if the message conveyed on that television ad is nothing but trash talk, then that money is more than wasted, for the ad has not contributed to the debate, but only caused it to degenerate further.

By some standards of comparison, political advertising is relatively cheap. The Microsoft Windows 95 campaign cost the software giant some $300 million. That is about the same amount spent by all the candidates for congressional seats in the 1994 cycle, and all general election candidates in the 1996 cycle through October 16, 1996. Although we spend more on political races than most other countries, campaign costs are much higher in Japan (as, apparently, is everything). The total cost to run for a seat in the Japanese Diet is around $3.5 million, compared to $600,000 here. Some scholars have estimated that the Japanese elections spent between $50 and $100 per constituent, while congressional incumbents spend a little more than one dollar.[10]

In congressional elections, the rise in campaign costs has been meteoric. In 1992, House incumbents spent an average of almost $600,000 per campaign. That is a 41 percent increase over 1990. In 1992, it cost an average of $3.8 million for a Senate incumbent to defend his or her seat. The figures for 1996 are sure to be far higher. Through October 16, 1996—the latest date for which figures were available at press time—the average House incumbent had already raised more than $700,000, and the average Senate incumbent up for reelection had raised $4.8 million.[11]

The cost of television advertising has had a significant impact on this campaign inflation. But the access and political influence expected from contributions to incumbents have also been a factor. Money accrues to political candidates in an inverse proportion to how much they need it. Contributors flock to incumbents, because they have a better chance of winning. Then, their challengers need equal amounts of money just to stay in the race. And potential competitors see early on that they cannot raise the requisite dough and stay out of the election altogether.

In open races, money affects political campaigns not so much in determining who wins, but in deciding who gets to run in the first place. Ross Perot and Steve Forbes proved that you need more than just money to get elected president. But they also proved that anybody willing to spend a whole lot of cash is automatically a legitimate contender. In the 1996 Republican primaries, candidates had to raise $10–$20 million just to get into the race. A campaign for major statewide office in California costs about the same amount, due to the size of the state and its far-flung and expensive media markets.

Underfunded candidates are shut out of the process entirely, unless they possess the high visibility, committed constituency, and knack for getting free media attention of a Jesse Jackson. Other candidates who are not so well known or controversial do not even get into the race. If we had meaningful campaign finance reform, then the advantages of both money and incumbency would diminish, the playing field would be leveled somewhat, and we could have a broader and more diverse range of candidates. Under these circumstances, many contenders might be more careful in launching stridently negative ads, knowing their opponents would have the wherewithal to fire back. But right now, the entry fee for American politics is simply too high. Politicians spend too much time asking for money instead of speaking to the voters. And the problem is not just the amount of money spent on political campaigns, but whose money gets spent. Fifty percent of all campaign contributions come from the wealthiest 10 percent of Americans. Guess who has the most influence? It should not be that way.

The *laissez-faire* political market has given fantastic advantages to the well funded and well connected. It has also created great inequities among different regions of the country. For example, a congressional candidate in New York City simply cannot get his or her message on television. It is too expensive to buy airtime, and the ads would have to be broadcast throughout the huge tristate market. Spot time in smaller markets is much cheaper, so a senator from Wyoming does not have to spend as much time fund-raising to pay for campaign spots as does a senator from California. And political campaigns are often charged the highest price for spot time. Knowing that campaigns have to get their message out, often on very short notice, television stations gouge candidates with exorbitant rates. And the candidates pay, because they have no other options. Faced with such extortionist costs, and wishing to make the most impact with their media buys, candidates go on the attack, often airing ads that are exclusively, and harshly, negative. Without some form of public financing and mandated media access for candidates, these problems will only get worse.

NEGATIVE SPOTS HAVE INCREASED AND BECOME INCREASINGLY SHRILL AND IRRESPONSIBLE

Unfortunately, this is not a myth, but a reality.

Anyone who has watched and listened to the last few campaigns cannot help but notice the increasing prevalence and bitterness of attack ads. Twenty years ago, only one in five political advertisements was negative. Now, approximately one-half are. And some campaigns only run negative spots.

This deplorable turn of events has come about because of two major changes in political campaigns. First, the communications strategy has changed; now, attack ads are often the weapon of first resort, rather than simply being one element in a campaign's arsenal. The second is a "win-at-any-cost attitude" that, like so many areas of our economy and culture, has infected the entire campaign structure. Decent and dignified campaigning has become not merely an anachronism, but a liability, as those who refuse to follow the latest slash-and-burn tactics are often unable to compete in this harsh new electoral arena.

The old approach to political advertising held that campaign communications ran in four cycles, starting 12 weeks before election day. The first four weeks were devoted to building name identification. The second four weeks established the candidate's credibility, qualifications, and vision for the office. The next two weeks were devoted to an *optional* third cycle, an attack on the opponent. And the final two weeks were a return to the positive, candidate-credibility cycle.

There was a logic to this. Challengers should become known by the voters and establish a positive image before they could credibly attack their opponents. Incumbents should not attack challengers who are not close in the polls, because they would just help the challengers gain name recognition. And any attack would carry the risk of backfiring against the attacker.

Then everything changed. Campaign consultants threw out the rule book, candidates gave in to pressures of expediency, and the press played along, reporting each new low in campaign standards with the same ironic detachment with which they treat every other degenerate practice. The electorate became increasingly volatile, or, at least, unpredictable, and the cost of getting elected made it too expensive to lose. Finally, the 1980s ethos that gave us insider trading, the savings-and-loan debacle, and the various scandals of the Reagan Administration caught on in politics itself, making the bottom line the only standard, and dismissing any sense of dignity, fairness, or social responsibility. All that matters now is winning.

The traditional campaign strategy was jettisoned in favor of this new one:

1. Advertise early if you have the money, even a year or more before election day, especially if you'll have the airwaves to yourself. (The Clinton campaign, via the Democratic National Committee, did this brilliantly in 1995.)
2. Go negative early, often, and right through election day, if necessary.
3. Appeal to the heart and the gut, rather than to the head.
4. Define your opponent to the voters before he or she can define him-/herself or you.
5. If attacked, hit back even harder.
6. It's easier to give voters a negative impression of your opponent than it is to improve their image of you, espe-

cially if you are already viewed negatively. The best way to win is by bringing the other guy down, not by bringing yourself up.

It is too bad, but these are the new rules of engagement.

MAKING NOISE

The problem is not with spots themselves, it is how they are being used. Too many campaigners are taking the low road, eschewing traditional forms of campaigning in order to concentrate solely on television ads and the fund-raising necessary to pay for them. And the content of those ads is often misleading, divisive, irrelevant, or just plain stupid. Some critics have suggested controlling negative ads or cutting the campaign short. What we need is not less campaigning but more of it, and of a different sort.

"Campaigns cannot deal with anything substantive if they cannot get the electorate's attention and interest people in listening to their music. Campaigns need to make noise."[12] So says political scientist Samuel Popkin. And he is right. There ought to be more debates, more rallies, more candidate appearances, more discussions on the talk shows, more in-depth reporting on the news, and yes, even more advertising. But we need to hold campaigners to higher standards, to demand that when they do attack their opponents, they do so honestly and fairly, raising issues and asking questions that are relevant to the debate, and do not simply trivialize or degrade it.

For good and for bad, the way to make noise in today's media campaigns is through television, in spots. If we are to reinvigorate our democratic system, bring the uninvolved voter into the picture, and help the undecideds make an informed decision, television ads are the way we have to do it. There is a lot wrong with television ads, and a lot wrong with television itself. But television is not going away, and unless we do something to change the way we talk on it, our sad state of political discourse will only get worse.

The Infamous Daisy Spot

The most famous political ad—the one that truly defined "the spot"—only ran once. It was September 7, 1964. "David and Bathsheba" was playing on *Monday Night at the Movies*. Just before 10:00 P.M., a political commercial came on the screen. The original title was "Peace, Little Girl," but it has since come to be remembered as "Daisy."

Video

Camera on little girl in field, picking petals off a daisy.

Audio

LITTLE GIRL (sound on film): "One, two, three, four, five, seven, six, six, eight, nine, nine—" (*sic*)

Video

Girl looks up, startled; freeze frame on girl; move into extreme close-up of her eye, until screen is black.

Audio

Man's voice, very loud, as if heard over a loudspeaker at a test site: "Ten, nine, eight, seven, six, five, four, three, two, one ..."

Video

Cut to atom bomb exploding. Move into close-up of explosion.

Audio

JOHNSON (voice-over): "These are the stakes—to make a world in which all God's children can live, or to go into the dark. We must love each other, or we must die."

Video

Cut to white letters on black background: "Vote for President Johnson on November 3."

Audio

ANNOUNCER (voice-over): "Vote for President Johnson on November 3. The stakes are too high for you to stay home."

The ad used powerful imagery: a little girl picking flowers in what looked like a field (but was actually Manhattan's Henry Hudson Parkway), the mushroom cloud, the poetry of W. H. Auden. And it worked. Once the commercial was over, the White House switchboard lit up with calls protesting the ad. Privately pleased with the spot's effectiveness, yet sensitive to the shifting winds of electoral politics, President Johnson ordered it taken off the air.

But that was only the beginning of the "Daisy" controversy. Some 50 million people were watching NBC when it came on. And over the next couple days, almost every American had seen it, or thought they had seen it, or at least had heard about it. The spot was shown several times on network news programs and discussed in the press. The Republican National Committee lodged a formal complaint against it. But publicity, even negative publicity, only helped strengthen the ad's message.

The conventional wisdom among political consultants is that an ad's exposure on a newscast is worth at least three times the same exposure in paid slots. Once an ad has appeared in the news, even if the coverage is critical, its credibility is enhanced. Certainly the "Daisy" ad was seen by more people secondhand in news broadcasts than in the original airing. The echo effect of this mediated repetition of the ad has also distorted people's memory of it. Many remembered the ad as specifically attacking Goldwater, even though he was never mentioned. Some viewers, even political and advertising professionals, seem to recall Goldwater's face on screen, with the mushroom cloud billowing behind him. One writer for the *New York Times* remembered the spot this way:

In 1964, the Democrats demolished Goldwater with a simple one-shot television spot. A little girl gently picking daisies moved happily across an open field. Suddenly, a mushroom cloud filled the air and the announcer asked sternly: "Whose finger do you want on the trigger?"[13]

Aside from the internal contradictions — calling the spot a one shot and then describing two separate images, a mistake which should, at least, have been caught at the copydesk of the paper of record — this recollection of the ad, written some eight years later, shows how time, memory, and mediated repetition can distort an image almost beyond recognition. But not only journalists are prone to such distortions.

One of the reasons why "Daisy" worked so well is that it was particularly artful, tugging at the emotions by contrasting the innocence of a little girl against the evil of nuclear devastation. It also worked because there was something to it. "Daisy" used strong symbolic language in order to evoke and enhance what the voters already felt about Goldwater.

But how effective was "Daisy" as a campaign technique?

Sidney Blumenthal thinks that the ad "vaporized Barry Goldwater's presidential campaign."[14] And he is not alone in his opinion. Ask just about any political junkies, and they will tell you the ad catapulted Johnson to victory. Unfortunately, they are mistaken. "Daisy" probably had little impact on the campaign, and it certainly did not change the course of the election.

"Daisy" was not the only negative ad run by either side. In fact, the 1964 election was one of the nastiest media campaigns ever. The Democrats ran several other attack ads, none of them nearly as well put together or as well remembered as "Daisy." In one ad, another little girl licked an ice-cream cone while a female announcer spoke of how atomic testing had released strontium 90 and cesium 137 into the atmosphere. This spot was also run only once, but who remembers it?

Other anti-Goldwater ads tried to link the Republican nominee to the Ku Klux Klan, claimed he would destroy Social Security, or made an issue out of his remark that America should "saw off the Eastern Seaboard and let it float into the Atlantic." They attacked Goldwater for suggesting that tactical nuclear weapons be used in Vietnam. Another atomic blast was used as a visual, with the announcer reminding voters that Goldwater had called the nuclear bomb "just another weapon." And they did the first "hot-line" spot, a genre that has been used in almost every sub-sequent presidential campaign, calling into question Gold-water's diplomatic ability, especially in a time of crisis.

The Republicans fought back. They filmed their candi-date visiting Eisenhower at his farm in Gettysburg, where the former president called criticisms of Goldwater "actual tommyrot." The Eisenhower spot originally ran as a half-hour show, but it got lower ratings than *Petticoat Junction* and *Peyton Place*. Even cut down to a 30-second spot, it did not do much better.

Another long film, entitled *Choice*, attempted to portray the Democrats' America as decadent and depraved. Images of racial strife, naked dancers, and a car speeding through a ranch (supposedly Johnson's) with beer cans flying out the window, were contrasted with Goldwater's "decent, God-fearing, peace-loving" Americans.

None of these ads had the resonance of "Daisy," and they exist now only in dusty archives, instead of our collec-tive memory. But it must be pointed out that all of these ads, even the famous "Daisy," were merely part of a larger cam-paign, one that Goldwater had little chance of winning from the start.

Johnson was the incumbent president, an extremely powerful leader. The nation still mourned the death of John F. Kennedy, and liberals and conservatives alike gave John-son a great deal of residual sympathy as the man who was sworn in on Air Force One the day the president died. Gold-water was the underdog from the beginning; he did not even enjoy the full support of his own party, as many Republicans felt that the primary had been hijacked by a cadre of right-wing ideologues and little old ladies in tennis shoes. And his line, "Extremism in the defense of liberty is no vice," cer-tainly added credibility to Democrats' protrayal of him as "right—far right."

In 1964, the political mood of the country was predomi-nantly liberal. Even many of Goldwater's fellow Republicans were in basic agreement with the Democrats on a series of fundamental issues such as civil rights and an expanded role of the federal government in providing social services.

Americans were enjoying a long, and seemingly endless, economic boom. Vietnam was just a skirmish somewhere far away. It is difficult to imagine how Johnson could have lost.

The ''Daisy'' ad certainly did not propel Johnson to victory. But, as we will see throughout this book, it is much easier to ascribe political defeat to one identifiable cause, and much more comforting to believe in vast political conspiracies or the mysterious powers of the media, than to admit that perhaps a campaign was out of sync with the times, and out of touch with the voters.

Chapter 5

Antipolitics

One of the key factors turning the legitimate tactics of negative campaigning into poison politics is the troubling phenomenon of antipolitics—the increasing distrust of government, particularly the federal government, coupled with a disdain for the sometimes messy business of elections. This attitude rose from a genuine and understandable public disillusionment in the wake of Vietnam and Watergate. However, it has also been exploited by cynical politicians and consultants, and encouraged by the media.

Unfortunately, like the attack ads it frequently relies on, antipolitics works—at least in the short term. But the long-term damage to our political system is significant. Antipolitics has created a vicious circle in which public debate is cheapened by trash talk, political institutions themselves—rather than just the individuals who serve in them—are attacked as inadequate or corrupt, and the very process of politics is increasingly seen as degenerate.

What these antipoliticians seek to replace politics with is unclear, for they rarely make any positive suggestions, offering only a crude nihilism that creates nothing but a growing sense of ugliness and despair, and strips our politics of that most essential democratic virtue—hope.

THE RISE OF ANTIPOLITICS

In 1964, while the nation was still reeling from the assassination of John F. Kennedy, 62 percent of Americans felt that the federal government could be trusted to "do what is right" most of the time, according to the Gallup Poll. Fourteen percent were even more optimistic, believing that the government would always do the right thing. Ten years later, after the traumas of the late 1960s, Vietnam and Watergate, only 34 percent responded positively when asked the same question. By 1992, the percentage of Americans who trusted their own government had fallen to only 21 percent. Another study showed that more than 50 percent of Americans feel they have no impact on the way their government is run. Seventy five percent said that government is operated for the benefit of a few powerful interests. Nearly two-thirds believe that public officials do not care what ordinary citizens think, and the same percentage say that government wastes their tax dollars. About 50 percent of Americans think that government officials are corrupt.[1]

Clearly, it was not just the national catastrophes of the late 1960s and early 1970s that created this poisonous atmosphere. What happened to the American people that made them develop such a negative attitude toward their own government? Tracking these public attitudes through the Gallup Poll, Matthew Robert Kerbel shows that distrust in government rose steadily through the 1960s and 1970s, peaking in 1980 at rates very close to the ones we are experiencing today.

Why were public attitudes toward government so negative during the late 1970s? Whether a cause, a reflection, or some combination of the two, one place to find some answers is in the campaigns and presidency of a Democrat, Jimmy Carter.

JIMMY CARTER

Meeting with his media adviser Gerald Rafshoon in the Georgia governor's mansion during his last year in office,

Jimmy Carter sketched out what he felt were his personal assets in his run for the presidency:

> not a lawyer
> Southerner
> 300 days a year to campaign (would be out of office)
> ethics
> not part of Washington scene
> religious[2]

Carter turned his perceived outsider status into powerful campaign themes. As Rafshoon remembers, "What the conventional wisdom perceived as negative was all positive, because everything he had to do had to be against conventional wisdom."[3]

The Carter campaign slowly and quietly gained momentum, and soon people began realizing that the one-term governor of Georgia was actually a viable candidate. Running in a crowded field of Democratic candidates, he soon surged ahead of the pack, reciting as his mantra a résumé full of negative constructions: "I'm not a lawyer.... I've never worked in Washington. I'm not a senator or congressman. I've never met a Democratic president."[4] Carter often defined himself by what he was not. When he did describe himself positively, his labels were no more informative. He was a Southerner, a Christian, a farmer. Well, so were many different people. Throughout the campaign, people kept asking who Jimmy Carter was, and for a long time he got away without having to give a definitive answer. In the end, he went to Washington on little more than a smile and a promise: "I will not lie to you." In 1976, that was enough.

In one of his early campaign ads, Carter stressed his antipolitician stance. The ad "Non Lawyer" emphasized the fact that Carter was not a lawyer and implicitly attacked all the lawyers in Washington. It is not all that odd or conspiratorial that Washington is inhabited by lawyers; after all, the government writes and interprets laws, and by stating his lack of a legal degree, Carter was, in a way, making a positive issue out of his own lack of experience.

This ad is also significant for being one of the first documented uses of the now inescapable, populist, sartorial campaign technique—the plaid shirt. Jimmy Carter wore the plaid shirt in his first commercials to reinforce the difference between himself and his dark-suited opponents. Later on, in the general election, however, he dressed only in suits, as he felt he had to appear more like people expect a president to look.

As is typical of most presidential candidates assuming "outsider" status (see Bill Clinton in 1992, Pat Buchanan, Lamar Alexander, even Ross Perot, who had intensive dealings with many administrations and made his fortune from the federal government), this was rather exaggerated—Carter had been governor of a large state, had a sophisticated campaign team, was well off financially and able to borrow against substantial assets. In the Democratic primaries, Carter rarely singled out his opponents for direct attack; instead, he fought the whole system. "Washington" became a code word of sorts, one that meant bureaucracy, corruption, and politics as usual. Constitutionally prevented from running for a second term as governor of Georgia, and now in the race for the presidency of the United States, somehow Jimmy Carter was not a "politician."

Of course, the country was still reeling from Watergate, and bad memories of Vietnam were vivid. Carter was running against veteran insiders and hardy perennials such as Scoop Jackson, Mo Udall, Birch Bayh, Frank Church, and Sargent Shriver. Hubert Humphrey and Jerry Brown became the favorite sons of the ABC (Anybody but Carter) movement. And George Wallace, the last demagogue of the Old South, entered the race, winning a few primaries in the South. So, Carter could claim with some accuracy, and often did, that he was the least qualified candidate of the field.

He won the Democratic nomination on the first ballot and went back to Georgia, where his campaign would be headquartered. Throughout the race, the Carter camp would find itself in the difficult position of running against established authority and yet cozying up to it at the same time. "It was hard to judge where the balance was," Press Secretary Jody Powell said, "between getting the support of Democratic organizations on the one hand and not appearing to be their captive on the other."[5]

In a time when people were fed up with politics, as it had been practiced, and looking for honesty and sincerity in their leaders, Carter's homespun candor was appealing. Throughout his campaign for president, Carter positioned himself as an outsider, the antipolitician. Although it got him elected, the strategy ultimately failed, for it rendered him ineffective as president. And by advancing the phenomenon of antipolitics, he harmed the long-term interests of the one political party whose belief in government as an instrument of social good requires reducing—not increasing—antigovernment sentiment.

THE POLITICS OF RAGE

In many ways, Carter's candidacy resembled that of another Southern governor who also ran for president as an outsider—George Wallace. Unlike Carter, Wallace, during the years he ran for president, was a racist who succeeded by fomenting white resentment of African Americans. But what is relevant to Carter is that the success of Wallace's three presidential campaigns showed that a Southerner could win the Democratic nomination, and possibly the presidency, by positioning himself as a populist outsider and running to the right of the Northern wing of the party. Wallace himself polled more votes in the 1972 primaries than the eventual nominee, George McGovern, but the assassination attempt by Arthur Bremer and his supporters' inability to successfully manipulate, or even understand, the Democrats' new delegate selection procedures kept him from gaining nomination.

Wallace was the first politician to take the techniques of Southern demagoguery and successfully exploit them on a national level. Although Southern populists, ranging from economic progressives like Huey Long to reactionary racists like Theodore Bilbo and Eugene Talmadge, rose to power by attacking "the establishment," particularly the federal government, they were unable to broaden their base outside their own home states. Even Long's "Every Man a King" program had little appeal beyond Louisiana, and had he not been assassinated, the bibulous dictator would probably not have been taken seriously beyond his little dominion.

But George Wallace changed all that. He turned the rhetoric of racial hatred into a critique of big government. In his first gubernatorial inaugural speech—written by Ku Klux Klan thug Ace Carter, who later wrote the spurious "autobiography," *The Education of Little Tree*—Wallace promised "Segregation now ... segregation tomorrow ... segregation forever." But he was careful to frame his argument not as a direct attack on African Americans so much as angry invective against the federal government informed by the crude hostility of class antagonism. "We will tolerate their boot in our face no longer.... [The federal] government has become our god.... A system that ... encourages everything degenerate and base."[6] Thus did government-bashing become code for race baiting.

From the statehouse in Montgomery, Wallace launched four presidential campaigns and established himself as the political leader of white backlash. His antigovernment rhetoric was often acerbic to the point of comedy: "Take those bearded bureaucrats and throw them in the Potomac." But the response Wallace received was significant, tapping the latent anger of the important swing voters and making him a candidate that politicians attacked or ignored at their own peril.[7] After Wallace dropped out of the 1976 race, Carter courted the Alabama governor, and his endorsement put Jimmy over the top.

Of course, Carter was not a racist like Wallace, but the Georgian did modify the Alabaman's critique of big government into a message that sought to attract Wallace supporters without alienating Northern liberals. And Carter's strategy succeeded, at least, the first time around. Then, he came up against a candidate far more smooth and expert at delivering

Wallace's antipolitical message with a smiling face and sooth-
ing voice.

Ronald Reagan was the consummate antipolitician, railing
against Washington as if it were a sinkhole of sloth, corruption,
and depravity. "Government isn't the solution. Government is
the problem," the former governor of the largest state government said, while running for the highest office in the land. His
antigovernment rhetoric, and its incredible electoral success,
taught a whole generation of rising politicians that the way to
political success in a cynical age is to despise the very office you
aspire to and campaign against the institutions you wish to
serve.

But antipolitics was not just created by ambitious politicians seeking to gain office by any means necessary. The media
had a great impact on the souring national mood. Flush from
their successes with Watergate and the Pentagon Papers, the
media began testing the limits of their newfound powers. Soon
every minor scandal was another Watergate, and sneering
hairdos were seen on the nightly news, disparaging the latest
act of Congress as "mere politics" or handicapping a political
election as if it were some low-stakes harness race. The rise of
media power coincides exactly with the increase in antipolitical
attitudes. And during the Reagan years, while the press waited
in the West Wing like trained seals to be tossed a few dead fish
from the White House prop boys, the public accepted their rosy
vision of reality and softened their attitudes toward government.

But all that is changed now. Candidates and the media try
to outdo each other, setting new standards for cynicism, and
turning what was once a healthy skepticism toward government into a virulent distrust.

THE NEW ANTIPOLITICS

Newt Gingrich rose to one of the highest offices in U. S.
government by running against government itself. Learning
from the campaigns of Wallace, Carter, and Reagan, Gingrich

has cranked up the volume, turning inflammatory rhetoric into revolutionary policies that seek to undermine and roll back much of our political progress.

Former Representative Mickey Edwards is no liberal. As a Republican, he represented a conservative district in Oklahoma before he was defeated in the 1992 primary, following his involvement in the House banking scandal. Now at Harvard's John F. Kennedy School of Government, Edwards believes that Gingrich created his own image as a revolutionary right-winger through careful exploitation of harsh rhetoric. "I told him at the time it was *he* who was whipping up the system, creating the anger," Edwards told *The New Yorker*. "I kept saying, 'Newt, attack the Democrats, don't attack Congress! It's the single main institution of American government.'" Edwards called Gingrich's rhetoric "a case of exaggerating. He oversimplified to the point of creating discontent with government, with the ability of Americans to govern themselves."[8]

Of course, Gingrich's solution is not to do away with Congress or the government but to have him run the show. He is not so much opposed to politics as he is opposed to politics practiced by anyone but himself. And he likes government just fine, so long as he is in charge of it. Unfortunately, he is not just some freebooter on the political fringe. He is the Speaker of the House—if now somewhat discredited due to scandal and sinking approval ratings—with a formidable (though ill-gotten) political organization still surrounding him.

Almost from the beginning, Gingrich has positioned himself as the leader of a new breed of Republican leaders, vehemently ideological, media savvy, ferocious, and uncompromising, making what he called "a third party," which shows that his loyalty is less to the Republicans than to his own cause. And ever since C-SPAN put the first camera in the House, and Gingrich pontificated to an empty assembly, he has been playing his radical blend of revolutionary conservativism to the media, and teaching his followers to do the same. In 1984, he told a group of conservative activists, "The number one fact about the news media is they love fights. You have to give them confrontations."[9] Unfortunately, Gingrich's fights are not the normal contests of democratic compromise and conciliation. He believes in total victory or total devastation and would rather paralyze the entire government than compromise his own agenda.

He has been training a whole generation of Republican politicians to follow his scorched-earth tactics. GOPAC, his political action committee that acted as fund-raiser, organizer, and political educator to the Republicans' class of 1994, is an organization fashioned after its leader. A series of audiotapes trained GOPAC candidates to think, act, and even talk like Newt. The GOPAC pols were taught a whole vocabulary of abusive rhetoric—words like *sick*, *traitors*, *corrupt*, *bizarre*, *cheat*, *steal*, *devour*, *self-serving*, and *criminal rights* were used to define Democrats.[10]

While Gingrich did ride the tiger of antipolitics to end 40 consecutive years of Democratic control of the House, it then turned around and bit him back. That is because antipolitics is akin to a parasite—ultimately, it kills itself by killing its host. In other words, if turned into a form of governance, it dies of its own contradictions. Antipolitics saw its ultimate form in the government shutdowns of 1995 and 1996. The impact was to make clear to Americans that there are many things government does that they like and rely upon in their daily lives, and that Gingrich's bomb-throwing approach to government and politics was not what they wanted in a national leader. While Gingrich barely held onto control after the 1996 elections, it was only by abandoning antipolitics for the type of mushy, moderate-sounding politics Gingrich used to deplore.

ANTIPOLITICS AND NEGATIVE SPOTS

It is one thing to attack a political opponent, something else entirely to attack politics itself. Unfortunately, these days, politics has become a dirty word. In the 1994 and 1996 elections, we saw an increasing number of ads attacking not merely individual candidates, but the institutions they served. Washington was seen as a wicked and distant place, out of touch with the rest of the country. The Capitol dome was used as "a symbol of corruption and government gone awry."[11] One Democratic political consultant said of the various graphic devices that were used to distort the Capitol's image: "It rattles, it shakes, it opens up, money is poured into it; it's clear that it's become demonized."[12] Republican consultant Frank Luntz said that outsider campaigns are so prevalent these days that "the best candidate of all would be an astronaut. He can say, 'I was floating in outer space the whole time.'"[13]

In Tennessee, in 1994, Republican Senate candidate Bill Frist linked experienced politicians with the criminal class, saying that he "supports term limits to stop career politicians, and the death penalty to stop career criminals." Frist unexpectedly unseated incumbent Democrat Jim Sasser in the election. Wearing the traditional plaid shirt, Washington lawyer-turned-actor Fred Thompson, running for the remainder of Al Gore's old Senate seat in Tennessee, said, "Congress is more the problem than the solution; they're out of touch and we're out of patience."

Even veteran Senator Bob Kerrey (D–Neb.) felt obliged to engage in antipolitical rhetoric. In one spot, he looked square into the camera and said, "The government is the most formidable enemy of all, sometimes."

There is a difference between running against your opponent and running against politics itself. Unfortunately, antipolitics has poisoned the well of democratic debate, so that almost every candidate feels it necessary to weigh in against the very institutions in which he or she wishes to serve. It is like going into a job interview and saying, "I have no respect for this company or its managers. I don't like what you do, and I don't like how you do it. But I want the job anyway." Unfortunately, in today's despairing political atmosphere, many of these can-

didates actually get elected, perpetuating what Jean Bethke
Elshtain calls the "spiral of delegitimation," as candidates gain
office on platforms of attack and negation, and arrive in Washington with no mandate from the voters and no faith in the
institutions in which they are about to serve.[14]

ANTIPOLITICS HIGH AND LOW

Antipolitics comes from two different schools, vastly dissimilar in tone and outlook, but which ultimately work together
to cripple our politics and demoralize the electorate. They can
be labeled high antipolitics and low antipolitics.

Low antipolitics is populism run amuck. It can be seen in
what is left of the term limits movement, where cynical leaders
and political neophytes rail against "career politicians" as if
politics were the one profession where experience was actually
a detriment. It is heard in the language of demagogues who rail
against Washington as if it were the foreign capital of some
nation with which we are at war. Americans' shaken faith in
government has been exploited by antipoliticians eager to gain
power in a system they profess to despise and promise to
dismantle. Some of these antipoliticians have served in public
office for years, but no matter, they are still committed to debasing our institutions, even the ones of which they are a part.

Low antipoliticians like Newt Gingrich often use the language of revolution, and they are indeed revolutionary, for they
want sweeping changes immediately; they are never satisfied
with compromise and do not attempt conciliation. They destroy
the bonds of democratic participation in two ways, by tearing
down the institutions of government, both rhetorically and
politically, and by creating a harsh and dogmatic tenor in our
public discourse, one that can only incite, and ultimately disap-
point, a people frustrated with business as usual and seeking
effective change in the way their country is governed. What
began as a healthy skepticism toward politics has degenerated

into an outright aggression toward government, which saw its most violent form of expression in the bombing of the federal building in Oklahoma City.

High antipolitics is progressivism run amuck. At the turn of the century, our politics needed reform. The parties were tightly controlled through patronage and graft, and voters had little real input, except for casting their ballots along party lines for preselected candidates. The progressives initiated a series of reforms that changed the way our country was run at all levels of government. From popular election of senators to declawing the tiger of Tammany Hall, progressive reforms gave us a democracy that better represented the will of the people.

However, from its inception the progressive movement had an aristocratic disdain for politics. Back when much of our politics was tightly controlled and inevitably corrupt, that disdain was somewhat understandable. Yet, what remains of the progressive impulse still has a whiff of the patrician, and it seems that many of those who would like to reform our politics do not really like politics in the first place.

High antipolitics can be seen today in many different forms: academic intellectuals, who construct exquisite political theories that share no understanding of how politics actually operates in the real world; news reporters, whose sneering "objectivity" keeps them from engaging in the issues, so they cover a political campaign as if it were a stakes race at Belmont Park; their colleagues in the opinion press, who rage, justifiably, about the content of public discourse and then suggest, unjustifiably, how to restrict or control its form; public interest groups, who seek to denude politics of all its rough-and-tumble aspects and turn our debate into sterile analyses of policy; sophisticated voters, who sit out elections, because no candidate meets all their exacting, and often contradictory, criteria.

High antipolitics is elitist. It is easily offended by the sometimes rugged and often unglamourous aspects of real-life politics. High antipolitics holds the voters in low regard, believing them to be, in the main, ignorant and easily manipulated. It has an unrealistic idea of what politics is and what it can achieve. Exalting individual virtue over the greater common good, high antipolitics would rather criticize than participate. High antipoliticians are the first to scream about negative campaigning and the last to actually get involved in campaigns themselves.

Both high and low antipoliticians like to state political questions, even relatively trivial ones, in terms of moral absolutes. This does not merely make solutions difficult but often makes politics itself impossible. John Bunzel put it this way: "When intricate political questions are reduced to simple moral ones, they are, in effect, put out of reach of practical solutions. The price that is paid is a deeper understanding of politics."[15] That is not to say morality has no place in politics—in fact, its increased presence is sorely needed—but when we approach issues such as tax policy in terms of absolutes ("Read my lips, no new taxes"), we make compromise, and thus governing, either impossible or tragic.

Antipoliticians want total conflict or none at all. Low antipolitics is by nature revolutionary, whereas high antipolitics wants our politics to be conducted like a tea party. But real politicians understand that conflict is inevitable, even integral to politics, and attempt to manage or ameliorate it. Low antipoliticians are dedicated solely to the ethic of ultimate ends— action is judged only by results. High antipoliticians are committed only to the ethic of responsibility—it is not so important what one does as how one does it. Both ethics, taken alone, are irreconcilable to democratic politics.

Antipolitics is irresponsible ideology of both the left and the right. Unsatisfied with the partial, gradual, and always incomplete successes of democratic compromise, antipoliticians hate politics, because it never gives them what they want, yet they still persist in it. Judge Learned Hand said: "The spirit of politics is the spirit which is not sure that it is right."[16] But irresponsible ideology, sure that it is right, attempts to transubstantiate the spirit of politics into the body of absolute certainty.

That is why antipoliticians do not have a sense of humor, at least, not about themselves. While they can mock and ridicule others, their own beliefs are no laughing matter.

Antipolitics polarizes and paralyzes democracy. In the end, we merely shout at each other across the great divide of ideological extremes; trying to achieve what we think is the only right outcome, we lose the chance of attaining the best possible good.

ANTIPOLITICS AND THE FUTURE OF DEMOCRACY

We are turning away from politics at a time when we need it most. With so many of the centrifugal forces of modern life pushing us farther and farther apart from each other, we need the centripetal forces of politics, especially election campaigns, to strengthen and restore our common bonds as citizens.

But that is not going to happen if the crude dynamic of antipolitics continues. We need to look at our government and its leaders in a new light, not through the treacly soft-focus of sentimentality, but with realistic expectations and a respect tempered by the understanding that they are our representatives, we have sent them to Washington to do a job, and their presence reflects our will. If anyone is to blame for the sorry state of our political system, it is all of us. Only when we stop pointing the finger at nefarious, invisible, and distant forces in Washington, and realize that in a democracy you get the government you deserve, can we make any real progress toward positive change.

Chapter 6

Poison Politics
and the Press

We have now looked at the role of "the spot" and antipolitics in contributing to poison politics. But those are not the only factors—not by a longshot. No examination of poison politics would be complete without an analysis of the changing role of the press and its impact on campaigning.

That is because politics is now played almost exclusively to the media. Consequently, the press has enormous power. In many ways, the press has taken over some of the traditional roles of political parties. It is more directly involved in the selection and election process than ever before. In decisions about how much air time or column inches to devote to individual candidates, it helps determine which ones are "electable" and whether personal or ethical problems are enough to derail their candidacy. A front-runner is given momentum by the press in the same way a favorite of the party bosses had a marked advantage over competitors. The press is often appealed to directly by candidates running outside of the party process, in the case of independents, or without the blessing of party leaders, in the case of outsider candidates.

As a source for political information, television news has clearly eclipsed the parties. According to Lichter and Noyes, two-thirds of Americans get most of their political information

67

from television news. Only 1 in 20 get their news from talking to other people, which was the standard method of political education back when the parties were dominant.[1] The two authors describe the media's influence over the political agenda this way: "No major event takes place in a presidential campaign whose format, substance, or effect is not influenced by whether or not major news organizations decide to cover it."[2]

You cannot win elective office without media attention. The press may not elect candidates, but it often decides who the contenders are. It also decides what the issues are by setting the political agenda. Unfortunately, the agenda is becoming increasingly mean-spirited and trivial, and for that, the news media share responsibility.

PACK AND ATTACK JOURNALISM

Contemporary journalism can be described as pack and attack. Pack journalism is basically beat journalism. Reporters are assigned to the White House or the State Department or Congress, or they follow the Vice-President or a front-running candidate. All the beat reporters get the same information; they speak to the same sources, attend the same briefings and press conferences, go to the same cocktail parties. There is little originality or investigation, and the news is mostly manufactured from the interested sources that the reporters rely on.

According to Stephen Hess of the Brookings Institute—one person to whom the pack turns when they want an "expert's" quote—Washington reporters do not use documents of any kind other than press releases in three-fourths of their stories. When they do use documents, one-third of those are other newspaper articles.[3] What they rely on most are interviews with sources, and these sources are usually interested parties, government officials, campaign aides, and advocacy groups, who all have specific agendas.

Who are journalists answerable to? Their producers and editors directly, and indirectly, the giant multinational corporations that own the broadcast networks, most cable channels and television stations, and the publishers who run the newspapers. Increasingly, this reflects itself in reporting designed—because of its emphasis on conflict, sensationalism, oversimplified choices, horse-race handicapping, and smug cynicism—to attract viewers and readers through entertainment rather than offering useful information to voters.

Attack journalism is not much different from attack ads, except that the press seems to think that it deserves a privileged position, right in the thick of things but, at the same time, above the fray. As Rich Galen, president of the American Campaign Academy, points out, "The columnists and reporters doing the complaining [about attack ads] often are the same people who break doors down in trying to report the story being told by negative ads."[4]

ADS AS NEWS

Political ads are a perfect source. They are partisan and often lively, even controversial. They are quotable, full of pre-packaged sound bites. They are objectively verifiable. They are a matter of public record. Often, they are the most interesting and sometimes the only information to come out of a campaign organization. For television journalism, they are packed with great visuals. It was only a matter of time before the press began using ads as sources and eventually as the subjects of news stories themselves.

Political campaigns take advantage of this by trying to make their ads into news stories. They unveil new ads in press conferences and make copies available to reporters. Those ads are often responded to, not just by other ads, but by other press conferences as well. The media report it all, happy with the controversy that will make for exciting, not to mention easy, news stories. Reporters can watch an ad, quote a few canned responses to it, find some other source to deplore it, and they have got a story. Journalist Tom Dworetzy wrote in *Omni* that "it's easier for a journalist like me to analyze an ad campaign in technical terms than to talk about the truth or wisdom of a political plan."[5]

Professor Darrell West of Brown University has studied television news stories about campaign ads, covering all of the CBS stories concerning political ads from 1972–1992. West found that, in general, "news reports generally placed much less emphasis on personal qualities, domestic performance, or specific policy statements than did the ads themselves."[6] And the news stories were more interested in negative than positive ads. According to West, 66 percent of the ads mentioned in news stories were negative, even though the ratio of positive to negative ads in campaigns is generally three to one. This not only reinforces the messages of the negative ads but gives voters the impression that negative messages predominate.

Press coverage of attack ads usually benefits the attackers, even when that coverage is critical. This is how Roger Ailes describes the process and a sophisticated consultant's strategy: "There are three things that the media are interested in: pictures, mistakes, and attacks.... If you need coverage, you attack, and you will get coverage."[7]

Being covered in the news makes a spot even more effective. As Ailes points out, "You get a 30 to 40 percent bump out of [an ad] by getting it on the news. You get more viewers, you get credibility, you get it in a framework."[8] All this, regardless of the critical commentary surrounding the ad.

On the *MacNeil–Lehrer NewsHour*, during the 1992 campaign, Democratic aide George Stephanopoulos and Republican advisor James Cicconi spent a full half-hour debating the various points raised by two ads that lasted a grand total of

90 seconds. Would we have been better served by a 30-minute debate on the issues?

TRUTH BOXES

After the trivial and ugly 1988 presidential campaign, the press decided that it would be more vigilant in its scrutiny of campaign advertisements. Many newspapers and television news programs instituted "ad watches" or "truth boxes" that analyzed campaign spots for accuracy and tone.

Although these features were initiated with the best intentions, they ran into some difficulties. Schooled in objective journalism based on source attribution, few ad analysts were willing to inject their own knowledge or perspective into their critiques. The result was something virtually identical to standard political reporting pegged on campaign advertisements.

Before truth boxes were first developed, the nascent form of media criticism was hampered by the method of sourcing traditional news stories, in which both sides are given equal weight, regardless of whether they deserve it. Writing in *Newsweek* after the 1988 election, Jonathan Alter pointed out:

> By almost any standard, Bush slung tons more mud than Dukakis, who for weeks was criticized for not fighting back. But misguided ideas of fairness required that reporters implicate both equally, lest they be seen as taking sides.... Fear of seeming slanted overcame any interest in reporting a larger truth.[9]

This "balance" only became more of a problem once truth boxes were formally instituted. For example, during the 1992 race, Richard Berke of the *New York Times* examined an ad by the Bush campaign that attacked Clinton on the credibility issue. First he described the visuals—a close-up of the *Time* magazine cover that read "Why Voters Don't Trust Clinton."

Then, he dutifully noted the producer, the November Company, and reprinted the script in full. In the section examining the spot's accuracy, Berke wrote: "The ad greatly oversimplifies Mr. Clinton's sometimes-contorted reasoning, but is not flatly inaccurate."

The rest of the article—and the longest single section—is spent analyzing the campaign tactics of the spot or simply recording each side's attempts at spin:

> The attack is in an area that many Republicans believe may be Mr. Clinton's most vulnerable.... some Republicans worry about detracting from the President's efforts to drive home his goals for the economy.... Clinton campaign officials said that they have already tested the ad with a research group of citizens and that it bombed. But Bush aides calculated that the ad would effectively complement the President's message during the blitz of debates this week.[10]

This truth box is little more than a standard election news article focusing on a single ad. Almost every statement is attributed, usually to anonymous and partisan sources, and the reporter is scrupulously evenhanded. But does it give us a new perspective on the ad?

Truth boxes rarely performed their most basic assumed responsibility: to correct factual errors or misrepresentations. As Lichter and Noyes write, "All too frequently, they simply replaced the campaigns' interpretations of ambiguous facts with their own."[11] And by focusing primarily on negative ads, they made the overall campaigns appear more negative and simply amplified the impact of negative ads instead of mitigating any pernicious effects.

Here is another truth box, same campaign, same newspaper, different reporter. Gwen Ifill (now with NBC News) took a look at a Clinton ad on the economy, in which the candidate's record as governor of Arkansas and plans for a tax on the rich, coupled with a vague promise for middle-class tax relief, are touted. Ifill investigated the accuracy of the ad by sourcing both camps.

> The Clinton campaign issued a flurry of documentation for the claims in this ad.... Officials of the Bush campaign said the ad emphasizes only the good news about Arkansas' record and Mr. Clinton's economic plan.[12]

Again, this truth box is little more than another campaign piece. Equivocation, anonymous sourcing, the Washington press pool two-step—it is all there.

A better example of campaign ad analysis was done by *The Times*'s Todd Purdum, who took a close look at the nasty race for senator between the incumbent Republican Alfonse D'Amato and Democratic challenger Robert Abrams. Instead of following the standard truth-box format of analyzing one ad in detail, Purdum looked at several spots, and rather than quoting them complete and verbatim, broke them down into four categories: claim, facts, distortion, and goal.

In the claims section, Purdum recounted the argument made in each spot. Then, he investigated the sources of the facts in the argument and pointed out the discrepancies or misleading information. Finally, he examined the goal of the spot in terms issue strategies, not campaign tactics. Here is Purdum's analysis of a D'Amato ad that claimed his opponent was soft on defense:

> Mr. D'Amato seeks to scare voters—especially middle-class and blue-collar workers like those on his home turf on Long Island—and persuade them that Mr. Abrams will hurt them. The attack also tars Mr. Abrams as soft on defense.[13]

Here is one of Purdum's examples of distortion: "Mr. D'Amato repeatedly accuses Mr. Abrams of planning to raise taxes, without specifying the purpose, leaving it to Mr. Abrams to respond that money would be for health insurance."[14] Finally, here is a quote from the introduction of the article, in which Purdum discusses some of the trash talk engaged in by both candidates:

> The distortions and side issues have surfaced in several
> different forms, including the use of code words, from Mr.
> D'Amato's sneering references to his rival as "hopelessly
> liberal" and "a sissy" who "deserted his people" to Mr.
> Abrams's calling Mr. D'Amato a "bully" and likening his
> campaign tactics to the Nazi "big lie" technique.[15]

Purdum was not afraid to inject his own analyses, draw his
own conclusions, and even state a few facts without attributing
them to sources. He was fair without being obsequious, evenhanded without resorting to equivocation, and tough without
being obnoxious.

Another example of effective campaign oversight by the
media comes from Florida during the 1986 Senate campaign.
Republican Paula Hawkins was running for reelection, and her
campaign produced an ad that featured the senator meeting
with President Reagan in the Oval Office. The ad went on to
suggest that Reagan had agreed to go along with a cost-of-
living increase in Social Security only after the personal inter-
cession of Hawkins. The *Miami Herald* (this was two years prior
to its much less exemplary stakeout of Gary Hart and Donna
Rice) ran a story headlined "Spot Doesn't Tell the Whole Story,"
which pointed out that the increase had passed two months
prior to Hawkins's meeting with the president. Hawkins's opponent, Bob Graham, was not spared either. The *Herald* ran a
story on page one that reprinted a letter from the commandant
of the United States Coast Guard asking Graham to stop using a
campaign ad that showed Coast Guard personnel in it.

This is the kind of journalism that is needed if the press is
going to become an effective critic of campaign advertising.
Whether campaigners would listen is another matter entirely,
but, at least, the critique would be part of public record. Unfortunately, ad watchers are often unwilling to submit material to
tough and critical analysis. CNN's Brooks Jackson is an intelligent, perceptive, and acute critic—as he was in analyzing
campaign finance for the *Wall Street Journal* prior to joining the
electronic media. But there are too few others. As Leo C.

Wolinsky, an editor of the *Los Angeles Times*, remarked, "Debunking commercials proved a more complex and subtle task than had been envisioned."[16]

SETTING THE AGENDA

The press began criticizing campaign ads, because it felt that negative campaigning had gotten out of hand, and therefore they needed to assert more control over the campaign messages. They were half-right. Negative campaigning has gotten out of control, but the press is not going to make things any better by simply struggling to control the agenda. It already has too much influence over every aspect of our political campaigns, without any corresponding responsibility.

Nowhere is this struggle for control more clearly illustrated than the case of the shrinking sound bite. Kiku Adatto of Harvard's Barone Center made a study of sound bites on network news programs that shows the average length of a politician's quote decreasing from 45 seconds in 1968 to 9 seconds in 1988. Further studies by the Center for Media and Public Affairs show the sound bite has shrunk even further, to an average of 7.3 seconds. This incredible shrinking debate is in part due to what appears to be an ever-decreasing national attention span, but it is also a result of the struggle between the candidates and the news media over control of the agenda.

Adatto remarked that

> [t]he more the campaigns sought to control the images that appeared on the nightly news, the more the reporters tried to beat them at their own game, to deflate their media events by magnifying a minor mishap into a central feature of the event itself.[17]

Not letting the candidates speak for themselves means journalists have more airtime to voice their own opinions. Adatto writes that "political reporters began to sound like theater critics, reporting more on the stagecraft than the substance of politics."[18] As Lichter and Noyes point out, "Short sound bites are a mechanism that allow the reporters, not the candidates, to have the final say."[19]

While the press and politicians fight over a few precious seconds of air time, public debate is diminished or even disregarded.

FRONT-RUNNERS AND THE BIG MO

Part of the media's agenda-setting power is their ability to decide which candidates are viable and push the forces of electoral momentum either for or against them. This certainly is not a conscious decision. Reporters do not get together in hotel bars on the campaign trail and agree to build one candidate up while knocking another one down. But the pressures of having to come up with exciting stories often result in just that.

Instead of focusing on the issues, the media like to report on the horse-race elements of a campaign. Lichter and Noyes's analysis of the 1988 early primaries—the last time both nominations were open—showed that "news about the strength or prospects of each candidacy was the focus of nearly 70 percent of all campaign stories between Iowa and New Hampshire."[20] And they found that more than one-third of *all* primary news coverage focused on those two early contests, giving these small states enormous political leverage, and creating a primary system that favors high-profile and well-financed front-runners. Focus on the competitive elements rather than the issues, particularly this early in the campaign, has an enormous impact on shaping the dynamics of the race itself. During this time, front-runners are created largely by the media, before a single voter has cast a ballot, and then these leading candidates have to live up to media expectations or else they suffer symbolic losses, even if they win.

In the 1984 Democratic primaries, Walter Mondale was the clear front-runner. As former vice-president and veteran senator, his status within the party was preeminent. Before the primaries even started, the press had grown bored with what seemed to be an uncompetitive race. So when Gary Hart made a surprising second-place showing in the Iowa caucuses with 16 percent of the vote, suddenly he was the candidate of the moment. Never mind that Mondale won the contest with 49 percent, a high plurality for an early primary. The media had decided that Mondale's victory was actually a loss, and they started giving Hart vastly increased, and mostly positive, coverage. He then beat Mondale in the New Hampshire primary by 37 to 28 percent and seemed to be on his way to a possible upset.

But the media giveth and the media taketh away. Once Hart became a significant candidate, he soon suffered harsh critical scrutiny. And when he did not meet the newly created media expectations in a series of primaries, suddenly his balloon burst, and Mondale went on to a fairly easy victory.

Another candidate, Jesse Jackson, made strong showings in both the 1984 and 1988 primaries. But the media, while lavishing attention on him because of his oratorical skills, never took him seriously as a contender, and he was considered more of a colorful novelty rather than a serious aspirant to high political office. While not explicitly racist, this treatment of candidate Jackson reflects implicitly racist assumptions of the society at large—that a black candidate can never be elected president, or even seriously considered for vice-president.

Front-runner journalism also hinders the fund-raising efforts of challengers. The perception of viability, or better yet, inevitability, is literally money in the bank, as contributors eagerly give to front-runners and are unwilling to support a candidate who the media do not think has a chance. This is a vicious circle—the press uses a candidate's ability to raise money as a measuring stick in deciding whom to cover, but without ample coverage, it is hard to raise money. So, without engaging in a conscious conspiracy, the media play a significant role in deciding who gets elected.

If reporters focused more on the issues rather than the horse-race aspects of a campaign, they would not have such enormous power in deciding which candidates are viable, and creating both momentum and expectations for front-runners and challengers. Before sitting down to write an article or produce a story, journalists should ask themselves: What information can I provide that would help a voter make an intelligent, informed decision? Perhaps then the Fourth Estate would begin to fulfill its role as sentinel of democracy.

HORSE-RACE JOURNALISM

Horse-race journalism does not just affect the campaigns and who gets elected. It also has an ill effect on the business of government itself.

Matthew Robert Kerbel points out that the same forces that govern campaign coverage apply to policy reporting as well. "[T]he media approach governance as if it were electoral politics, applying the same horse race-oriented, character-based, scandal-laden coverage standards to news about policy and development."[21] Issues such as healthcare, Medicare, and the budget are discussed in terms of who is winning and who is losing, and which groups stand to benefit from which political outcome, rather than how our country and its citizens would be affected by such change.

Journalists tend to see politics as competition rather than common endeavor. Political conflict, essential to democratic governance, is portrayed as turmoil or controversy. Describing policy as politics, the media forget the larger aims of political figures. Journalists speculate on who will win a certain struggle in Congress, rather than fleshing out the issues that animate the debate.

Anita Dunn sees this as a natural outgrowth of horse-race campaign journalism. "The American political process has evolved into one in which government is seen as a continuance of the campaign, rather than the campaign being seen as a part of the dialogue of governance."[22] So, for example, in the 1988 election, we heard a great deal about the Republican campaign strategy and the Democrats' lack of one, but the looming savings-and-loan scandal—and its exorbitant cost to taxpayers—was never discussed.

So, instead of important information about the issues that affect their lives, mass media audiences only get tactical discussions about the political process. The result is an electorate that—unless it seeks out information from other sources—is inevitably less informed than it needs to be in order to fully participate in our democracy.

Here is just one example of that knowledge deficit: A poll taken by Luntz Research found that while 59 percent of Americans can name the Three Stooges, only 17 percent can name three Supreme Court Justices. Justice John Paul Stevens, a 20-year veteran of the Court, was named by only 1 percent of respondents, the same percentage that could name Justice Stephen Breyer, the newest member of the Court. Clarence Thomas was named by 30 percent responding, such high recognition due to media exposure during his tabloid-scandal confirmation hearings.[23]

But ignorance is only one side effect of horse-race journalism. Today's journalists do give the voters a thorough education—in political cynicism. Reviewing scholarly research on the subject, Robert Lichter and Richard Noyes of the Center for Media and Public Affairs found that "voters tend to reflect the language and agenda of journalists who cover politics." Voters are more aware of candidates' positions in the horse race than their stand on the issues. "Increasing numbers cast their votes not with an eye toward each candidate's relative merits, but with a strategic sense of each candidate's viability." This might be useful if politics was a betting sport, but since voters are the *players* in a democracy, not gamblers or spectators, such journalism is a disservice. Lichter and Noyes conclude that "journalists aren't training citizens to become better voters. Instead they are training them to think about politics as journalists do—cynically and superficially."[24]

Horse-race journalism gives news reporters the illusion of professional objectivity. If, instead of discussing such subjective topics as issues, personalities, and ideas, they talk simply of who is ahead and who is behind, they can maintain a certain detachment. Ironically, though, the evaluation of who is ahead and who is behind *is* subjective until the votes have been cast.

Reporters do not want to seem naive or unsophisticated to their colleagues, both in the media and on the campaign staffs. The result is a jaded insider's perspective that casts all workings of government in a jaundiced light.

Rather than having a pronounced liberal or conservative bias, the press seems to have an antipolitical bias. They are "equal opportunity destroyers," as Barbara Matusow so aptly put it.[25] Journalists are not just reflecting the increasing cynicism and distrust throughout society, they are also contributing to it.

Thus does the media contribute to antipolitics.

Some journalists recognize the media's role in this vicious circle of cynicism. When he stepped down from the *MacNeil– Lehrer NewsHour* after 20 years of substantive and responsible television journalism, Robert MacNeil said,

> [J]ournalists are citizens of this country. I feel myself as a journalist, not somebody who stands on the sides watching the idiots screw it up. Every journalist in this country has a stake in the democratic institutions working, and I think institutions of democracy are worth taking seriously.

Unfortunately, if their reporting is any indication, such attitudes are not shared by many of his former colleagues. MacNeil acknowledged that "it's a very old-fashioned, corny view."[26]

TELLING TALES

In the media, news events are told as stories. And the narrative form has certain rules—a story must have a beginning, a middle, and an end. Almost from the start, television news has been fashioned to fit into an exciting yet tidy narrative, letting form dictate content. In a 1963 memo to his staff on the launch of their 30-minute network news program, Reuven Frank, then executive producer of the *NBC Evening News*, described the essentials of a good news story:

> Every news story should, without any sacrifice of probity or responsibility, display the attributes of fiction, of drama. It should have a structure and conflict, problem and denouement, rising action and falling action, a beginning, a middle and an end. These are not only the essentials of drama; they are the essentials of narrative.[27]

Not only do these rules still apply to television journalism, but now they also seem to be the only rules that do apply, and Frank's important qualification that the story not sacrifice "probity or responsibility" has often been ignored.

With the demands of ever-higher profits and the needs of entertainment outweighing the responsibility of public service, television news has been turned into one big shouting match, as journalists go for the easy drama of raging controversy instead of trying to explain the important details of our public life in a way that we can appreciate and understand. So many politicians talk trash these days because that is what gets them on television. Detailed, reasoned, and responsible debate just is not entertaining enough.

In a speech to the National Press Club, James Baker related how the network news refused to cover a policy address by then-Vice-President and candidate George Bush because, as a producer told him: "You didn't have any sound bites, and you didn't attack Dukakis." Baker said that any substantial messages from candidates "is too often lost in the noise."[28] In response to such criticisms, television journalists simply explain yet again the technological demands of their media, as if they had nothing to do with its content. "It frankly makes better television when they beat up on each other," explains Carl Cameron, who, as political reporter for New Hampshire's only statewide television station, is, for several months every four years, one of the most powerful journalists in the business.[29]

To be sure, candidates and campaigns are responsible for their messages, but the media has a powerful effect on how those messages are shaped. As Lichter and Noyes write of journalists, "Their *modus operandi* are *intended* to distort reality—to make it more condensed, interesting, understandable, and dramatic." [emphasis in original][30] This distortion is not going to stop unless the journalists take a close and honest look at their increasing power over the terms and content of the debate, critically reexamine their priorities, and finally assume the responsibilities that should be demanded of a responsible media in a democratic society.

But so long as news is judged only as a means by which to attract advertisers, we will have a trivialized and mean-spirited political discourse. Substantive discussion is being crowded out by trash talk and scandal, and the supposedly "serious" news programs are increasingly resembling their tabloid colleagues. (The most telling example was the juxtaposition of the O. J. Simpson civil trial verdict with President Clinton's 1997 State of the Union address.) Even a relatively in-depth and journalistically responsible show like Ted Koppel's *Nightline* gets higher ratings when he is interviewing Jim Bakker rather than Jim Baker. Those who own and operate the media do not see any difference between news and entertainment; in fact, they simply view news as just another form of entertainment, slightly dull and bound by the ever-loosening standards of truth and accuracy, but entertainment first and last. Indeed, they require news operations to be profit centers, rather than treat them as a public service to be performed in exchange for the right to use a public resource—the broadcast spectrum—to make bucketloads of money the other 23½ hours per day they broadcast.

In 1966, Fred Friendly quit his position as president of CBS News because the network insisted on showing the fifth rerun of an episode of *I Love Lucy* instead of a crucial Senate hearing on the Vietnam War. Today's networks have apparently solved the dilemma of providing either entertainment or information by making the two virtually indistinguishable from each other. Serious issues are discussed in sitcoms and movies of the week; tabloid television news magazines such as *Dateline NBC* interview celebrities, exploit human tragedy, and manufacture "news"; the political events of the day are turned into a soap opera.

The confusion of information and entertainment has crippled our public debate and made our political rhetoric both more cruel and more infantile. Every night, the network newscasts go up against *Jeopardy* and reruns of *Roseanne* in the continuous and often brutal fight over ratings. Quality newspapers compete with tabloids for a dwindling number of newspaper readers. Except for the dim voice of civility inhabiting a narrow frequency at the left end of the dial, radio is filled with pop music and angry talk-show hosts. The media are going tabloid.

THE TABLOIDING OF THE NEWS

Tabloid shows are cheap to produce and make a great deal of money. *A Current Affair* costs about $260,000 per week to produce and brings in $850,000 in revenues. Serious news operations are slightly more expensive and less profitable. Still, for today's competitive media conglomerates, that is too high a price to pay for public service. So, they try to make the news shows more like the tabloids. What results is a Gresham's Law of broadcasting, where bad programming crowds out good programming.

At the same time that news programs began to resemble tabloid shows, the tabloid shows themselves started challenging the news shows on their own turf.

In the 1970s, President Carter's mother Lillian appeared on *Donahue*, where she asked her host: "I don't wear an IUD, I'm not a homosexual, and I don't smoke pot—just what am I going to talk about?"[31] It took some time for Phil to become a seriously considered broadcast journalist, but in the 1992 campaign, he was able to hector Bill Clinton about his sex life, a line of questioning the candidate quickly stopped. A woman in the audience complained: "I can't believe you spent a half an hour of airtime attacking this man's character."[32] In order to seem at least fair, Donahue asked Clinton's opponent Jerry Brown the same questions. Brown responded: "If you want to know, do I go out with girls, yes I do."[33] After increasing criticism from both candidates, the establishment press, and his own audience, Donahue set up one of the more substantive (yet still lively) debates of the campaign between Clinton and Brown. (The irony here is that the now-retired Donahue looks like Edward R. Murrow compared to the Ricki Lakes and Jenny Joneses of TV land.)

As tabloid shows and tabloid values increasingly dominate politics, the very language and images of scandal become prevalent in political discourse. On the *McLaughlin Group*, a show that has raised shrill discourse to an art form, Fred Barnes stated: "If NAFTA goes down, President Clinton will be in, metaphorically speaking, the same condition John Bobbitt was in after the attack"[34] Appearing on MTV, President Clinton was asked the question the whole world was dying to know: "Is it boxers or briefs?"

His wife has certainly not been spared the tabloid treatment. Commenting on CNBC, Sally Quinn compared the First Lady to the figure-skating queens of then-current tabloid fame: "She's either got to be Tonya or Nancy." The *New York Post*, a tabloid paper that has achieved national prominence and even some respectability, despite its hysterical headlines and often irresponsible news standards, said that Hillary was "starting to resemble an Ozark Leona Helmsley."[35] Even when they want to say something good about her, the denizens of tabloid land cannot help but be crude and insulting. This is how Larry King discussed his interview with Hillary in *USA Today*: "She was funny, charming, sexy—yes, gang, sexy. We are both Scorpios, which tells you a lot."[36]

By turning serious news into tabloid scandal, politics has been reduced to merely another story line in our national soap opera. Thus, the bitter, personality-driven conflict that underlies most soap operas (who shot J. R.?) permeates—and poisons—politics as well. Who is to blame for this deplorable state of affairs? Certainly the media professionals who decide what is news are responsible for their portrayal of information and events. But could the problem with contemporary journalism be more deeply rooted in media technology—specifically television—itself?

Chapter 7

The Video Culture

Dr. Oliver Sacks was making his rounds one night when he heard a roar of laughter from the aphasia ward. He did not know what was going on in there, though he did remember that President Reagan was about to make one of his televised speeches that night. He looked into the television room, and there were his patients, racked with laughter as the President spoke with his characteristic charm and sincerity on a subject of great importance.

These patients were brain-damaged. They could not make sense of words, but they understood voice tone and emphasis, body language, and all the other sense perceptions that accompany speech communication. So they were hypersensitive to the "feeling-tone" of the president's speech. This is what the Great Communicator was supposed to be so skilled at, those little gestures and inflections that made voters love him even if they disagreed with his policies, or, in other words, the content of his speech. But the aphasiacs were not buying it. They found Reagan so patently bogus that he made them laugh out loud.

Sacks, a professor of clinical neurology, who is also the author of several best-selling books (and was portrayed by Robin Williams in the movie *Awakenings*), believes that you cannot lie to aphasiacs. When they heard the president's speech, "it was the false grimaces, the histrionisms, the false gestures and, above all, the false tones and cadences of the voice, which rang false to these wordless but immensely sensitive patients."[1] In other words, it was precisely Reagan's alleged acting talents that tripped off their BS detectors. And they reacted, as we often react to that which is sincere yet unauthentic, with laughter.

However, one patient in the ward was not laughing. Emily D., a former English teacher, had "an exceptional feeling for language, and strong powers of analysis and expression."[2] But she also suffered from total agnosia, meaning she only understood the literal meanings of words, without any of the sensory nuances that were so acutely developed in the other patients. She could not recognize any emotion in a person's voice, and when she heard words, they were mere prose. As the aphasiacs compensated for their lack of literal understanding with razor-sharp sense perception, Emily's literal understanding was enhanced by her lack of sense perception. She paid extremely close attention to the words that were being uttered. So, when she listened to the President's speech, she sat there stony faced and unmoved. " 'He is not cogent,' she said. 'He does not speak good prose. His word use is improper. Either he is brain-damaged, or he has something to conceal.' "[3]

If President Reagan could not fool the brain-damaged, how could he put it over the rest of us? As Dr. Sacks puts it: "We normals—aided, doubtless, by our wish to be fooled—were indeed well and truly fooled."[4]

Leaving aside the troubling questions that this anecdote raises about the eight-year national daydream known as the Reagan years, and whether we as a country were not well and truly fooled, what does this anecdote say about television?

A common assumption is that television is poisoning American politics and culture; that it turns us into a nation of couch potatoes who spend every waking hour tuned in to the "plug-in drug"; that it brainwashes us into being docile consumers, violent psychopaths, sexual perverts, and, finally, vapid voters who can no longer make informed political decisions. How true are these assumptions? Could it be possible, as illustrated in the Sacks story, that television can actually present a vivid and accurate picture of reality—more vivid and more accurate in ways than other forms of representation?

Of course, television is being used, particularly in attack ads, for poison politics. However, as I have argued previously, blaming the medium is akin to blaming the car for drunk driving. Television is a powerful technology that has, for the most part, failed to live up to its potential and its promise, because it has too often been "driven" by those with the same sense of social responsibility of a drunk driver.

WORDS AND IMAGES

Critics of television often complain that the video culture is replacing the written culture, and although they are right in saying that people should watch less television and read more, the argument is often overstated.

The word is essential to our understanding of the world around us and the world inside our heads, but so, too, are images. The power of visual images has literally reshaped our world, and television has been the major agent of that transformation. The Vietnam War was being reported by print journalists for years, but once television cameras started sending pictures home, public attitudes toward the conflict changed. For years, cases of police brutality often came down to the victim's word against the blue wall of silence, until George Holliday crawled out of bed to videotape Los Angeles Police Department officers clubbing Rodney King. The collapse of both communism and apartheid was dramatically aided and abetted by the technology of the global village. Television is not just a powerful medium but also an essential one. In many ways, visual images give us a larger dimension of the truth (as we saw in the Sacks story, television can be an effective BS detector).

The word and the image do not necessarily contradict each other, nor do they stand for different values, or even different eras in history. Instead, they should be used together, as we use all our senses together, to compose a full perception of life. Together, words and images can give us a clearer idea of the truth. And the medium best suited for combining words and images is television.

Television is a tool, a very powerful tool, and one that we should use with care, even caution. But it is only as good or bad as the uses to which it is put. And, unfortunately, it is currently being operated in a way that frequently contributes to the poisoning of our politics and culture.

THE VAST WASTELAND

Addressing a convention of television broadcasters in 1961, Newton Minow, then chairman of the Federal Communication Commission, gave his complacent audience the following challenge:

> I invite you to sit down in front of your television set when your station goes on the air and stay there without a book, magazine, newspaper, profit-and-loss sheet or rating book to distract you—and keep your eyes glued to that set until the station goes off. I can assure you that you will observe a vast wasteland.[5]

Minow was describing television at the end of its "Golden Age," when documentaries by Edward R. Murrow and Fred Friendly shared the airwaves with dramas written by Paddy Chayevsky and Gore Vidal. Since his speech, the wasteland has only grown vaster. Television is no longer run by "broadcasters"—the three networks are owned by the giant multinational corporations General Electric, Disney, and Westinghouse; most of cable television is divided up among these three, the Time/Warner/Turner conglomerate, Australian tabloid baron Rupert Murdoch, and TCI. Thus, television has been corrupted and abused by the same economic and corporate forces that have poisoned our environment, turned our forests into deserts, abused and exploited workers, shipped jobs overseas, and otherwise squandered and destroyed our great national resources. By valuing short-term profits over long-term responsibilities, television's corporate officers have kept the medium from realizing its true potential as a positive force in our world.

The first image ever broadcast on a television screen was a picture of the dollar sign. In 1927, Philo Farnsworth demonstrated his new invention by showing that symbol for 60 seconds, in effect, the first television commercial. Since then, commercial television has extended that legacy through thousands of hours of programming which, despite its wide variety of topics, has all been geared toward one thing—selling an audience to advertisers.

Television stations sell programming to the viewers and, in turn, sell the viewers to advertisers. This process is efficient and to a certain degree democratic—television does not have any direct or immediate costs to the viewer. However, the commercial imperative of television, *unrestrained by public interest or government regulation*, has created a system of communications so depraved and revolting that its critics commonly assume the technology itself must be inherently evil. But the culprit is not the technology of television; rather, it is those who own and operate it.

With few exceptions, television executives are concerned with profits and stock prices, and could not give a damn about any broader public responsibility. This is not some hidden or subconscious agenda; it is explicit corporate policy, no different from the way other businesses operate, and it is often expressed in crude terms by television executives themselves. Arnold Becker, vice-president for research at CBS, said,

> I'm not interested in culture. I'm not interested in pro-social values. I have only one interest. That's whether people watch the program. That's my definition of good, that's my definition of bad.[6]

David Sarnoff, the former head of NBC, "defined 'public inter-est' as whatever the public chooses to watch on television."[7] And Frank Stanton, late of CBS, said, "A program in which a large part of the audience is interested is by that very fact … in the public interest."[8]

Obviously, if television was not profitable, no one would broadcast, and as a businessperson myself, I am certainly not going to argue that there is anything wrong with making money. However, communications is in many ways distinct from other forms of commerce and should be treated with greater respect and responsibility. Information is not just an-other commodity, and its use has a profound impact beyond just its interest value to an audience. It forms the substance of our public and, to some degree, private lives. Television is the primary source of information in our society, for better and for worse. And much of this information is vital. Unfortunately, our democratic debate is being treated by corporate television as either a profitless obligation it would sooner be rid of, or as something to be metamorphosed into entertainment in order to make more money. It is hard to say which attitude is worse.

Television is a semimonopoly, and even with the growth of cable, ownership is growing even more concentrated. The broadcast networks divide up the huge national market among themselves, offering only slightly different versions of the same, largely unimaginative product. Major market stations often operate in the same manner, much like the trusts of the Gilded Age, protecting their shared monopoly and then fight-ing like hell among themselves to increase profits. These sta-tions are licensed by the government and make free use of an invaluable public resource—the broadcast spectrum—with very little public obligation attached to that enormously prof-itable privilege.

The same day that Newton Minow described "the vast wasteland," President Kennedy also spoke to the broadcasters' convention. And his words, although less critical, emphasized the great responsibility of public trust placed in the hands of those assembled:

> The flow of ideas, the capacity to make informed choices, the ability to criticize, all of the assumptions on which political democracy rests, depend largely on communications. And you are the guardians of the most powerful and effective means of communication ever designed.[9]

How do the owners of television stations respond to this vast beneficence and great public trust? By assaulting their audience with words and images of breathtaking vulgarity, by appealing not only to the lowest common denominator, but also to people's worst instincts. Flip through the various offerings on commercial television and you will see an endless parade of idiocy, greed, perversion, and violence. And it shows few signs of improvement; indeed, most indications are that television is only getting worse.

As mergers occur like rabbits in reverse and the means of communication are owned by a shrinking number of companies, television and other media will only become more vulgar and more trivial. While the technological capabilities of television have been expanded beyond the wildest fantasies of Philo Farnsworth, his original idea that television could be an enormously profitable commercial venture has become not just the dominant ethos, but also the sole motivating factor in programming.

Giddy futurists such as Newt Gingrich and his technoguru George Gilder keep proclaiming how new developments in television and telecommunications will solve all our problems. Their predictions are not just silly, but dangerous, since they form the core argument for a deregulated marketplace. What difference will 200, 500, even 1,000 television channels make if they are all owned by Rupert Murdoch and Michael Eisner? The same corporate and economic pressures will prevail, and we will simply have more, much more, of the same sleazy trash.

Right now there are some 11,000 cable systems in the United States, but only seven companies own 60 percent of the total cable market.[10] So much for a diversity of views in the free market of information.

Cable television is a sad example of a new technology failing to live up to its promise because of corporate greed and government inaction. Eager to win lucrative monopoly contracts in new markets, the cable corporations promised substantial commitments to local programming. However, many companies soon began renegotiating their contracts to reduce what they felt were costly obligations, whereas others simply neglected their public-service promises. The reckless deregulation of the cable industry has diminished community control over cable systems. The result has often been higher cable fees, combined with diminished public access and other community services. Now cable is filled with reruns and idiot movies, home shopping, and other smarmy sales pitches. And while there is now potential for competition among local cable providers, and telephone companies can start getting into the business, it remains to be seen whether this will give consumers real alternatives and lower prices, or whether it will just lead to cable companies buying telephone companies and vice versa.

Perhaps the most illustrative—and scary—development in the cable industry is the incredible shrinking of C-SPAN, the one place where citizens are guaranteed to learn about how their government works and what it is doing, free from analysis, commentary, and cynical spin. The *Washington Post* reported that over the past four years, C-SPAN and C-SPAN2 have been eliminated or reduced to part-time status in cable companies serving 5.2 million households. This is due primarily to corporate greed. For example, other channels such as the Fox News Network pay local cable systems to get on the air so operators will pick them up and make room by dropping C-SPAN. Then we have Time/Warner's increased domination of the industry since its buyout of Turner Broadcasting (whose for-profit CNN is something of a competitor to the nonprofit

C-SPAN). The Federal Trade Commission forced Time/Warner–owned local cable systems to run a competing news service to CNN, so they added MS-NBC (here we have another monopoly, Microsoft) and dropped C-SPAN in exchange. And another giant cable operator, TCI, dropped C-SPAN from 40 systems. Of note, in more than a few instances, this occurred so that TCI could add cable channels in which it has a financial stake.[11]

As C-SPAN President Brian Lamb said,

> In recent years over-the-air television has basically made its news operation into entertainment. So as they become more and more entertaining, it's more and more important that you have some place to go where you can get the basics—and, in our case, long-form television which covers the political system.
>
> Congressional legislation in '92 and '96 changed the economics of the cable business. On occasion the cable industry looks for ways to improve their bottom line and we don't make money for anyone. We're the only network that doesn't…. So on those occasions where we have been either dropped or cut back it's because of money.[12]

It does not have to be this way. The success of C-SPAN shows that community programming does not have to be high tech or high budget. It does not cost much to put a camera in a city council meeting or to arrange a talk show on local issues or a debate among political candidates. However, as long as cable companies view public access and community programming as contractual obligations that must be fulfilled with the minimum of expense, instead of as their responsibility to the society that allows them to earn exorbitant profits, then the promise of cable will remain hollow. And as long as cable systems are owned by a few companies competing for an ever-growing profit margin, then the larger public obligations are bound to be neglected. A small but dedicated investment in public programming may seem to be an outlay with no visible return, but, in fact, companies will eventually profit by sustaining an active and involved community.

The same holds for broadcasters as well. In many ways, communication franchises are entitlements, hugely profitable, many legally protected from competition and virtually immune to regulation of content. Yet, the operators of these franchises are unwilling to give back to the communities from which they are reaping great profits. It is time for television executives to recognize and act upon their broader public responsibilities, not only in creating more quality programming, but also by using the powerful technology of television to encourage and support democratic participation.

More than just distorting or ignoring the public debate, television has become a powerful force with a profound impact not only on the transmission of words and images, but also reality itself. Just one example of this phenomenon can be seen in the local news programs of many major cities, where parent companies are ordering the downsizing of news organizations, not because they do not make a profit, but because they do not make one that executives feel is big enough. As a result, news teams are cut down to a handful of mobile units, and in order to cover enough events to fill the hour-long time slot, they simply appear at several crime scenes and report on the latest acts of violence and depravity, mostly in poor communities. The only exceptions are during sweeps months, when elaborate, week-long specials on sensationalistic subjects, designed to scare or titillate viewers but having virtually no news value, are produced. That is much more cost-effective than putting a crew on the city council for an entire day to try and make sense of a complicated bond issue. It is also a whole lot sexier and easier to spike ratings by showing graphic reports exploiting human tragedy. The result is not only vulgar programming—worthy of the new "TV14" rating at a minimum —but also vulgarized audiences, who, since their primary source of information is television, are led to believe that crime is rampant, that they are not safe on the streets, and finally, that the world is a violent and ugly place. Soon they behave accordingly, either acting in a violent and ugly manner themselves or simply hiding behind locked doors, watching more television. More about that later.

The mass media's ability not just to portray reality, but in some ways to create it, is a force that must be controlled either by regulation or competition, or a mixture of both. Without a responsible media, we are in big trouble as a society, and the growing monopolization of the means of communication is only making an already deplorable situation worse.

TELEVISION AND POLITICS

Democracy is based on information. Representative, elective government developed only once there were adequate means of transmitting information through books, pamphlets, newspapers, and personal correspondence. Two hundred years ago, Americans communicated solely through printed material that had to be physically delivered to its destination. It took over a week for a message to get from Boston to Washington. The battle of New Orleans was fought long after the War of 1812 was over, due to the fact that no one there knew an armistice had been signed. Technological change has made communication easier, more accurate, and more effective, allowing our government to develop into a truer and more representative system as the means of political communication became accessible to more citizens.

Television is just one phase of this development, but an important phase, and one that has already had both a positive and a negative impact on democracy. But if television only lived up to a fraction of its promise, our public life would be much healthier.

Television can inform the electorate. Compared with voters 100, or even 50 years ago, the electorate is much better educated, more politically sophisticated, and more able to make decisions based on information rather than ignorance.

When American politics was controlled by party bosses, voters did as they were told. Political choices were made on political terms, narrowly defined, such as patronage, fealty to the ward boss or party leader, or class interest. Leaders were chosen in back rooms, and voters had no voice in the nominating process. Voter turnout was high, but that was in a large part due to the pressures applied by party activists and the fact that, for many, the election was the most exciting event of the year.

Today, most voters make their decisions based on the information, both substantive and symbolic, that they receive mostly from television. Much of this information is incomplete, irrelevant, even degrading. But a lot of it is relevant, even essential, and the voters are making their decisions based on deliberation rather than blind loyalty. To say that commercial television is an imperfect means of conveying political information is an understatement, but in many ways, it is better than the saloons and "social clubs" where most political education once took place.

Television can make politics more honest. C-SPAN has cameras covering every minute of the House and Senate sessions, and many committee meetings. Television has taken politics out of the back rooms and into our living rooms. Decisions are now made in full view of the public, and while the horse trading and arm twisting that animates the political process has not been completely eliminated, it has at least been subjected to a more rigorous scrutiny. But too much of the coverage of our democratic institutions is overmediated, as the messengers have become more important than the message itself.

Television can make democracy more democratic. By creating a direct feedback loop of information, voters and their leaders could be more plugged in to each other. Voters would be better informed and more involved. Politicians would be more aware of their constituents not just during the election cycle, but also throughout the political season. Rather than being an inherently conspiratorial or manipulative technology, television has the ability to be a profoundly democratic technology, if only we would use it correctly. Unfortunately, too much of the political message these days is as ugly and trivial as most everything else on television.

LIGHT AND WIRES IN A BOX

When it was first developed, television showed an almost limitless potential. And in many ways, it has failed in delivering that promise. Right now, television is dumbing down democracy, creating a false picture of reality, and dispiriting an already cynical populace. And unless we make some serious changes, things are only going to get worse.

Ronald Reagan's TV America

The presidency of Ronald Wilson Reagan was an escape into the realm of fantasy and delusion, in which the problems that faced our country were quietly ignored while we celebrated our hollow triumphs, such as an economic expansion that benefited those who needed it least, the barely successful execution of a war against a tiny Caribbean island, and an Olympics in which our chief competitors stayed home.

In the first years of Reagan's presidency, the country experienced the worst recession since the Great Depression itself. Then, both the economy and Reagan's approval ratings began to rise, but he still faced what most political observers anticipated would be a tough reelection battle. Even though the national mood was buoyant, there were still significant social, economic, and political problems. In his reelection bid, Reagan campaigned hard against the Democrats and against reality. He won on both counts.

The 1984 election has been remembered for soft-focus ads extolling America's return to greatness, particularly the series of schmaltzy spots known as "Morning Again in America." In fact, Reagan ran a tough campaign, with lots of

continued

negative ads. But he let his surrogates and other supporters do most of the trash talking, including such well-financed independent expenditure organizations such as the National Conservative Political Action Committee (NCPAC) and several agencies of the Christian Right.

The 1984 campaign was, on the whole, extremely negative. Both Reagan and Democratic nominee Walter Mondale ran a large proportion of attack ads. As Ed Rollins, Reagan's campaign manager, put it: "The decision was to go with two negative commercials for every positive commercial.... Let me say the commercials clearly worked, we drove (Mondale's) negatives back up."[13] While the "Morning in America" ads may be what lingered in people's minds, certainly the attack ads had an impact.

Whereas some of the negative spots were hard hitting, others were more subtle. Case in point, "The Bear," a sophisticated allegory arguing in support of Reagan's massive defense buildup.

Video

Camera upon a grizzly bear. It lumbers across a hilltop, crosses a stream, and forges through underbrush.

Cut to a slightly blurry image of the bear (shot through a diffusion filter). It walks slowly along a ridge, silhouetted against sky. It looks up, stops suddenly, and takes a step backwards. The camera pulls back to show a man standing a few yards away, facing the bear. He, too, is silhouetted. A gun is slung over his shoulder.

Cut to closing graphic: "President Reagan: Prepared for Peace."

Audio

(Under announcer, a drum plays incessantly, like a heartbeat.)

ANNOUNCER (RAINEY) (voice-over): "There's a bear in the woods. For some people the bear is easy to see. Others don't see it at all. Some people say the bear is tame. Others say it's vicious and dangerous. Since no one can really be sure who's right, isn't it smart to be as strong as the bear? (*Pause.*) If there is a bear."

It was a clever—at the time, groundbreaking—ad defending the military buildup in allegorical rather than literal terms. And the Soviet threat is reinstated by underemphasis. Perhaps the Democrats are right, and the Soviets are not out to get us, the ad says, but should we not be ready just in case they are? Then there is that final pause ... "If there is a bear." We hear this while the bear has been on screen for 30 seconds, sending the not-so-subliminal message that, of course, there is a bear, the threat is real, and we should be spending hundreds of billions of dollars a year building up a deadly and redundant nuclear arsenal. If "Bear" were to be translated into foreign policy, it would be one of ambivalent vigilance.

Another successful negative spot focused on the economy. Three average Americans were asked by an announcer how they would cope with the proposed Democratic tax increase. Needless to say, they were not enthusiastic about Mondale's tax plan.

The Mondale campaign fought back with its own negative spots, but the Reagan campaign had already framed the terms of the debate, much in the same way that the administration framed the news stories coming out of the White House press room. The Reagan handlers were savvy in the ways of the media. But they also understood the power of incumbency, and the power of silence. If the president only spoke in controlled situations, and if that was all the West Wing reporters were given, then that is what they would report on.

In his first four years in the White House, Reagan gave fewer press conferences than any president since Calvin Coolidge. At the same time, he made more television addresses than any president before him. The Reagan administration not only tightly controlled the words and images coming out of the White House, but also by restricting their man to scripted monologues rather than press conferences, they controlled the media coverage.

continued

A case in point is the film *Morning Again in America* made for the Republican convention in Dallas. Clearly, it was another of the series of campaign spots, 18 minutes of gauzy tripe about how America was back—though where we had been was only darkly hinted at—all because of Ronald Reagan, a great American hero, the amalgamation of so many of our national myths; the cowboy on horseback, the self-made man, the citizen politician, the gentleman farmer, the guy next door, the Hollywood star, in short, anything Americans wanted him to be.

The film was to be shown as an introduction to Reagan's acceptance speech, and the Republicans assumed that the networks would run it uncut. But the Democrats protested; their campaign film on Mondale had not been shown by the networks. In light of this, the networks decided not to show the Reagan film after all. However, the Democrats' complaint, which they unwisely made public, created a controversy about the film and its television airing. In the end, as former NBC News president Lawrence Grossman describes it, "NBC News was the only network to televise *Morning in America* and the audience responded by turning to us in record numbers."[14] NBC showed the film because they thought it had become an item of genuine controversy, but the Republicans were able to get 18 minutes of free airtime for a commercial.

"Morning Again in America" was also the title of a series of television spots created by the Reagan media team. The spots were among the most artfully crafted campaign advertisements ever made. To this day, they remain the standard as far as production quality is concerned. But with regard to content, they are the political equivalent of Hallmark greeting cards. Though they only mention the opponent obliquely, it is not too far off the mark to characterize them as attack ads, for they insult the viewer's credulity and attack reality itself.

"It's morning again in America," Hal Rainey's avuncular voice intoned over the image of dawn breaking on another day in the heartland, as people of every creed and color go about their daily business, smiling, cheerful, restored of vigor and pride. America is a clean, well-lit place; nothing is unsightly or troubling, and everything is for the best in the best of all possible worlds.

Audio

Announcer (voice-over): "It's morning again in America …
"Today more men and women will go to work …
"Than ever before in our country's history.
"With interest rates and inflation down, more people are buying new homes and …
"Our new families can have confidence in their future.
"America today is prouder …
"And stronger …
"Than ever before.
"Why would we want to return to where we were less than four short years ago?"

Video

Boat crossing harbor in early morning.
Yuppie with briefcase getting out of cab.
Rancher herding horses.
Station wagon pulling up in front of quaint, white frame house with picket fence.
Bride hugging grandmother in slow motion.
Man raising flag.
Fireman raising flag.
Ethnic children looking up at flag.
Flag waving in wind.
Slide—picture of President Reagan with slogan "President Reagan: Leadership That's Working."

The spots were created by a team of advertising and political professionals whose credits included Bartles & Jaymes wine coolers and Meow-Mix cat food. They are beautifully photographed, skillfully crafted, with every element designed to work together, eliciting a powerful resonance of comfort, happiness, hope, and patriotism.

In Ronald Reagan's America there was nothing unacceptable. All our problems were behind us, the future

continued

looked bright, and everyone was happy, or at least content. The "Morning Again in America" ads are *kitsch* on a large scale; they represent a powerful, controlled, sustained, and sophisticated denial of the many painful realities that our country was unwilling to acknowledge.

Watching the "Morning Again in America" ads, you may argue against the false sense of serenity that the commercials create. You may remind yourself that while the camera pans the New York skyline, thousands of homeless wandered the streets. You may reflect that the economic expansion of the 1980s was little more than a speculative bubble of paper profits and plastic money. You may remember, as you see cheerful farmers working in their fields, that the Reagan economic policies helped ruin thousands of family farms. You may recall that most of the new jobs created were in fast-food restaurants in the strip malls that destroyed the Main Streets of countless small cities and towns, making them look remarkably dissimilar from the Norman Rockwell towns in the ads. You may find yourself cringing in revulsion at the patently phony symbolism of flags and sunrises, and smiling, happy people. You may become physically ill at the sheer dishonesty of it all. But you also get goose bumps watching these spots.

Because the problem with *kitsch* is that it works, not just on those unnamed others who are always susceptible to emotional manipulation, but also on just about anyone who is not dead from the neck down. As much as these ads may offend your sense of taste, your political beliefs, even your personal dignity, they are affecting. And that is the worst thing about them.

Reagan was a man deeply informed by *kitsch*. His commitment to *kitsch* went deeper than simply his political advertisements and televised homilies. He governed by *kitsch*, evading tough questions with *Reader's Digest* anecdotes, approaching, or worse yet, avoiding difficult problems with an almost pathological optimism. According to his biographer Lou Cannon, Reagan "expected concord, and the appearance of concord, to prevail among his staff."[15] His wife Nancy, who was more hard-edged but similarly devoted to the appearance of concord, put it in suitably kitschy language: "He likes everyone to like one another and get along."

Ronald Reagan wanted us all to like each other and to get along. Yet, his policies and rhetoric only drove us further apart. As we watched those stirring images on television and listened to Hal Rainey's reassuring words, the fabric of our nation quietly unraveled.

Chapter 8

Fear and Loathing in Suburbia

In New York, murder rates are as low as they were in 1970. Houston reports a 37 percent decrease in the murder rate. According to a survey by the Justice Department, after a brief rise in the 1980s, violent crime has fallen to the same level as in 1973.[1] Yet, according to a *U.S. News & World Report* poll in November 1994, when people were asked to name the biggest problem facing our nation, 34 percent said it was crime. No other problem came close.

Why do people not feel safe any more? Partly because there is a new kind of violence: random, vicious, and often drug related. Partly because people do not get out enough, and they get a steady assault of graphic violence on the television, both in fictive programs and, as we have seen in previous chapters, on news that either leaves the viewer terrorized or completely numb. And partly because they have been listening to politicians, who keep running negative ads exploiting the fear of crime to get themselves reelected.

One of the reasons the infamous 1988 Willie Horton spot was so powerful, and so odious, was that it exploited the fear of crime, specifically the fear of white suburbanites that they will be victims of violent crime at the hands of a black man. It is difficult to distinguish between paranoia, racism, and the very real fears that a perceived increase in violent crime and a very real breakdown in social order have created. However, the apparent success of the Willie Horton and other crime-related spots by the 1988 Bush campaign have spawned a whole generation of negative advertising attempting to capitalize on crime.

In many campaigns, crime is not just the dominant issue, it is the only issue. Candidates trade sound bites and attack ads, escalating the war of words, promising tougher sentencing and more executions, claiming that their opponents are "soft" on crime. The result is not just impoverished discourse, but a serious issue deficiency in which candidates are elected on platforms of little more than punitive vengeance, and are unprepared or unwilling to address the many other problems facing their constituents. Demagoguery on this issue often does not stop at campaign's end, and many disastrous laws and misguided policies are enacted because of the promises made by crime-obsessed campaigns, and by politicians afraid of being tarred as "soft on crime" in future races.

CRIME WARS

Of course, it did not start with Willie Horton. As Thomas and Mary Edsall write in their book *Chain Reaction*,

> To an extraordinary degree, the presidential campaigns of Barry Goldwater, George Wallace, and Richard Nixon in the 1960s and 1970s shaped the rhetoric, themes, and tactics of the Reagan and Bush campaigns of the 1980s.[2]

Many of the veterans of these early campaigns worked on the later ones, and the new blood always had a close eye on recent political history. Of course, the Goldwater, Wallace, and Nixon campaigns embraced a whole range of populist rhetoric that was often thinly veiled racism or class warfare; the issue of crime was only one aspect of these bitter and predominantly negative campaigns. However, crime has been a consistent theme throughout. Unchanged by economic or political vicissitudes, undaunted by actual facts of whether crime rates are rising or falling, and unwilling to address the social problems that create and encourage crime, the rhetoric of crime has remained an unrelenting drumbeat in our political discourse.

Nixon was quite effective in his use of crime as a wedge issue in 1968. He was the first to promise a "war on crime" and constantly used the phrase "law and order," or sometimes just "order," to evoke an image of social control that resonated with his "Silent Majority." One of the earliest and most chilling anticrime spots came out of his 1968 campaign; it became known simply as "Crime."

Video

Middle-aged white woman walking alone down a city street.

Audio

ANNOUNCER [Voice over sound of footsteps]: "Crimes of violence in the United States have almost doubled in recent years. Today a violent crime is committed almost every 60 seconds. A robbery every 2½ minutes. A mugging every 6 minutes. A murder every 43 minutes. And it will get worse unless we take the offensive. Freedom from fear is a basic right of every American. We must restore it."

The "Crime" spot evoked images of fear while keeping the threat mysterious and oblique. The female victim, dressed in red, white and blue, symbolized Americans, innocent, vulnerable, alone, and threatened by the Other, who is neither mentioned nor shown but assumed to be violent, and no doubt dark. The specter of assaults by black males on white female victims has a long and despicable history in American culture, and this ad certainly draws upon that imagery, if only by inference.

Of course, the Nixon campaign was about more than crime, but crime also became a symbol for many other issues that Nixon and subsequent politicians of polarization have been able to exploit. According to the Edsalls,

> "Crime" became a shorthand signal to a crucial group of white voters, for broader issues of social disorder, evoking powerful ideas about authority, status, morality, self-control and race.[3]

Crime spots appeal to voter fear rather than addressing the issues. What makes appeals to fear so despicable? Kathleen Hall Jamieson writes: "Messages that induce fear dampen our disposition to scrutinize them for gaps in logic. When the message is fear arousing, personal involvement and interest in it minimizes systematic evaluation."[4] They make us react unthinkingly, appealing to our most primitive emotions. They are not arguments so much as taunts, and cannot be responded to, only echoed. The result is that political argument is replaced by terrifying hysteria, as candidates compete with each other to see who can scare the voters more, who can make greater promises of punishment, who can hold such fundamental legal institutions as the Bill of Rights and the presumption of innocence in greater contempt.

CRIME WARS

Recently the crime war has escalated, and it has only gotten more ugly. California politicians have raised crime baiting to an art form, and it has crowded out many of the other pressing problems that have tarnished the Golden State.

In his 1994 reelection campaign for governor, Pete Wilson ran on two issues: crime and immigration, which was a form of crime, and of which the perpetrators—in the public's mind at least—were largely nonwhite. One of his ads sounded like the teaser for a tabloid television show: "Rape. An ugly word, a devastating crime." Wilson pilloried his opponent Kathleen Brown for her lack of enthusiasm for the death penalty and accused her of opposing his proposal that rapists and child molesters get life imprisonment on their first conviction. The Brown camp countered by describing how their candidate had supported a revised bill, which passed the state legislature, that called for stiffer sentences. A spot for Brown charged that "Pete Wilson is exploiting the pain of rape victims to cover up his failed record." Brown then tried to stick Wilson with his own Willie Horton—Melvin Carter, a white serial rapist, whose release was required by law. The tactic backfired, with the press calling it "demagoguery," a "cheap shot," and a "bum rap."[5]

Wilson also ran hard on a recently passed "three strikes and you're out" mandatory sentencing law. Caught up in the fervor of a campaign rally, Wilson upped the ante. "Not three strikes you're out," the governor shouted. "But one strike you're out." The crowd responded enthusiastically. In fact, the three-strikes law has proved to be almost unworkable. The first felon put away for 25 years to life was convicted for stealing a slice of pizza, and another got the sentence for forging a check.[6] The law is so broadly written that the father of Polly Klaas, one of the victims on whose behalf the campaign was waged, lobbied to have it changed. Of course, that did not stop the "fry 'em" crowd from grotesquely using Klaas's murderer in an appalling ad used against several Democratic congressional candidates in 1996 (see the Epilogue for more detail).

But it is not just California. Throughout the country, politicians have been running hard against crime and trying to use the issue to beat their opponents. "Crime in Illinois: More random, more violent. Criminals younger and younger," ran one spot for Governor Jim Edgar (R). A 1994 ad for Ted Kennedy claimed, "He fought successfully for the bill that put 2,300 new police on Massachusetts streets. And imposed life sentences for three-time violent offenders."[7] Republican James Inhofe, who defeated Democrat Dave McCurdy for the Oklahoma Senate seat vacated by retiring Democrat David Boren in 1994, ran a spot with look-alikes of hardened convicts dressed up in pink tutus and dancing around a ballet studio. The ad was supposed to be an attack on "lenient" treatment of criminals, though it

worked better as slapstick comedy. The *Washington Post*'s Howard Kurtz described the general focus of campaigning thus:
"The meat, in 1994 terms, is rather raw: for the death penalty,
longer prison terms and cutting off welfare benefits."[8]

VICTIM ADS

One of the more troubling developments of recent political
campaigns against crime has been the use in political spots of
victims of crime, recounting their traumatic experiences and
endorsing a candidate. Both liberals and conservatives have
taken their genuine grief and attempted to turn it into political
capital. But these arguments are not always equally despicable.
Liberals often use victim appeals as an argument for gun control, whereas conservatives simply use them to stir up anger,
fear, hatred, and the taste for revenge.

When Jeb Bush (R) ran for governor of Florida in 1994
against incumbent Lawton Chiles (D), Bush wanted to brand
his opponent as being soft on crime. So he ran a spot starring
the mother of a 10-year-old murder victim. The bereaved
mother said that Larry Mann, the man convicted of killing her
daughter 14 years previously, "is still on death row and we're
still waiting for justice." Then she said, "We won't get it from
Lawton Chiles because he's too liberal on crime."[9] Bush's argument was that Chiles had not signed a new death warrant to
replace one that had expired in 1986. But what Bush neglected
to mention was that the case was still on appeal, and Chiles
could not have executed Mann even if he wanted to. Most
relevant, Chiles himself is not opposed to capital punishment.
Eight criminals were executed during his first term.

The ad is not just misleading, it is odious. You cannot argue
with the grief of a mother whose child was taken from her by a
violent act. But you cannot blame Chiles for something he has
no control over. He most certainly would have signed Mann's
death warrant had he been able to. Moreover, if we are going to

have capital punishment, then we have to be extremely careful in meting it out. Although our system of justice may be the best in the world, it is not foolproof. Innocent people are sometimes convicted—often because of inadequate legal representation (especially for the poor), witnesses who lie and later recant their testimony, or even police frame-ups (witness the recent case of evidence planting by New York State Troopers). When new evidence comes to light, the innocent can be let out of jail. But modern technology has yet to devise a means of bringing back the dead. If that means some criminals wait for years on death row while their appeals are being processed, that seems to be a price worth paying for the guarantee of justice.

Sometimes politicians are directly blamed not only for the inadequate administration of justice, but also for the crimes themselves. This was the implication of the Willie Horton ad— that Dukakis's furlough policy, even though it was initiated by a Republican predecessor, created a rape and kidnap. In the 1994 New York gubernatorial race, Republican George Pataki blamed Mario Cuomo's parole policies on the murder of a young man.

"I blame it all on Cuomo and his policies," said Carol McCauliff, whose son was murdered. "Cuomo doesn't care about the victims of crime. He cares about the criminals."[10]

This is a powerful appeal. Unfortunately, it is wildly inaccurate. The *New York Times* pointed out that "the killer, though he had been paroled, was not on parole at the time of the crime; his full sentence had ended before the murder, so he would have been free in any event."[11] However, it is difficult to make that distinction in a highly charged atmosphere, and one does not want to diminish or disregard the real pain of the crime victim's survivors. Hence, irresponsible arguments such as Pataki's go unchallenged, or at least unrefuted, and are often quite successful. Pataki defeated Cuomo in that election, and his media campaign focused almost exclusively on crime and the governor's opposition to the death penalty.

But Cuomo himself used crime victims as advocates. One

television spot for the Cuomo campaign used a victim and the relative of two other victims of the Long Island Railroad shooting in which Colin Ferguson killed 6 people and wounded 19. "Carolyn McCarthy, whose husband was killed and whose son was partly paralyzed, argues not for capital punishment, but for a state ban on assault weapons that the Governor seeks."[12] (Of note, in 1996, longtime Republican McCarthy ran for Congress as a Democrat on the issue of gun control and unseated a Republican incumbent who had voted against the assault weapons ban.) Cuomo's policy approach may make more sense than Pataki's, but his using victims to make his arguments is still highly exploitative.

Sometimes the victim is close to the candidate. Dukakis refused to use the violent assault of one of his parents as an issue in the 1988 campaign, and his reluctance to do so, along with his weirdly detached, cerebral response to Bernard Shaw's question in the debate about what he would do if his wife were raped, seemed to give credence to Bush's irresponsible attacks. In his gubernatorial race in Georgia, Republican Guy Millner ran an ad in which his daughter described how she was confronted by a knife-wielding burglar. In a 1994 debate with Wilson, Kathleen Brown mentioned her daughter's rape. Tennessee senatorial candidate Jim Cooper (D) did a spot recounting a terrifying brush with crime. "Some time ago a man with a pitchfork tried to break through my basement door while my wife, Martha, was alone at home, pregnant with our first child." The assailant "got off, even though he was already a wanted criminal." In fact, the assailant was extradited to Missouri, where he was wanted on more serious charges.

Sometimes the message is policy driven. Other times, the message is simply an emotional appeal to fear and vengeance. But in both aspects, the use of victims as political advocates is cynical and exploitative. The victims of violent crime have suffered enough. Yet, in their quest for justice, or simple vengeance, they have been used by candidates for political purposes. And that is wrong.

CRIME RHETORIC AND POLICY

When candidates run on little more than promises to be "tough on crime," they often get elected. Then they have to act on their mandates. Bad politics often results in bad policy, and the campaigns against crime have created a series of crime laws that are, at best, futile and, at worst, racist and counterproductive.

Since 1984, Congress has passed a new crime bill every two years. Some of these laws have been beneficial, addressing the social problems that create crime in the first place, and seeking to stop or reverse the cycle of deprivation and despair that initially leads so many into a life of crime. However, many of the laws that make up the various crime bills are either merely symbolic gestures or else punitive measures that sometimes retard society's attempts to deal with crime.

Federal crime bills are messy, patched-together laws. First of all, there is little that the federal government can do about crime, except give the state and local governments more money to hire new policemen or build new prisons, or create mandatory sentencing laws for federal crimes. Mandatory sentencing has been a disaster, filling our prisons with often nonviolent drug offenders and choking the courts with accused criminals who cannot plea bargain and therefore insist on a trial. Sometimes overcrowding is so bad that violent and dangerous criminals get out early to make room for new inmates. And the convict class is increasingly African American. While accounting for only 13 percent of the general population, African Americans make up over half of the prison population. Many of those incarcerations are drug related. Between 1980 and 1990, the proportion of drug offenders in federal prisons increased from 22 percent to 40 percent. Meanwhile, the proportion of African Americans arrested for drugs, out of all drug arrests, rose from 24 percent to 41 percent. Much of this increase in drug arrests and incarcerations is the result of new drug laws requiring mandatory sentencing. Perhaps the most egregious among them is the law that imposed penalties for crack cocaine—used disproportionately by African Americans—many times more severe than those for powder cocaine, which is used just as disproportionately by whites.

While politicians realize the failure of these laws, they keep on voting for increased strictures. No one wants to point out the problems of mandatory sentencing. "There's a perception that you pay a big price for being soft on drugs," says Representative Barney Frank (D–Mass.). "People are afraid of the 30-second spot."[13]

In general, politicians are afraid of voting against crime measures; they do not want their opponents to use the vote against them in the next campaign. "Mandatory minimums are a political response to violent crime," Senate Judiciary Committee Chair Orrin Hatch (R-Utah) says. "Let's be honest about it. It's awfully difficult for politicians to vote against them."[14] That is why crime bills pass without much scrutiny and with such overwhelming majorities. And the sources of much of this legislation are dubious at best.

One hundred thousand policemen were added to local forces in the 1994 crime bill proposed by President Clinton. How did Clinton come up with that number? He had to make a big speech on crime, and his aides "had no idea how many cops would be a good thing." Then a twenty-something aide asked, "Would 100,000 be enough?"[15] The number was nice and round and easy to remember, and despite the fact that several law enforcement officials protested that it was too many new officers to train and assimilate, it soon became law. Another part of the 1994 act, a provision for background checks on child-care workers, may have been useful, but it was proposed by television talk-show host Oprah Winfrey.

Wendy Kaminer links the passage of the 1994 crime bill with two elections the previous fall. Republican George Allen ran for governor of Virginia and GOP former prosecutor Rudy Giuliani ran for mayor of New York. Both campaigned hard with negative advertising attacking their Democratic opponents' position on crime. Both supported abolishing parole for violent offenders. They both won, and their polling and other data showed that crime was an increasingly important issue, creating an atmosphere in Washington where, as Senator Joe Biden (D–Del.) put it, "If someone came to the Senate floor and said we should barbwire the ankles of anyone who jaywalks, I suspect it would pass." Biden himself voted for the crime bill and was author of the death penalty amendments, even though he admitted that "they are not going to have much effect."

Despite evidence that many of these anticrime measures are not working, are not fair, or actually increase the incidence of crime, and the fact that crime rates, particularly violent crime rates, are declining and will probably continue to decline, every campaign season, Congress can be counted on to pass more laws. In the debate over criminal justice, as Kaminer says, "Knowledge is irrelevant."[16] What is important is emotion—not only the voters, but also politicians have ceased thinking about crime. Now they only feel.

In many ways, federal crime bills are not meant to prevent crime but are only symbolic expressions of frustration and disgust. The *New York Times* editorial writer David Anderson calls the laws "expressive justice." These policies "are designed more to vent communal outrage than to reduce crime." Expressive justice is a primitive form of punishment found in such displays as public executions or floggings or holding a criminal in stocks. When the Constitution prohibited "cruel and unusual punishments," those were exactly the practices they sought to eliminate. But now we seem to be reverting.

Although no one has seriously suggested bringing back the stocks or the pillory, there have been proposals to televise executions and bring back corporal punishment. Now the death penalty is no longer seen by its proponents as a deterrent to murder, but rather as righteous vengeance. The effectiveness and morality of capital punishment are almost never argued anymore; instead, candidates simply try to outdo each other in their avidity to implement it. And the public is responding positively to the increased savagery of our criminal justice system. As Anderson points out, "Once upon a time, executions in the United States were attended by solemn candlelight vigils of protest. Now they are also likely to draw raucous celebrations of support."[17] Outside the Florida prison where the long-awaited execution of serial killer Ted Bundy took place, people turned the event into a ghoulish party, drinking beer and carrying signs that read "Roast in Peace" and "This Buzz Is for You."

CODE WORDS

Crime is a serious problem. But it is not the only problem that faces our country, and it is not going to get solved by simply building more prisons or executing more criminals. We have to address the social conditions that create crime, to make our country more equitable, both economically and socially, extending the benefits of good schools, good healthcare, good jobs, and hope in a better future to everyone equally. And that is not going to happen with the politics of vengeance and polarization. Instead, crude political messages about crime are only making things worse, as white middle-class voters secure themselves in Fortress Suburbia and leave minority city dwellers—the primary victims of crime—to cope with violence alone and unprotected. We are all in this together, but the demagogic rhetoric that attempts to exploit the fear of crime only pushes us apart and makes this difficult problem even more challenging than it already is.

The Willie Horton Story

In 1988, George Bush was a man in search of a message. He desperately wanted to be president, but he could not give a very compelling reason why he should be.

Throughout his political career, Bush ran on personality, experience, and political connections, avoiding issues and casting himself as basically a nice guy who works real hard. But he never defined himself politically, which is one of the reasons why, after a strong showing in Iowa, his race for the presidency in 1980 had faltered. George Bush was diligent, amiable, and vague on the issues. Polite almost to the point of obsequiousness, Bush always returned phone calls and sent thank-you notes.

But as he began the 1988 campaign, his advisers knew that Bush could not run just on thank-you notes. When Michael Dukakis came out of the Democratic convention with an 18-point lead, they began searching for issues that their candidate could run on. And if George Bush could not come up with a reason for Americans to vote for him, at least he could think of a few reasons why they should not vote for his opponent. The Bush camp found several negatives to hit Dukakis with: the pledge of allegiance, the environmental mess in Boston Harbor, the charge that he was weak on defense, his membership in the American Civil Liberties Union, and his supposedly lenient policies on crime. The Republicans also hoped to counter the public impression that Bush was some upper-class twit, a preppy wimp whose watchbands always matched his ties, with a series of tough negative ads.

Of course, the most famous of those ads involved a paroled felon named Willie Horton. The issue was first raised by a Democrat, then-Senator Al Gore (Tenn.), in a debate with Dukakis before the New York primary. James Pinkerton, head of the opposition research team for the Bush campaign, saw the debate and knew they had an issue. He followed the Horton saga back to a series of stories in the Lawrence (Mass.) *Eagle-Tribune*, which recounted Horton's murder trial and subsequent escape from the prison furlough program, followed by the rape of a woman and the

continued

kidnaping and assault of her boyfriend in their home in suburban Maryland. The newspaper articles were sensationalistic and often inaccurate, creating several misperceptions about the case that persist to this day. For example, Willie Horton was convicted of murder, but it was never proven that he was the one who actually stabbed the victim to death. And the victim was not sexually dismembered, a claim repeated so often that no one is even sure where it originated.

Just before the Memorial Day weekend, top strategists of the Bush campaign met with focus groups at a shopping mall in Paramus, New Jersey, to test out possible campaign themes on conservative Democratic voters who were supporting Dukakis. They brought up the pledge of allegiance, Boston Harbor, and prison furloughs, and by the end of the session, half the voters had changed their minds; now they were against Dukakis. "I realized then and there that we had the wherewithal to win," Lee Atwater said later. "The sky was the limit on Dukakis's negatives."

Still, the candidate had to be convinced. Ailes and Atwater went up to Kennebunkport and showed Bush tapes from the focus groups. They wanted him to go negative hard and early. "Bush stared into the abyss," a campaign aide recalled. Then, Bush decided, " 'yes, I will engage, and I will do it sooner than later.' " When he went back out on the campaign trail, Bush started using the furlough issue, bringing up the Willie Horton case as evidence that "Michael Dukakis on crime is standard old-style sixties liberalism."[18]

Atwater claimed that, at first, they did not know Horton was black, but that once it came to their attention, "we made a conscious decision ... not to use him in any of our paid advertising, on television or in brochures." They had to be careful of backlash or charges that they were exploiting a racial wedge issue.

Then, the conservative *Reader's Digest* got a hold of the story. Editor Kenneth Tomlinson, a Republican former director of the Voice of America (who left the magazine in 1996 to work on Steve Forbes' presidential campaign), rushed an article on Willie Horton into publication, claiming that he wanted to get it out before the election really heated up. In late June, Cliff Barnes, the man whose girlfriend was raped by Horton, appeared on the *Geraldo* show, along with the author of the *Reader's Digest* article and an antifurlough activist named Donna Cuomo. The team went on to make several more television appearances and press conferences on behalf of the Republicans.

But the campaign had not yet made Willie Horton into a star. It took a television spot to do that.

Willie Horton's mug shot shows a mean-looking character. He has a sullen expression, hard eyes, a scruffy beard, and a high, wild Afro. He is also black; in the grainy, out-of-focus shot in the television ad, he looks very black.

"This is every suburban mother's greatest fear," Larry McCarthy said, recalling his decision to use the mug shot in his now-famous spot. McCarthy was a former vice-president of Roger Ailes's company, but in the 1988 campaign he was freelancing for an organization called Americans for Bush. The group was part of the National Security Political Action Committee (NSPAC), which was run by Admiral Thomas Moorer, former chairman of the Joint Chiefs of Staff. NSPAC and Americans for Bush had no formal ties to the Bush campaign, and the campaign even publicly disavowed the groups, but McCarthy developed an ad campaign that would fit nicely with the strategies of his former boss and Atwater.

"I know Roger very well," McCarthy told reporter Martin Schram. "I just tried to run it as if I were Roger. I tried to spare him from doing some of these things. I figured they'll go negative by mid-September. So I said, 'I'm going to lead them by about a week or two.' "[19]

Looking at the mug shots of Horton, McCarthy thought long and hard, not about whether he should use the photos, but how he could get them past television officials. Race was obviously the issue. McCarthy explained,

> If he looked like Ted Bundy, I probably wouldn't have used his picture, because he looks perfectly normal. But then I said, as an advertising guy, I should have been shot if I didn't use Horton's picture, because the picture says it all. It says this is a bad guy
>
> *continued*

and Dukakis let him out. If it was a picture of a guy who looked like a crazy — an animal — but was white or Hispanic or Oriental, you'd use it. So I decided to put a criminal's picture on the screen.[20]

But McCarthy still had several obstacles. The organization did not have much money, and they would not be able to afford broadcast network television. It would have to air on cable. And McCarthy knew that even the officials on cable networks would scrutinize the ad for inflammatory content. (Although broadcasters have to run the ads of candidates, independent-expenditure campaigns can have their ads rejected for content.) So he made two separate versions of the ad. The first version mentioned the Horton incident, but only as a brief and vague detail, and it did not show his photo. McCarthy sent that version to CNN, Christian Broadcasting Network, Lifeline, and A&E, knowing that the first version of an ad always got closer scrutiny. Then he quickly followed with a second version of the ad — campaigns often update or revise their spots at the last moment. And McCarthy knew that the replacement would not be looked at so closely, if at all. The second version had the mug shot and a detailed, though erroneous, description of events.

Video

Still of Bush: "Supports Death Penalty."

Audio

"Bush supports the death penalty for first-degree murderers."

Video

Still of Dukakis: "Opposes Death Penalty."

Audio

"Dukakis not only opposes the death penalty, he allowed first-degree murderers to have weekend passes from prison."

Video

Mugshot of Willie Horton. "One was Willie Horton, who murdered a boy in a robbery, stabbing him 19 times."

Video

Still of Horton being led in handcuffs by policeman: "Horton Received 10 Weekend Passes from Prison."

Audio

"Despite a life sentence, Horton received 10 weekend passes from prison."

Video

Horton in handcuffs: "Kidnapping Stabbing Raping."

Audio

"Horton fled, kidnapping a young couple, stabbing the man, and repeatedly raping his girlfriend."

Video

Still of Dukakis: "Weekend Prison Passes."

Audio

"Weekend prison passes. Dukakis on crime."

The ad was shown several times on the cable stations, but its real impact came from the news media. First, McCarthy gave a copy of the ad to the producers of *The McLaughlin Group*. The ad was shown on the program in its entirety, and the panelists then discussed it at length. Suddenly, the ad itself was a news item. The broadcast networks, which McCarthy notes probably would not even have approved the ad, gave it free airtime in news stories, which is much more effective than running in a commercial spot, because viewers pay more attention to the news, and press scrutiny of an ad, even when critical, lends the spot credibility and makes it more memorable.

Although the Willie Horton spot was only aired on cable

continued

as an advertisement, network news programs showed it 10 times. Only once was it ever mentioned that the ad contained a gross inaccuracy. Overall, network newscasts showed 125 excerpts of campaign advertisements in 1988. In only 8 percent of those broadcasts was the factual accuracy of the ads even addressed. The result was free publicity for the most controversial—in other words, the most irresponsible—examples of campaign propaganda.

When the Bush campaign first decided to attack Dukakis using the Horton issue, Atwater bragged that by the end of the campaign, voters would think the convict was Dukakis's running mate. Indeed, that bravado proved eerily true. Two-thirds of the American public recognized Willie Horton's name; that is about the same percentage that knew who the vice-presidential candidates were. The press frenzy over Willie Horton reached such a hysterical pitch that *ABC World News Tonight* broadcast their correspondent Sam Donaldson asking Dukakis whether he thought Willie Horton would vote for him. Dukakis had to point out to Donaldson that as a convicted and jailed felon Horton could not vote.

The Bush campaign dissociated themselves from the Willie Horton ad, protesting, in Martin Schram's words, "with all the anguish of a pro wrestler pounding the mat in feigned pain." Americans for Bush said that they would take the ad out of circulation only if asked to do so by the Bush campaign. Elizabeth Feiday, the founder of NSPAC, told the *New York Times*, "Officially, the campaign had to disavow themselves from me. Unofficially, I hear that they're thrilled about what we're doing." She proudly passed around a letter from Dan Quayle, praising the organization as "a source of real encouragement as well as a great boon to our efforts."[21]

Bush campaign chairman James Baker finally sent NSPAC a letter complaining that the group was raising money in George Bush's name without the candidate's permission. This letter was seen as an attempt to get them to pull the ad, without mentioning it specifically. The spot was finally yanked, but only after it had already run for 25 days and had just three days left in circulation. As Floyd Brown, a colleague of McCarthy's and later perpetrator of even sleazier attacks on Bill Clinton, told the *New York Times*: "If they were really interested in stopping this, do you think they would have waited that long to send us a letter?"[22]

What did the Bush campaign know about the Willie Horton ad, and when did they know it? The evidence is insubstantial, and perhaps we will never find conclusive proof that they approved of the spot, either tacitly or implicitly. The Bush people had learned from the expert himself, Ronald Reagan, the power of deniability and executive ignorance. McCarthy claims that when he started working for Americans for Bush (and before the Horton ad) Ailes "called me up and he said: too bad, he wanted to hire me to do negative spots, but he couldn't now." Perhaps that was all the hint McCarthy needed to go on a freelance smear campaign. Or maybe it was just a friendly phone call. Either way, the ad remains seared in the memory of American voters, establishing a bitter precedent for the use of racial fear and hatred in political advertising.

Chapter 9

The Hate That Dare Not Speak Its Name

While *crime* is frequently used as a code word for *race*, it is not the only one. Many issues, such as affirmative action, welfare, immigration, even taxes, are racially charged and used in negative ads to polarize the electorate and pander to the fears of white voters. This tactic is odious in the extreme. Unfortunately, it has also been extremely effective.

Racism is America's original sin. It was institutionalized with the creation of our government, written into many of our founding documents, and it took almost 200 years for our political system to begin to recognize African Americans and other people of color as citizens who deserved full and equal protection under the law. Throughout our history, race has been used as a political tactic, exploiting fear and hatred, spreading the evil doctrines of racial superiority, and pitting Americans against Americans in a cruel and divisive grasp for power.

Thomas Jefferson was accused of miscegenation. In his arguments against slavery, Abraham Lincoln had to repeatedly state his opposition to "race mixing" and his belief in the natural superiority of white men. After Teddy Roosevelt invited Booker T. Washington to a White House dinner, his opponents circulated buttons with TR in blackface, seated next to the

African American leader. Racist pamphlets said presidential candidate Warren Harding was "not a White man."

THE EMERGENCE OF RULING-CLASS POPULISM

George Wallace made race baiting a successful tactic in the age of media politics. By pitting white middle- and working-class voters against African Americans and other people of color, Wallace helped break up Roosevelt's New Deal coalition and repudiated FDR's vision of unity with his own message of hatred and polarization. Although he was a Democrat, Wallace helped begin the process of Republican hegemony in the South by fomenting animosity toward the national Democratic Party's embrace of civil rights. And he helped elect Republican presidents, both by dividing his own party and drawing a strategic blueprint for successful right-wing-populist demagoguery.

At first, his appeals were crude and obvious. "Vote right—vote white—vote for the Fighting Judge," went one of Wallace's early radio ads. His slogan "White Supremacy" was printed on all Alabama primary ballots. Soon, he learned to make his pitch a bit more subtly. During his 1964 presidential campaign, Wallace gave a series of speeches in Maryland, hammering away at the Civil Rights Act without specifically mentioning African Americans. It was, as Wallace biographer Dan T. Carter describes it, "as if T. E. Lawrence had sat down to write *The Seven Pillars of Wisdom* without mentioning Arabs."[1]

After achieving national prominence by opposing integration—including his infamous and well-staged "stand in the schoolroom door"—Wallace no longer had to use explicit racial appeals, at least not when campaigning nationally. But in order to shore up support in Alabama, he still had to make his race hatred clear enough for rednecks to notice. When a black leader demanded the hiring of African American state troopers, Wallace countered with a radio ad: "Suppose your wife is driving home at 11 o'clock at night. She is stopped by a highway patrolman. He turns out to be black. Think about it.... Elect George C. Wallace."[2] One 1970 campaign leaflet showed a little white girl on a beach, surrounded by black boys. "Wake up, Alabama!" the leaflet read. "Is this the image you want? Blacks vow to take over Alabama."[3]

Richard Nixon was afraid of Wallace, but he also learned a great deal from him. In 1968, he worked to outdo Wallace with his law-and-order message to keep him from pulling enough Nixon votes to swing the election to Humphrey. Throughout Nixon's first term, with his vaunted "Southern Strategy," he worked to preempt Wallace, to make sure that he would get the 14 percent that the Alabama governor received in 1968. Polls after the 1968 election showed that four out of five Wallace voters would have voted for Nixon if Wallace was not in the race. In 1972, after Wallace was shot, Nixon no longer had to worry about direct competition and could concentrate on fashioning Wallace's techniques toward his own purposes.

Nixon gave lip-service to unity, as one of this 1968 campaign slogans was "Bring Us Together." But he also scapegoated blacks and used divisive wedge issues while carefully avoiding explicitly racist remarks. John Ehrlichman believed that his boss "always couched his views in such a way that a citizen could avoid admitting to himself that he was attracted by a racist appeal."[4] In private, Nixon's crude racial views were not so craftily hid. He told Ehrlichman, "America's blacks could only marginally benefit from Federal programs because blacks were *genetically inferior* to whites." [emphasis in original][5] After viewing a spot produced in his 1968 campaign on the decline of "law and order," Nixon exclaimed that the ad "hits it right on the nose.... It's all about law and order and the damn Negro–Puerto Rican groups out there."[6] As Dan Carter describes it, there was an irony to the party of Lincoln adopting the politics of Southern demagoguery:

> For nearly a hundred years after the Civil War, politicians had manipulated the racial phobias of whites below the Mason–Dixon line to maintain a solidly Democratic

South. To Nixon it seemed only poetic justice that the
tables should be turned. The challenge lay in appealing to
the fears of angry whites without appearing to become an
extremist and driving away moderates.[7]

Nixon successfully met this challenge by playing the middle against both ends, portraying himself as a Wallace who was
smart enough to cover his tracks with high-sounding but meaningless platitudes. At the same time, he appealed to every
racial, ethnic, and religious difference that could possibly be
distinguished, uniting his Silent Majority with the common
glue of hatred and suspicion.

After Nixon's first year in office, the Silent Majority was
silent no longer. In a feature eerily similar to today's examination of the angry white male, *Newsweek* devoted almost an
entire issue to "The Troubled American: A Special Report on
the White Majority." Now the majority was given official status
as a persecuted class, and given free rein to express its hostility
without qualification, or even remorse. And politicians, realizing that they could win by appealing to this majority, adopted
Barry Goldwater's tactic of "hunting where the ducks are."
(During Goldwater's campaign, American Nazi Gerald L. K.
Smith said, "The Republican Party has become the white man's
party.")[8] They could ignore blacks and other minorities, and
win on with almost exclusively white support. John Mitchell
called this strategy "positive polarization"—positive in the
sense that it won elections. And Kevin Phillips wrote a book
(*The Emerging Republican Majority*) predicting how, if they
played the race card right, the GOP could control the then
solidly Democratic South. After reading Phillips's book, Nixon
told H. R. Haldeman, "Study his strategy.... Don't go for Jews
and Blacks."[9]

After Nixon went down in ignominy, Reagan rebuilt the
Republican coalition much along these lines, with a message of
greedy populism and a willful ignorance about the problems of
black America. He simultaneously exploited racial stereotypes
with his story about the fictitious "welfare queen," whom

everyone "knew" was black, while also downplaying white economic hostility against the poor by promising them all a larger slice of the pie through the just-as-fictitious supply-side economics. Even if it was delusional, the tactic was clever, and it worked for a while. More pertinent to this discussion, however, is that the Reagan era marked a significant shift in the populist alliance. Now middle- and working-class whites were told, and soon came to believe, that they had more in common with the rich than they did with the poor, particularly the African American underclass. When times turned bad, they would no longer blame Wall Street; now they would look to Martin Luther King Boulevard as the source of their economic disenfranchisement.

Today, Reagan's ruling-class populism still dominates the political debate, not just in the Republican party, but among many Democrats as well. The Contract With America was a typically ruling-class populist document, mixing deregulation with welfare cuts, giving aid and succor to the rich while blaming the poor, not just for their own problems, but for everyone else's as well. Between 1973 and 1993, household incomes of the two lowest quintiles of the population declined in actual dollars, the middle fifth stayed virtually the same, and the two top groups, especially the very rich, got much richer. Ruling-class populism has succeeded in blaming the poor for this economic catastrophe that has virtually destroyed that bulwark of democracy, the American middle class, partly by casting the problems that face our country in racial rather than economic terms.

At first the message of ruling-class populism was subtle, as candidates couched racial appeals on the grounds of policy debate or tried to cover their divisive tactics with meaningless rhetorical froth. Then, it gradually became more blatant, and more vile. Nixon used the code words "law and order" to prey upon whites' fear of violent crime and summon up images of black rioting in the inner cities. In 1976, Jimmy Carter criticized welfare to attract Wallace voters. Reagan beat Carter at his own game with his aforementioned "welfare queen." Bush, of course, gave us Willie Horton. In 1994, the GOP ran hard on crime, welfare, immigration, and affirmative action—all issues that have transcended their original policy significance to become powerful symbols of race antagonism. All four of these issues were also used in 1996, although President Clinton's spineless signing of the welfare "reform" bill in 1996 effectively removed this from the presidential contest.

Two pioneers of the new populism were David Duke and Jesse Helms. While these racebaiters are often perceived as extremists, in fact, their message of hatred and division has entered mainstream political debate as the rhetorical legacy of George Wallace becomes increasingly acceptable.

THE MAN FROM THE KLAN

David Duke is a Nazi, former national director of the Ku Klux Klan, and founder of the National Association for the Advancement of White People. He picketed the Chicago Seven trial dressed in a Nazi uniform. He posed in front of London's Houses of Parliament in the white robes of the Ku Klux Klan. Although he tried to dismiss his racist past as the mere pranks of a callow youth, he remained a right-wing extremist, selling books such as *Hitler Was My Friend* out of his district office during his short stint as state legislator. The various racist, anti-Semitic, and crackpot statements he has made over the years, and even quite recently, include suggestions that "there are genetic differences between races.... There's differences in I.Q."; that welfare mothers should be given Norplant, an implanted contraceptive, to keep them from having more babies; that "the Jewish people have been a blight.... And, they probably deserve to go in the ashbin of history"; and advocating that North America be divided into separate ethnic nations for whites, blacks, Jews, Asians, Hispanics, and other groups.

Duke was a slick manipulator of the media, couching his racist rhetoric in code words and smooth talk, his boyish features refined by cosmetic surgery and a blow-dried hairdo, his reasonable, even affable, manner belying the message of hate that he spread. In the beginning, at least, he got a great deal of media coverage for the simple fact that here was a racial extremist who was also telegenic, who did not look or talk or act like a bridge troll. When he ran for a seat in the Louisiana state legislature and won (by 227 votes), he became a national political figure for no other reason than that he was the highest elected Nazi in the country.

He ran for the U.S. Senate in 1990 against J. Bennett Johnston (D) and won 44 percent of the vote. Suddenly, Duke began to look like a real threat. Then, he set his sights on the statehouse. Governor Buddy Roemer (D turned R) was finishing a lackluster first term, and the crowded field of challengers included Edwin Edwards (D), a former governor who had beaten a series of corruption charges and was running for office again.

Duke ran on one issue: race. He used the policy pretexts of welfare and affirmative action as code words, but what he was really trying to do was stir up racial antagonism between middle- to low-income whites and African Americans. Duke would say in his stump speech,

> I'm not blaming blacks for our problems, but earlier I did.
> The greatest problem facing the state today is the liberal
> social welfare system that doesn't encourage people to
> work and doesn't encourage people to be responsible.[10]

He addressed his Nazi and KKK activities, saying "I've done things in my life I'd take back." But he characterized this as if it was the distant past, not things he had done and said in the last two years. And he never seemed to recognize that his statements and actions were morally repugnant and could not be excused as the silly mistakes of an enthusiastic young man. "I may be controversial but I'm the only candidate with no skeletons in my closet." Duke said. Yes, but while Edwards had been accused of the rather common, at least in Louisiana, practice of collecting graft, Duke's skeletons wore the colors of racial hatred and had flesh on their bones.

Every speech that Duke gave, and just about every ad he

put on television and radio (all of which were written by him), mentioned affirmative action and welfare. Of course, Duke never mentioned that very few Louisiana businesses even practiced affirmative action, or that welfare made up a minuscule percentage of the state budget. Duke supporters were not interested in welfare and affirmative actions as issues of policy—they understood that when their candidate used those words, he really meant to raise the issue of race. White voters, particularly among the middle and working classes, who had seen the oil bust turn their state's economy into one of the worst in the nation, wanted someone to blame. And blacks in Louisiana were a convenient target for populist hate speech, as they had been for earlier racist demagogues like Leander Perez.

The mood in Louisiana was poisonous during the primary and later in the runoff. Duke came in second to Edwards with 31 percent of the vote. There were several racist attacks on black people, including one woman who was beaten, kicked, and spat upon as she walked alone on the Louisiana State University (LSU) campus. Her male attacker said, "More of the same's gonna happen when Duke gets elected!" A group of anti-Duke activists organized to form the Louisiana Coalition against Racism and Nazism (LCARN). They collected and disseminated information about Duke and ran a series of ads in independent-expenditure campaigns highlighting the candidate's public record of hate mongering. One of them was called "Nazi."

Audio

ANNOUNCER [voice-over]: "In 1969 David Duke said, 'I am a national socialist. You can call me a Nazi if you wish.' In 1976 he organized the meeting of a Nazi group which called for the release of all Nazi war criminals. In 1978 he hired a former American Nazi party captain to manage his presidential campaign. And in 1989 David Duke was caught selling Nazi books and tapes from his legislative office."

Music up.
Crowd shouting "Sieg heil!"

Video

Film of Nazis marching in Nuremburg rally framed with words top and bottom.

"David Duke, Nov. 13, 1969
'I am a national socialist. You can call me a Nazi if you wish.'
LSU *Daily Reveille*, 11/13/69."

"David Duke, Sept. 9, 1976
Organized a meeting of a Nazi group which called for the release of all Nazi war criminals."

"David Duke, Spring 1988
Hired a former American Nazi party captain to manage his presidential campaign.
Times-Picayune, 2/17/88."

"David Duke, June 1988
Caught selling Nazi books and tapes from his legislative office.
Times-Picayune, 5/8/89."

Film of Hitler addressing the rally.
"Vote for David Duke.
Create a Fuhrer."

(In the interests of disclosure, I should note that this and other anti-Duke ads were produced for LCARN by my firm's campaign consulting subsidiary, Politics, Inc. They are harsh, they are negative, and whether they are fair or foul is a subject that is open for debate. But I would argue with anyone that they are within bounds. They are factual and fully documented, and provide voters with information they ought to know about Duke that he would rather they did not know.)

Even though many Louisiana voters did not want to return to the *bon temps* politics of Edwin Edwards, a populist whose penchant for gambling was just one way in which he liked to play fast and loose, the alternative was much worse. Soon there were lawn signs and bumper stickers saying "No Dukes," "Republicans for Edwards," and "Vote for the Crook, It's Important." Election day saw a record turnout, especially strong among black voters, and Edwards won by a 61 to 39 margin. At the Edwards victory party in the Monteleone Hotel in New Orleans's French Quarter that night, the mood was festive. But the next morning, many Louisianans were sobered by the thought that a Nazi was almost elected governor. He might have lost, but David Duke got 55 percent of the white vote.

Duke tried to run for the Republican presidential nomination in 1992. During his announcement speech, he called the Democrats the party of "Ron Brown and Jesse Jackson." And he expanded his narrow repertoire of issues to include illegal immigration. "This country is overwhelmingly European descent and overwhelmingly Christian. And if we lose our underpinning, I think we're going to lose the foundations of America."[11] But the critical exposure he received from the media and public interest groups had made the former Klansman unacceptable, or at least embarrassing, and many of his new populist supporters went to Pat Buchanan instead. However, the 1992 Republican message was not much different from Duke's. Republican National Committee Chair Clayton Yeutter could point to only one issue—trade—on which Duke disagreed with GOP policies.

Now Duke is a member of the Republican Parish (county) Executive Committee in the second largest parish in Louisiana, has a World Wide Web site where he solicits for money and volunteers, and is trying to get back in the public eye. But the media no longer pay him much attention; his novelty has worn off. As Gary Esolen of LCARN described Duke's brief appeal as a media demagogue:

> The paradox is that although Duke's TV message is that he has cleaned up his act, he cannot in fact leave his original politics too far behind or he will fizzle out. A scoundrel who goes straight will soon lose the attention of the news media.[12]

Sam Jones, the mayor of Franklin, Louisiana, who ran for governor in 1991, explained Duke's appeal this way:

> We've been in a ten year depression here and it's only
> going to get worse. Everyone is on the edge and they're
> just angry. If he didn't have the baggage, [Duke] could
> have blown the race wide open.[13]

Duke had some nasty baggage, yet he was able to transform economic hardship into racial antagonism and nearly get
elected governor. Other race baiters who use the same pernicious techniques do not have Duke's ignominious public
record. Instead, they are respected and successful politicians
such as Senate Foreign Relations Committee Chairman Jesse
Helms.

HELMS–GANTT

In 1990, Senator Jesse Helms (R–N.C.) was challenged by
Harvey Gantt, an African American. Gantt was a city council
member in Charlotte, who was elected the first African American mayor of that predominantly white city in 1979 after an
extremely well-organized campaign that mixed traditional
grassroots strategies with the latest in affordable high technology (the campaign used Apple personal computers). But when
he went up against Helms, he faced an opponent who was able
to combine the time-tested strategies of Southern demagoguery
with the latest in television wizardry.

The Helms campaign attacked Gantt for being prochoice,
producing a spot in which a white woman talked about how
Gantt supported third-trimester and sex-selection abortions. The
charges were not true, and Gantt answered them. But Helms
kept attacking. In one spot, Gantt's face takes up a portion of
the screen while the announcer says, "Let's set the record
straight. Harvey Gantt denied he would allow abortion for sex
selection, when parents want a boy and not a girl. But Gantt
told the press he would allow abortions ..." Here, the still of
Gantt grows to fill the screen and turns into video. Then Gantt
himself says, in a statement taken out of context: "... whether

for sex selection or for whatever reason." The videotape goes on rewind as the announcer asks, "Did he say even for sex selection?" Gantt is shown repeating his truncated statement. The tape rewinds for a final time, and the announcer says, "Read his lips." This time, Gantt's video image is slowed down and his voice sounds dull and slurred as he makes the statement yet again.

Focus groups seeing this ad characterized Gantt's altered voice as "stupid," "definitely black," "the kind of really dumb black you used to see in the movies."[14] Sound distortion was used in another Helms spot, this time changing Gantt's campaign manager Mel Watt's voice to make him sound weak and indecisive. Then Helms tried to make an issue out of Gantt's support from gay-rights activists, a group with no great love for the North Carolina homophobe. In a 30-second television spot for Helms, an announcer charged:

> Gantt has run fund-raising ads in gay newspapers. Gantt has raised thousands of dollars in gay and lesbian bars in San Francisco, New York and Washington. And Harvey Gantt promised to back mandatory gay rights laws.

As Gantt himself said in response, "If this were 25 years ago, he'd be talking about blacks. If this were 18 years ago, he'd be talking about the communists or those civil rights agitators."[15]

Coming into the last week of the race, Gantt had a narrow lead. Then, Helms pulled out all the racial stops, attacking Gantt for profiting from a minority set-aside broadcasting contract and airing an incendiary ad that was ostensibly about affirmative action but really only about fomenting white hatred of blacks.

Audio

ANNOUNCER [voice-over]: "You needed that job, and you were the best qualified. But they had to give it to a minority because of a racial quota. Is that really fair? Harvey Gantt says it is. Gantt supports Ted Kennedy's racial quota law that makes the color of your skin more important than your qualifications. You'll vote on this issue next Tuesday. For racial quotas: Harvey Gantt. Against racial quotas: Jesse Helms."

Video

A white man sitting at a desk. We only see his hands and arms. He reads a letter and then crumples it up.

Slides of Harvey Gantt and Ted Kennedy.
"Harvey Gantt supports Ted Kennedy's racial quota law."

Slides of Harvey Gantt and Jesse Helms.
"For   Against
Racial Quotas."

The ad seemed to say that the entire election was about affirmative action. In fact, the entire election was about race. Gantt's lead slipped away from him in those final days, and he lost to Helms by less than four points.

In 1996, Helms and Gantt squared off again, and if that race was tamer than six years earlier, by any other standards it would have to be labeled poisonous. Helms again played the race- and sexual-orientation cards, with an ad showing newspaper clips in which Gantt details his support of gay rights, and another raising the minority broadcasting issue.[17] The latter ad prompted Duke University political scientist David Paletz to tell Associated Press, "We're back to 1990. Race has always been there. Race is now there in black and white."[18] Helms also attacked Gantt for trying to hide the Democrats' alleged support for "more taxes and more welfare." However, Gantt said he would have voted for welfare reform and supported a middle-class tax cut.[19]

Unlike 1990, though, Gantt fired back hard, with ads accusing Helms of being a millionaire slumlord, lying to the Senate Ethics Committee, taking secret donations from foreign governments, and cutting Medicare. Gantt, at least, had the advantage of accuracy. Helms is worth more than 1 million dollars and owns rental properties that are substandard and have no heat. The Senator twice underreported his assets to the Ethics Committee but claimed each was a mistake. A foundation Helms runs has taken money from Kuwait and Taiwan. And Helms has criticized Medicare since 1965.[20]

In the end, Helms won again.

Duke's and Helms' nasty political rhetoric seemed radical at the time they first used it. But in just a few short years, the message of code words and race baiting has gone mainstream. Appealing exclusively to white voters, and only to their most despicable emotions, politicians of both parties beat up on affirmative action and welfare as if these were really the source of our problems. Eager to enjoy the electoral majority that the ruling-class populist coalition often provides, politicians who race-bait and code-word may be winning in the short term, but over the long run, they're poisoning politics and making America a less civil society.

WHITE FRIGHT – WHITE FLIGHT

Ever since the 1960s—in other words, ever since the passage of the landmark civil rights bills, and ever since crime became a divisive political issue—whites have been fleeing the cities for the suburbs. No doubt, this exodus is not solely motivated by race—many city dwellers want the usually cleaner air, safer streets, better schools, and living space that suburbia provides—but we would be kidding ourselves if we did not admit that race often has a great deal to do with it. Now, more than 40 percent of Americans live in the suburbs, less than one-third live in cities, and about one-fourth live in the country.

How does that translate politically? In 1988, 48 percent of the vote came from the suburbs, and that vote was split 28 to 20 in favor of the Republicans. The GOP's lead in the suburbs was greater than the Democrats' edge in the cities. Plus, the suburbs had more voters. George Bush's margin of victory in Michigan was larger than the entire Democratic vote tally in Detroit, the same for Ohio and Cleveland, Georgia and Atlanta, Louisiana and New Orleans. This meant Bush could ignore the cities and win on his margin in the suburbs. As William Schneider, who provided this analysis, put it, "The suburbs had arrived, politically."[21]

The suburban strategy is the politics of polarization: white versus black, have versus have not, private versus public, antipolitics versus government. And polarization has worked. In 1990, Democratic candidates for the House got 78 percent of the black vote. In 1994, they got 92 percent and lost control of the House for the first time in 40 years. In 1996, with comparable African American support, Democrats gained 10 seats, which was not enough to recapture a majority. Despite the rhetoric of a few Republicans such as Jack Kemp and Jim Pinkerton, the GOP has basically given up on the black vote, and given up on blacks as a whole, even when they are running for office as Republicans.

In 1988, Alan Keyes, an African American, was running for Senate in Maryland on the Republican ticket. Then-President Reagan helped Keyes with fund-raising and even starred in a political spot for the campaign. But the ad did not show the candidate's face. Why could they not have used Keyes's face in his own spot in a state with one of the highest percentages of African Americans in the country, and one that is probably more racially tolerant than most? If your party's time-tested strategy for success is premised on racial polarization, you cannot suddenly turn around and present a black face to people accustomed to voting against blacks.

Not only are African Americans getting ignored, but they are also becoming disgusted by the increasingly negative tone of political campaigns. "It took us black people so long to get to vote," T. J. Smith, a handyman in Philadelphia told the *New York Times*. "Now, they're making us not want to vote."[22] That is the flip side to the GOP approach—they not only motivate white voters to vote along racial lines, but they also seek to depress black turnout and participation. That is not the least bit unintentional, and sometimes they do it overtly. Witness the flap involving Ed Rollins's claims that he had black ministers paid to keep voters away from the polls in Republican Christine Todd Whitman's successful 1993 gubernatorial race.

Some African Americans are reacting to this increasing marginalization—not with apathy but anger. And this anger often translates into a distorted view of the way our nation is run. A recent survey by the polling firm Marttila and Kiley found that 63 percent of African Americans believe "the U.S. government deliberately makes sure that drugs are available in poor black neighborhoods." That same survey found that 58 percent believe "the U.S. government is deliberately allowing the black community to be destroyed."[23] These data and others, including the 85 percent of African Americans who believe O. J. Simpson was innocent, show how significantly the effects of bigotry have alienated African Americans from the political mainstream and pushed them toward conspiratorial views.

The result of all this racial politicking is an increasingly polarized electorate and campaign-driven policies such as crime bills, lower aid to cities, and the rejection of affirmative action. Clearly, these policies hurt African Americans. But that does not matter, because the Republicans have written them off anyway. So, the Democrats are left to represent the urban blacks in a country that is increasingly suburban and, for the moment, significantly conservative, or at least antigovernment. As our public spheres diminish, our private enclaves prosper, making our entire nation—the cities, suburbs, and country—a more savage place in the process.

IMMIGRATION

Not all racism in American is white on black. As immigrants from Asia, Latin America, and the Middle and Near East come to this country in increasing numbers, animosities toward resident foreigners are emerging once again. While the economy continues to grow at a lackluster pace, and good jobs become scarce, some white workers are beginning to resent the presence of these new Americans, despite the fact that most are hardworking and law-abiding, and even illegal immigrants pay approximately $25–30 billion per year in property and income taxes, according to a study by the Urban Institute. The impression exists, and is exploited by demagogues, that most immigrants are on welfare, when, in fact, illegal immigrants are barred from all social services except emergency medical care, and legal immigrants, who make up 9 percent of the total population, comprised only 5 percent of all families on welfare. This disinformation is what led to the 1996 Welfare Reform bill's ban on aid to *legal* immigrants, an outrage that should be repealed. Illegal immigration in Texas and California has reached almost-crisis proportions, but much of the impetus behind anti-immigration legislation is not so much reasoned deliberation over public policy as crude and hostile nativism—which would lose its explosive power if the immigrants were from Europe rather than from countries where people are not white.

One of the more pernicious referenda to come out of California recently was Proposition 187, a plan to cut off all social services to illegal immigrants. The 1994 referendum was mean-spirited, even deadly (immigrants could be denied emergency healthcare), not to mention patently unconstitutional. Incumbent Governor Pete Wilson (R) campaigned in support of it, whereas challenger Kathleen Brown (D) opposed it.

Wilson demanded that the federal government declare a state of emergency and fork over $2.4 billion to California, his estimated cost of providing social services for illegals. Later, he backed down from his initial demand and asked for a "downpayment" of $1.8 billion. "We cannot educate every child from here to Tierra del Fuego," Wilson said. Even though he acknowledged that the bill was unconstitutional, Wilson said, "The save-our-state initiative is the two-by-four we need to make them take notice in Washington and provoke a legal challenge that will go all the way to the Supreme Court."[24] Wilson hired a media firm that included Larry McCarthy of Willie Horton fame, and they produced a series of ads showing illegal immigrants—obviously not with white faces—scurrying across the border. He came back from a 23-point deficit to win reelection. Proposition 187 also won and is now being challenged in the courts.

GOP Senate candidate Michael Huffington supported Proposition 187, and he liked the issue so much that he attempted to exploit it, even after losing to Democratic Senator Dianne Feinstein. Following the election, a radio campaign asked listeners to call a toll-free number to report "suspicious activity" by illegal immigrants who may have voted for Huffington's opponent. A group called the Voter Fraud Task Force (VFTF) was responsible for the ad, but it was paid for by Huffington himself. "Everybody's heard stories," said VFTF president Harold Ezell, a former INS official, prominent immigrant basher, and coauthor of Proposition 187. But the group could offer no proof for its claim. Although the toll-free fraud line received more than 400 calls, Anthony L. Miller, acting Secretary of State, said, "There has not been a scintilla of evidence presented to this office with respect to illegal voting by non-citizens."[25] Huffington's pathetic and desperate move was plagiarized by a 1996 California GOP loser, former Representative Bob "B-1" Dornan, though his equally baseless charges were all the more inflammatory because he was beaten by a Latina, Representative Loretta Sanchez.

Illegal immigration is a real problem, but a lot of the screaming about it is simply the politics of hysteria and polarization. Chicago and New York both have large immigrant populations and many illegals, but it has not become nearly as much of an issue, because both cities have powerful minority groups and political systems committed to ethnic diversity. The issue of immigration is not going to go away, particularly given the 111 electoral votes in California, Texas, and Florida, and the compulsive political need for right-wing demagogues to frighten white suburban voters throughout the country.

THE RACE CARD

The ruling-class populist alliance has created a tenor of political debate in which racism is not only condoned but also encouraged. This tactic is cynical in the extreme. But, unfortunately, it also happens to work, at least in the short term.

Since whites are the majority in most districts, all states, and the nation as a whole, campaigns appealing on strictly racial lines can be political winners, though the cost is a nation that is irreparably divided and antagonized, and the creation of a political class that is recognized only as a target of hatred and frustration, or else simply ignored. Ultimately, minorities will only become increasingly disenfranchised, our cities will become uninhabitable, and our nation will be a society in name only, with nothing holding us together but a common fear of each other.

Chapter 10

Gender, Sexuality, and Religion

Of course, racism is not the only form of hatred that poisons our politics. The fears and prejudices surrounding gender, sexuality, and religion are often exploited by political messages. And these animosities are just as insidious as race hatred, for they are deeply personal issues that provoke deeply personal responses. Unfortunately, in today's climate of backlash and reaction, these issues are being used with increasing crudity, and often their exploitation is meeting with electoral success.

SEXISM

Women are slowly making inroads into electoral politics. The Senate now has 9 women; the House has 51. Women are becoming more powerful at the state and local levels as well. But they have still got a long way to go, baby.

Politics is a male-dominated profession. And women face significant disadvantages in campaigning. As Wendy Kaminer writes, "Women have a harder time than men in establishing their credibility as candidates, because our traditional images of political leadership are male."[1] Celinda Lake, a Democratic pollster, says that the three attributes on which women are

147

constantly challenged are competence, electability, and toughness.

Female candidates suffer from a variety of double standards and no-win situations. Strong women are often seen as threatening by insecure men. Female candidates are not taken as seriously as less-qualified males. A successful woman is often seen as being a cold-blooded professional, whereas women without much work experience are dismissed as amateurs. If women devote attention to their appearance, they're criticized as being fashion plates. But if they do not, they are called dowdy.

Hillary Rodham Clinton is the perfect example of a talented, intelligent woman who has been subjected to these contradictory expectations and then pilloried when she fails to meet them. Either she is too involved in her husband's job, or she is not involved enough. Either she is too high profile, or she is hiding from the press. When she changes her hairdo, she gets criticized. When she leaves it alone, she gets criticized. She decides to follow her heroine Eleanor Roosevelt's example and write a newspaper column, and suddenly her enemies become literary critics and complain about that, too. Every rumor sticks, even the ugliest slanders, such as the innuendo about herself and Vincent Foster. Hillary just cannot win, and it is not her fault. She, of all people, is no victim. But the sexist double standards that still prevail in this society make it difficult, even impossible, for a woman to succeed.

In order to survive in a political world that is not only male-dominated but also deeply informed by the various peculiarities of the Y chromosome, women have to adapt. At the 1988 Democratic Convention, Ann Richards offered the following analogy: "Ginger Rogers did everything Fred Astaire did. She just did it backwards and in high heels."[2]

One of the more pernicious double standards is "toughness." A woman who campaigns hard is often seen as that word that rhymes with *kitsch*, whereas a man who does the same thing is called tough. Therefore, female candidates are often more reluctant to go on the attack, especially when their opponents are men. Sometimes this reluctance can work to a candidate's advantage. As Cathy Allen, a political consultant in Washington state, points out, "Women are often perceived as being above the fray of negative campaigning." But in the sexist world of politics, even a positive perception has serious drawbacks. Going negative "may destroy this appearance of integrity."

Representative Patricia Schroeder (D–Colo.) was called "The Wicked Bitch of the West" for her investigation into the Tailhook scandal. "Bitch is the archetypal slur against the woman who talks with certainty, makes bold statements rather than hedged ones, acts with authority," says Deborah Tannen, Georgetown professor and author of *Talking from 9 to 5.* "The reaction is, 'Who does she think she is?' and she will be disliked." *Time* correspondent Margaret Carlson relates that after her appearances on CNN's *Capital Gang*, she gets hate mail if she so much as frowns at Robert Novak, whereas Novak gets fan mail for insulting her.

In attempting to respond to the "toughness" issue, some women candidates fall prey to the "Thelma and Louise" fallacy, in which females simply mimic male attitudes rather than developing unique virtues of their own. In that movie, the two women drove speeding cars, shot guns, and chucked each other on the shoulder. Although they took revenge on rapists and sexual harassers, and in many ways were classic feminist characters on one level, they acted more in accordance with the male stereotype. Female candidates who heft assault rifles to assert their toughness do not do themselves or their gender any good. American politics could benefit from a perspective that values cooperation more than conflict, tolerance more than hatred, compassion more than callousness, especially when we are debating crucial issues such as foreign policy, crime, war, and economic equity. We do not need any more testosterone in politics, particularly not in political argument.

Female candidates' spouses often get far more attention

than they deserve. Part of this is lingering patriarchy, a society that still believes only a man can support a family. But part of it is simple political opportunism. It started with Geraldine Ferraro, whose husband, John Zaccaro, owned rental properties in New York neighborhoods where it would be impossible *not* to be renting to shady characters. The feeding frenzy over Zaccaro's finances reached hysterical proportions. The *Philadelphia Inquirer* assigned 30 reporters to investigate the story. Ferraro was forced to respond with an hour-and-a-half news conference. Ultimately, nothing was found.

Much of the $28 million that Michael Huffington spent on his 1994 Senate campaign went toward trying to prove Dianne Feinstein and her husband were crooks. Running for a Pennsylvania U.S. Senate seat, Democrat Lynn Yeakel was attacked for comments her pastor made on Israel and for her husband's membership in a club that excluded minorities. She soon realized, "What [GOP Senator Arlen Spector] is doing to me is what people have done to women through history, and that is to define them in terms of other people in their lives, particularly men."[3]

Despite the fact that many journalists are women, and some of them are feminists, the press has not been exempt from sexist stereotyping and double standards. When the *Washington Post* profiled Lynn Yeakel, the story led with a description of her hair and her wardrobe, and called her "an unlikely standard bearer." Not until halfway through the article did the *Post* mention that Yeakel was the Democratic nominee for Senate, or describe her political experience. The next day the *Post*'s profile of her opponent, Arlen Spector (R–Penn.), led with the fact that he had been "a crimebusting district attorney and a mayoral hopeful." Carol Moseley-Braun got similar treatment from the *New York Times* in her race against Richard Williamson. "She is commanding and ebullient, a den mother with a cheerleader's smile; he, by comparison, is all business, like the corporate lawyer he is." Twenty-two paragraphs into the piece, the *New York Times* finally acknowledged that Moseley-Braun was a lawyer herself, as well as a former federal prosecutor and veteran state senator.[4]

And there is always the threat of sexual innuendo, which is more damaging to women than to men in a society still governed by sexual double standards. Female candidates who are unmarried often face whispering campaigns about their sexual orientation or promiscuity. Women who are married have to tote their husbands around the campaign trail to a degree that political wives are seldom subjected—rarely do political husbands campaign for their spouses alone. Women with young children are often accused of neglect for campaigning instead of staying at home. When the National Women's Political Caucus held its first convention in Houston in 1973, members were told by the hotel staff that a woman could not be paged, since only prostitutes would answer such a summons.

Women are seen as a special interest group rather than more than half of the world's population. "[T]he defeat of one woman is often read as a judgment on all women," Ferraro wrote in her memoirs. When Schroeder tested the waters for a presidential race in 1988, she was asked, "Are you running as a woman?" Schroeder responded: "Do I have an option?"

Let us hope that after enough women get elected—like maybe 52 percent of all officeholders—women will be able to run just as candidates, and we will have a more thoughtful and compassionate nation.

HOMOPHOBIA

The politics of homophobia is usually only played in whispering campaigns and rarely makes it into advertisements, although we have already seen how Jesse Helms tried to smear Harvey Gantt by linking him to gays and lesbians. Of course, only Helms and his ilk would think it is a sin to have gay and lesbian friends and supporters, but the smear is evil, at least in intent.

When Ed Koch was running against Mario Cuomo for governor of New York, a slogan made the rounds, slandering the bachelor Koch: "Vote for Cuomo, not the homo." Cuomo had nothing to do with the slogan, we assume, and it was soon squelched.

In the 1986 campaign for a Maryland senate seat, Republican Linda Chavez tried to smear her opponent Barbara Mikulski as a "San-Francisco–style liberal," using that city's reputation as a haven for homosexuals to insinuate that the unmarried Mikulski was a lesbian. The fact that lifelong Baltimorean Mikulski had never lived in or had any association with San Francisco had nothing to do with it. Chavez also ran a spot criticizing a staffer of Mikulski's for being a "radical feminist" and "anti-male." Fortunately, both attacks fell flat. Mikulski was a homegrown political star, who got her start in politics organizing a Baltimore neighborhood to block construction of a highway. An authentic political character, her marital status was not an electoral handicap because, as she put it, she reminded ethnic Marylanders of the unmarried aunt who was common to many families. More important, as someone whose politics has always been populist, colorful, and progressive, voters saw her as an effective, dynamic, and proworker public servant.

Pat Buchanan managed to use both racism and homophobia in a spot broadcast during the 1992 Georgia primary. The advertisement, entitled "Freedom Abused," blamed Bush for a documentary film about gay African American men called "Tongues Untied," which was broadcast on PBS and partially funded by the National Endowment for the Arts (NEA). "In the past three years," the ad announced, "the Bush administration has invested our tax dollars in pornographic and blasphemous art, too shocking to show." The ad did show clips from the film, clearly designed to inflame (or possibly titillate) voters. On his ad-watch program, Brooks Jackson pointed out that the film was actually funded by the Reagan administration. Howard Kurtz, in the *Washington Post*, showed that filmmaker Marlon Riggs did not get direct NEA funding; instead, the grants were made to the American Film Institute and then the Rocky Mountain Film Institute before he was awarded them. The accuracy of Buchanan's claims aside, the ad created a backlash. According to a CNN–Gallup poll, 23 percent of voters said the ad made it more likely they would vote for George Bush, and Buchanan got thrashed in Georgia.[5]

Before Representative Barney Frank (D–Mass.) officially came out of the closet, most political insiders knew he was gay, and knew that it did not make any difference. Frank was and is one of Congress's most competent and effective members. In his first term, he was named "Rookie of the Year" by his colleagues in the House. But the sleazy whispers started when his district was reconfigured and he had to run against eight-term Republican incumbent Margaret Heckler. His media adviser, Dan Payne, shot an ad of Frank playing softball to both forestall the homophobic smears and show that the candidate was more than just a wonk. Frank won the election, and Heckler's consolation prize was being named Reagan's Secretary of Health and Human Services. But a gay man should not have to engage in macho preening just to prove that he is "one of the boys." I hope that Barney Frank's example of a being a great Congressman who just happens to be homosexual will motivate other gays and lesbians to run for office, and we can finally put the ghost of homophobia to rest, at least in electoral politics.

Unfortunately, as more gay and lesbian candidates come out of the closet and into the political realm, the hatred is only increasing. During the 1994 campaign, there were several openly gay candidates, many of whom were subjected to vicious homophobic slanders and smear campaigns.

"The Radical Right has stepped up its attacks on openly gay political figures as part of its overall strategy to undermine the strength of our community," says Kathleen DeBold, deputy director of the Gay and Lesbian Victory Fund. "They know qualified gay and lesbian officials dispel anti-gay stereotypes and increase our community's visibility in an extremely positive way—something they don't want to happen."[6]

When Tim Van Zandt ran for Missouri State Representative, his opponent Carl Wilson used the campaign motto "Straight Talk," but denied that it referred to Van Zandt's sexual orientation. Then, Wilson abandoned all pretense of subtlety, sending out a letter calling Van Zandt "a single-issue candidate," and stating that his "sole purpose for running is to *promote the gay rights agenda*." In a final mailer, planned to arrive on election day, Wilson inaccurately claimed that Van Zandt had been involved in a disruptive ACT-UP demonstration.

When Evonne Schultz fell behind Christine Kehoe in a race for San Diego's City Council, she came up with a comparison chart between herself and her openly lesbian opponent. Under the category "Family," Schultz listed her two sons. Under the same category for Kehoe was a large blank, ignoring Kehoe's long-term, committed relationship. Does this mean that gay candidates cannot have families, despite the fact that many gays are in stable, committed, and long-term relationships, and some have adopted children, or have children from previous marriages? When right-wing candidates talk about family values, are they actually invoking the love, trust, and commitment that many gays, as well as straights, share with their family members? Or are they simply using code words to smear people who want to be married but cannot because of the right-wingers' votes in Congress for the gay-marriage ban?

Homophobic politicians do not just beat up on gay and lesbian candidates; they are often on the forefront of the debate over serious issues, including the various attempts to pass state and local initiatives denying homosexuals equal rights, and the fight to allow gays to serve openly in the military. Before President Clinton abandoned his campaign promise by giving in to the "Don't ask, don't tell" policy, several Religious Right and antigay organizations led the fight against gays in the military. The Antelope Valley Springs of Life Ministries in Lancaster, California, a church where Jim Bakker preached a few sermons before heading off to jail, distributed a videotape entitled "The Gay Agenda." The tape was a viciously distorted view of gay life, used to suggest that homosexuals were unfit to serve in the military. Not only was the tape enormously popular—during the height of the controversy, the church was receiving orders for up to 500 tapes a day, and a total of 25,000 were distributed—but it also had an impact on the debate. Senate Armed Services Committee Chairman Sam Nunn and other key members of Congress received a copy, as did the members of the Joint Chiefs of Staff and a number of Pentagon officials. The controversy over gays in the military was a financial boon for the Religious Right. Jerry Falwell speculated that he might be able to revive his defunct Moral Majority as a result of the increased attention and fund-raising success that the issue generated.

Steve Gunderson (R–Wis.), a capable and conservative former congressman who happens to be gay, was attacked in the 1994 primary by ads that showed clips from "The Gay Agenda," even though Gunderson is nothing like the extravagant personalities shown on the video. He officially came out before 1994 and promised not to run for Congress again, although, if he had, he would probably have won. Gerry Studds (D–Mass.) and, most recently, Jim Kolbe (R–Ariz.), were the other openly gay members of Congress (Studds and Gunderson retired in 1996), but all four, Studds, Gunderson, Frank, and Kolbe, came out after they had already established themselves in Congress.

Once Jonathan Wilson, a 12-year member of the Des Moines, Iowa school board, announced that he was gay, he faced bitter opposition in his next election. Antigay activist Bill Horn moved to Iowa to attack Wilson, heading up a Des Moines branch of the Springs of Life Ministries. Hoping to get support among the hard right in this early caucus state, Senator Phil Gramm (R–Tex.) supported Horn's efforts, signing a fund-raising letter that read, "Thank God for Bill and the thousands of parents who will not be intimidated by the liberal media or the radical homosexual community." Gramm's presidential primary opponent, Senator Bob Dole (R–Kans.), countered by returning a $1,000 donation from the Log Cabin Club, a gay

Republican organization. Dole's calculated refusal of gay support was harshly criticized by Gunderson, who had already endorsed the Senate Leader.

Minnesota's Governor Arne Carlson (R) was attacked in an independent-expenditure campaign ad that simulated the wedding of two gay men. Carlson is straight himself, but he supported a statewide gay-rights initiative, and that was enough to bring out the gay-bashers. The local Christian Coalition criticized the governor and his administration for a pamphlet designed to help school officials to counsel gay and lesbian kids. The pamphlet, according to one Coalition leader, "clearly promotes homosexuality." His opponent said that men were "genetically predisposed" to head the household. Soon, the debate was joined by radio talk-show host Bob Larson, who fulminated in characteristic hate-radio hysteria about "the immoral homosexual propaganda aimed at our teenagers." For a small fee, he sent interested listeners a copy of the videotape "Secrets of the Homosexuals, Lesbians, and Lobbyists."

Principled conservatives can disagree with issues such as gay marriages or open military service. But that does not mean they should hate gays or foment public hatred. Vin Weber, the former Republican congressman who now heads Empower America, says, "I don't want to see the gay lifestyle promoted, but tolerance is an American value. There's a great danger in taking a single group of people and making them the enemy." Weber has already warned fellow Republicans to tone down the rhetoric and get rid of the hate. He thinks that gay-bashing could lead to violence. "It's an ugly thing," Weber says of antigay hysteria on the Right. "It makes me nervous."[7]

While campaigning in the New Hampshire presidential primary, then-Representative Bob Dornan (R–Calif.) praised a local school board's policy that barred schools from portraying gay and lesbian lifestyles "in a positive light." He went on to say that homosexuality "is basically a cult.... It's just wrong." Dornan said that lesbianism is adopted by women as a revulsion against the foul treatment by men in their society.... Men date rape, rape, disrespect, treat women in such a cruel way that women who are smart and go into college decide they don't want men in their lives.[8]

Dornan's remarks are fatuous enough to be left unremarked upon. But he and his Orange County colleague, former Representative William Dannemeyer (R), have been making political hay out of gay-bashing for some time now. Dannemeyer came up with a series of odious proposals concerning AIDS, including quarantining people who test positive for the HIV virus. He wrote in his book, *Shadow in the Land: Homosexuality in America*: "The homosexual blitzkrieg has been better planned and executed than Hitler's.... Unlike the French, who wept in the streets of Paris as the Germans marched by, we don't even know we've been conquered."[9]

This is a common rhetorical technique for hate-spewers, to take an oppressed group and turn them into some omnipowerful enemy, hoping to increase the fear and hatred that the larger society already feels toward them. Pat Robertson of the Christian Coalition likes using Nazi analogies himself. This is what he has to say about gays: "Many of the people involved in [*sic*] Adolf Hitler were Satanists, many of them were homosexuals—the two things seem to go together."[10]

Just when gays and lesbians are coming out all over, able to live their lives in openness and freedom, the forces of hatred and repression are trying to push them back into the closet. And chief among those forces are Pat Robertson and the other minions of the Religious Right.

THE RELIGIOUS RIGHT

The Religious Right likes to portray itself as a persecuted majority, using Nazi analogies to a frightening degree, and in doing so, insulting the memories of those who truly suffered. Texas newspaper columnist Molly Ivins quoted Pat Robertson as saying,

> Just what Nazi Germany did to the Jews, so liberal America is now doing to the evangelical Christians. It's the same thing. It is the Democratic Congress, the liberal-biased media and the homosexuals who want to destroy all Christians. Wholesale abuse and discrimination and the worst bigotry directed toward any group in America today.[11]

At times, his rhetoric is violent; he told his followers to prepare for "confrontations that will not only be unpleasant but at times physically bloody."[12]

Antiabortion extremist Randall Terry, the founder of Operation Rescue, a group that physically prevents women from exercising their rights to legal medical care, used similarly violent language in a speech to his supporters. "I want you to just let a wave of intolerance wash over you. I want you to let a wave of hatred wash over you. Yes, hate is good." This alleged Christian seems to have forgotten the Biblical injunction "Love thy neighbor"—indeed, he seems to have ignored all of the New Testament and a good bit of the Old. But his goals are religious only in the most narrow sense; he is basically a crusader for intolerance and theocracy. "Our goal is a Christian nation," he says. "We have a biblical duty, we are called by God, to conquer this country."[13]

During an interview on a St. Louis radio station on June 24, 1994, President Clinton compared evangelist Jerry Falwell with the moneychangers that Christ chased out of the temple. Clinton was angered by Falwell's hawking of a videotape that accuses the president of, among other things, ordering the murder of "countless people." The tape, which Falwell produced, promoted and was selling on his television show, *The Old Time Gospel Hour*, for $43 included a number of wild assertions for which it offered no evidence.

The fact that Clinton is a devout Baptist means nothing to

the proselytizers of the Religious Right, which shows that they are more concerned with matters secular than spiritual. Pat Robertson called Clinton's inauguration a "repudiation of our forefathers' covenant with God."[14] When Clinton stood up to Falwell on the radio, Bob Dole, trolling for votes among the troglodyte right, accused the president of "Christian bigotry."[15]

"Religious Right organizations have found it increasingly convenient to cry 'religious bigotry' when their political agenda is criticized," said the late Arthur Kropp, then president of People for the American Way. "It's an effective way to divert attention from their political goals and activities and portray themselves as victims of intolerance."[16] The Christian Right wants to have it both ways, to be a political actor, yet to hide behind its religious organizations, particularly when they provide tax-exempt status. But they are much more Right than they are Religious, and we ought to start calling them by a different name—how about right-wing bigots who happen to be Christians?

Rolling Stone reports that during the 1994 campaign, a branch of the Christian Coalition "published an editorial warning that the federal government was paving the way for a United Nations takeover of America."[17] The report was based on an article in *The Spotlight*, the newspaper of the anti-Semitic Liberty Lobby. Two Christian Coalition candidates elected to the school board in La Mesa, California, opposed a federally funded breakfast program, claiming that it "violated family values" and was "socialist." It seems that the Christian Right is more concerned with maintaining dogmatical adherence to their antigovernment agenda than it is worried about whether schoolchildren go hungry.

Operation Rescue distributed 140,000 copies of a brochure that warned: "To vote for Bill Clinton is to sin against God." It called Clinton "a neo-pagan" with only "a veneer of Christianity." The letter claimed, "If Bill Clinton is elected, he will help destroy three centuries of Christianity in America."[18]

During the 1992 Democratic Convention in New York,

Randall Terry helped a supporter attempt to hand Clinton a fetus. In Indiana, congressional candidate Michael Bailey used pictures of aborted fetuses in his campaign ads and said that the most important issue in the race was belief in Christ. Fortunately, he was defeated, and we were spared his morbid theocracy in Washington.

Let us take a look at the thorny issue of abortion. Instead of debating abortion as an important policy issue, the Religious Right states their opposition to abortion not just on moral but on spiritual grounds. How can you argue with someone whose motive intellectual force is faith? Now, clearly, the prochoice side needs to respect the religious views of people who oppose abortion on these grounds, just as those on the other side need to respect the religious views of prochoicers and the lack of unanimity among all religions on the subject. The problem is that rather than trying to engage in a dialogue, to find common ground—such as preventing unwanted pregnancies—the Religious Right casts its opponents as Satanic murderers. In the end, we get nowhere. In a democracy, we cannot endlessly argue first principles or seek to impose our religious beliefs on others whose faiths may tell them something completely different. If we cannot find some common ground, if we cannot agree to disagree, then our public debate will become poisonous. That is exactly what has happened with abortion.

Paul Weyrich, founder of the Heritage Foundation and many other New Right organizations, told the *Conservative Digest*: "We see the anti-family movement as an attempt to prevent souls from reaching eternal salvation."[19] There is a lot to consider in this brief statement. First let us look at the divisive epithet "anti-family." It assumes that whoever Weyrich's enemies are, they are politically engaged against families. To be more honest, Weyrich should call the movement the anti-Weyrich movement, because the only thing that all of these alleged political actors, if they do indeed exist, would have in common is that Weyrich does not like them, and the feeling is no doubt mutual. But by casting their rhetoric in such loaded terms—"pro-life," for example—they immediately put their opponents on the defensive. Now their opponents have to explain that they are not, after all, antifamily or prodeath. One way to fight the Christian Right is simply to refuse to use their terminology. In the beginning was the word.

But another point raised by Weyrich's comment is that the Christian Right often acts as if their political goals are, in the end, spiritual. If they are sincere, then there is no arguing with them—if you disagree with them, they believe you are damned and will go to hell. If they are not sincere, it is even worse, for they are using the deeply personal issues of belief, spirituality, and salvation as cheap rhetorical tactics.

Try as the Religious Right may to divide the world into the liberal-secular and the conservative-devout, religion is not a partisan issue. According to a 1992 Gallup poll, 41 percent of Republicans characterized themselves as "born-again." That is only a statistically insignificant margin over the 39 percent of "born-again" Democrats. And even though Robertson and his cronies keep painting the Democrats as a party of secular-atheists, in fact, 71 percent of Democrats go to church, while 79 percent of Republicans do.[20]

Religion has a place in public life. The religious and ethical beliefs of men and women of goodwill should inform the political debate. However, we cannot allow religious bigots to polarize our political discourse into the Manichean world of believers and unbelievers, the righteous and the evil, the followers of God and the devotees of Satan. Religious belief is too personal an issue to be debated publicly, and attempts to judge or convert voters on religious grounds through the political process is not just wrong, it is ugly.

Religious prejudice has no place in our democracy. The Bible teaches love, yet that virtue is sadly absent from the Religious Right's arguments and tactics. Instead of using their religion as a positive force to bring people together, they are using it as a negative force to divide and disrupt us, to sow their seeds of hatred in the freshly churned soil of political chaos. For all of their talk about Jesus, they are frightfully (perhaps intentionally) ignorant of many of his most important teachings and his example. Instead, their God is an angry God: the harsh, vain, and vindictive creator of the Old Testament. The Religious Right gives a very narrow reading to the Bible, focusing more on the code of Leviticus than the Gospel of Jesus. They ignore such Christian virtues as forgiveness, compassion, and charity.

For all of their talk about religion, their ambitions are almost purely secular. Instead of their religion informing their politics, their politics informs their religion. And in the realm of politics, the Christian Right repeatedly attempts to break down the constitutionally established wall between church and state, a distinction that Christ himself made clear by saying, "Render therefore unto Caesar the things which are Caesar's, and unto God the things that are God's."[21]

THE LEGACY OF HATRED

Too much political campaigning, and too much of our political discussion, is motivated by hatred and fear. We must stop the politics of polarization and begin appealing to voters of all races, colors, genders, sexual orientations, and religious faiths equally, not pitting them against each other in some atavistic war of rancor and exclusion, but bringing them together with a politics of inclusion—in other words, a real democracy.

Chapter 11

The Selling
of the Candidate

How are decisions made inside a campaign that lead to the poison politics of crime, race, gender, sexual orientation, and religion? One big factor is the influence of Madison Avenue on the road to Pennsylvania Avenue. And one of the first places to look is the successful 1968 presidential campaign of Richard Nixon.

Nixon was the Babe Ruth of negative politics. He changed the way the game was played. But while the Bambino made baseball a game of power and excitement, Nixon just made campaigning a game of sleaze and soap. He was the first inhabitant of a place Adlai Stevenson called "Nixonland—a land of slander and scare, of sly innuendo, of a poison pen, the anonymous phone call, and hustling, pushing, shoving—the land of smash and grab and anything to win."[1]

After a failed bid for the presidency, and then an embarrassing defeat in the California gubernatorial election of 1962, Nixon promised that we would not have him to kick around anymore. But, of course, he came back, this time as a new and improved version. But like many advertising renovations, the New Nixon proved to be the same product in different packaging.

"I am not going to barricade myself into a television studio and make this an antiseptic campaign," Nixon promised shortly after becoming the Republicans' presidential nominee in 1968.

But, of course, that is exactly what he did. During the campaign, voters saw very little of the "New Nixon," except on television appearances, made up mostly of staged panel interviews, in which carefully selected interrogators lobbed easy questions at the candidate.

Five of Nixon's key staffers came from the J. Walter Thompson (JWT) agency: H. R. Haldeman, Laurence Higby, Ron Ziegler, Dwight Chapin, and Ken Cole. And they tried to run the press operation like an ad account. Nixon once wrote the following memo to Haldeman:

> When I think of the millions of dollars that go into one lousy 30-second television spot advertising deodorant, it seems to me unbelievable that we don't do a better job in seeing that Presidential appearances always have the very best professional advice.[2]

Nixon and his JWT gang did a pretty good job of taking a second-rate politician and selling him to the American people through a sophisticated media campaign that kept the candidate at arm's length from the public and allowed him to run a nasty and divisive race from the comfortable settings of Roger Ailes's television studios.

Joe McGinniss turned Theodore White's campaign journalism on its ear by writing *The Selling of the President 1968*, the first backstage look at a political campaign in the television age. Pretty soon everyone was asking, "Should political candidates be sold like soap?"

Of course they should not. Political candidates are not a product, and any attempt to sell them that way is a mistake, both strategically and ethically.

MERCHANDISED CAMPAIGNING

Politics and commercial advertising have a long and uneasy history together. As advertising historian Stephen Fox points out, "The first politician to tack a sign on a tree or distribute a handbill was, of course, engaged in political advertising."[3] But as American advertising became more sophisticated and the techniques of mass marketing emerged, political campaigns began to adopt, in their own way, some tactics of commercial appeals.

As advertising became more prevalent throughout America, it eventually made its way into the political arena. When Theodore Roosevelt met Albert Lasker of the Lord and Thomas agency, he said, "They tell me you are America's greatest advertising man." Lasker replied, "No man can claim that distinction so long as you live."[4] Lasker was eventually hired by the Republicans to defeat the League of Nations, and he became a confidant of Warren Harding. The slogan "Keep Cool with Coolidge" was coined by Henry Ewald, a Detroit advertising man. Madison Avenue's Bruce Barton served two terms in Congress, and said, "Salesmen should really make excellent congressmen. They know people."[5] But in 1940, he lost a race for the Senate by almost a half-million votes and wound up back in advertising.

There were so many Madison Avenue types working on the 1940 Wendell Wilkie campaign that Dorothy Thompson told her radio listeners she was supporting FDR, "because I am at long last fed up with the glib copywriters who think they can slug this nation into an election."[6]

Eisenhower's chief advertising consultant was Rosser Reeves, creative maven at the Ted Bates Agency, who had come up with campaigns such as "M&Ms melt in your mouth, not in your hands" and "Wonder Bread helps build strong bodies twelve ways." His theory of marketing was called the Unique Selling Proposition. The USP is a claim that can pull in new customers, and one that the competitor cannot make. USP was supposed to be judged on functional, not aesthetic grounds. According to Reeves, the ad campaign "must be judged on whether it performs what it was designed to do."[7]

This functional approach was best illustrated in Reeves's campaign for Anacin, which featured a cartoon of a headache sufferer with three boxes in his head containing a pounding hammer, a coiling spring, and a jagged electric bolt, which were quickly "relieved by little bubbles of Anacin making their way up from the stomach."[8] The ad was not pretty. In fact, it was the most unpopular commercial on television at the time. But it worked, and Reeves often bragged that it had made more money than *Gone with the Wind*.

Applying the hard-sell and USP to a political candidate proved a little more dicey. Reeves could not isolate one, unique selling proposition for Eisenhower and instead focused on three separate issues: Korea, government corruption, and the high cost of living.

In the Reeves spots, the candidate really is being sold like soap. And the spots were shown repeatedly, on counsel of his ad consultants, schooled in the hard-sell marketing techniques in which repetition, even to the point of inanity, was essential to selling a product. (Repetition is also important in political communications, but there has to be more of a message than simply "Buy!") The spots had a negligible effect on Eisenhower's election; he was already revered as the hero of World War II, and he carried everything but the Solid South both times around.

Still, the idea persisted that a candidate was just another product and could be sold in the same manner as packaged goods. Many advertising people who worked in the early television campaigns referred to their candidates as "the product." There was no attempt at specialization in political ads; creative people were taken off commercial accounts to work on elections, and vice versa.

SOAP BUBBLES

Unlike commercial advertising, you cannot cover up a lousy candidate with slick packaging. Political advertising is about character and issues. Even some people on Nixon's media team realized that. Jim Howard, a public relations consultant who worked on the 1968 campaign, said:

> You can't sell a candidate like a product. A product, all you want to do is get attention. You only need two percent additional buyers to make the campaign worthwhile. In politics you need a flat 51 percent of the market and you can't get that through gimmicks.[9]

Political ad campaigns have markedly different strategies and tactics from commercial appeals. They are focused and run over only a short period of time. They have fixed end dates. They discuss matters of importance—to people personally and to society as a whole. And they are more memorable. According to one study, 79 percent of television viewers recall political spots, whereas only 20 percent remember product ads.[10]

The techniques necessary to discuss important issues are completely different from those of selling automobiles or toilet paper. As Patterson and McClure note:

> The issue appeals contained in political advertising bear little resemblance to the kind of product appeals typified by Coca-Cola ads. Where such product commercials are nonsensical, issue advertising is substantial. Where the product ad eschews conflict, the issue spot highlights it.... Where the product message simply tries to create awareness, the issue message tries to get the viewers to think.[11]

Even when political advertising is attempting to convey the more human aspects of a candidate, it is still far different from standard commercial approaches. The whole challenge of a commercial advertisement is to develop some value or a difference that may not be inherent to the product. Reeves's USP depended on creating a perceived advantage to a product that is probably not in any significant way distinguishable from its competitor. "Wonder Bread helps build strong bodies twelve ways." Which twelve ways are those? The claim, like the product itself, is mostly air.

In politics, you cannot create something that does not exist. The candidates are there, flesh and blood, and no amount of makeup or hairspray is going to change the way people feel about their character or the issues. Ads that attempt to portray a candidate as something other than who he or she is will usually fail. Think of Michael Dukakis riding a tank, or Richard Nixon walking down the beach in a business suit. Phony and contrived images just do not go over.

Because political ads do not create values or differences out of nothing, the style of the candidate dictates the style of the ads, and the message of the spot has to be consonant with the message of the campaign as a whole if it is to have any impact. Imagine if Barry Goldwater had run the "Daisy" ad. It simply would not have been credible. "The same commercial can be run by two different candidates and one would be seen as being fair and the other unfair," says consultant and *Hotline* publisher Doug Bailey.

And a candidate's record is always going to be more important than salesmanship, especially for incumbents. After his client Jimmy Carter lost in 1980, Gerald Rafshoon said he should have taken the $30 million spent in the campaign and bought three more helicopters for the Iran rescue mission.

In 1988, pollster Frank Luntz conducted a survey among political consultants asking, "What is the single most important factor in a political campaign today?" The overwhelming answer was the candidate, with 66 percent. Running a distant second was money, at 11 percent. Other answers included issues, television, and strategy, all in the single digits. Consultants know that if you do not have a candidate, you do not have a campaign. In 1994, Oliver North spent $20 million running for the Senate and lost. That same year, Michael Huffington spent $20 million and lost. John Connally, in 1980, and Phil Gramm and Steve Forbes, in 1996, spent millions running for the Republican presidential nomination, to no avail. The short-lived 1984 presidential campaign of John Glenn is an example of how you can arrange a great deal of consulting talent and give them a lot of money to spend, but if the candidate—even a national hero—cannot give the voters a reason to vote for him or her, you do not stand a chance.

Often what works on Madison Avenue will not work on the campaign trail and vice versa. "Where's the beef?" was a much more successful slogan for Walter Mondale than it was for Wendy's hamburgers.

Political spots are often held under closer scrutiny than commercial advertisements. The *New York Times* and *Washington Post* do not have truth boxes criticizing the various claims of commercial products. And competing brands rarely come out with response ads.

What if a good commercial ad campaign fails, or a bad or misleading one succeeds? The worst thing that happens is that a few consumers are stuck with products they do not want or do not really need. But the consequences of political advertising are much more lasting and more important. Although the effects of political advertising have certainly been exaggerated by its critics, no one is going to argue that they do not have an impact. And advertisers who work on political campaigns should be aware not only of their duty to the client, but of their greater civic responsibility as well. Politicians are not just product, they are our leaders, and we should choose them with infinitely more care than we would a bar of soap or a tube of toothpaste.

SELLING SOAP LIKE CANDIDATES

The question really is not whether we should sell candidates like soap, but whether we should sell soap like candidates. In fact, Madison Avenue is taking notice of how candidates are presented to the public, and they are trying to bring political tactics to the marketplace.

In a paper entitled "Different Reasons, Same Conclusions," an adman considered how politics can serve as a model for successful marketing. "Politicians recognized something most marketers have yet to come to grips with. People often do the same thing for very different reasons."[12] The author of the paper, Craig Middleton, a 27-year advertising veteran, who wrote the paper for McCann-Erickson and is now at Young and Rubicam (Y&R), noted: "Politicians build coalitions, create consensus and, important for our purpose, manage constituencies."

Middleton points out how a candidate appeals to separate constituencies by appealing to different issues.

> An American presidential candidate can build support among farmers for being for export subsidies; among autoworkers by being for restrictive import quotas; in the inner cities by being tough on crime; in the suburbs by talking aid to education.

Those appeals are focused and yet not contradictory. They can all belong to the same platform.

Advertisers could learn from these strategies, according to Middleton. "Marketers will need to address highly divergent consumer groups and join them together in a kind of coalition franchise." Rather than mass-marketing brand names to huge consumer groups, which may contain highly divergent constituents, or appealing to only narrow segments of the populace, Middleton suggests a multifaceted approach in which one brand can be different things to different people, without losing its core identity.

For example, instead of simply appealing to people who are concerned about their weight, the way Weight Watchers has, successful packaged-food companies have sought wider constituencies with products such as Lean Cuisine and Healthy Choice, broadening their base to people who want to reduce their fat intake—whether they are overweight or not—or simply to eat healthier. In the same way that a successful politician reaches out to as wide a coalition as possible, and runs a campaign of inclusion rather than exclusion, products should be marketed broadly rather than narrowly.

Madison Avenue could learn a lot from politics. Unfortunately, too many advertising mavens feel that they are above politics, that flogging laundry detergent is somehow morally superior to representing a candidate who seeks to lead our nation. As Tony Schwartz says of image meisters of Madison Avenue, "I wouldn't even sell soap the way they sell soap."[13]

FROM THE FOLKS WHO BROUGHT YOU JOE CAMEL

There are some people on Madison Avenue who do not like political advertisements. And while they, as voters, might have cause to complain about the content of negative ads, they are in no position as advertisers to claim the moral high ground. Some political ads may be sleazy, but nothing compares to the pernicious idiocy that pours out of Madison Avenue. From dancing cats to belching frogs, to cartoon camels teaching children how to smoke, Madison Avenue has created a culture of amoral salesmanship and mindless dreck that, by comparison, makes political ads seem like high-toned discourse. And worse than the sheer idiocy of much that passes for commercial advertising these days is the way that Madison Avenue values have come to dominate our culture. Everything is for sale, and one can barely make it through the day without being barraged by various commercial pitches, both the jackhammer repetition of hard-sell and the sleazy insinuation of soft-sell. The result is a culture where moral, ethical, and aesthetic values are replaced by the crucible of the marketplace, and everything is reduced to the status of commodity, even individuals.

Politics may be, at times, a rough business. But in a choice between the standards of Pennsylvania Avenue and Madison Avenue, I would take the former any day.

MR. ADMAN COMES TO WASHINGTON

Countless commercial advertising people have been unable to make the leap from packaged goods to politicians. Every campaign cycle, Madison Avenue hotshots find out that you cannot sell politicians like soap.

Martin Purvis, a Madison Avenue copywriter, who created ads for George Bush's 1992 campaign, says of political advertising, "People who go into this thinking it's just advertising are in for a shock."[14] Political campaigns have tighter budgets and time constraints. Purvis had four months to make his first ads for MasterCard. But the Bush campaign only gave him six days to produce one of their spots. MasterCard spent $60 million on advertising, all of which was controlled by Purvis, whereas the Bush campaign spent $40 million, which was divided among other agencies and consultants. A single political spot for Bush cost no more than $40,000, whereas commercial spots often run production budgets into several hundred thousand dollars.

For some advertising executives, campaign work is a status enhancer, the equivalent of high-visibility charity work. Much commercial advertising is not at all glamorous, but there is a lot of money for products such as canned cheese and adult diapers. Ad people like the publicity that follows a political campaign, and often electoral work will translate into more billings in the commercial sector. Most of the people who come from Madison Avenue to work in politics may believe in their candidate or their cause, but do not kid yourself for a minute that they would not rather have the Burger King account. As one advertising observer put it, "Given the choice between getting Bill Clinton and Proctor and Gamble, anybody would take P&G."

Advertising people are business people, plain and simple. Many will sell any product, even if it kills people. So it is a little bit troubling when Madison Avenue takes the high ground and starts complaining about the content of political ads, which is exactly what has happened in the last two national elections.

PROJECT RUN FAIR

It started in 1992, when Project Run Fair was established by the League of Women Voters, the American Association of

Advertising Agencies (AAAA), and the Markle Foundation. They began right before the New Hampshire primaries, hoping to serve as watchdog for the political ads during that campaign. The organization gave voters a telephone hotline to call and identify ads that they did not like.

The program was plagued with difficulties from the start. First of all, the telephone hotline was a 900 number and charged the caller $1.15 per minute. Ginger Culpepper, president of the New Hampshire chapter of the League, said that the telephone toll was established to offset the costs of the operation, and that they had hoped it would keep campaign organizations from flooding the phone banks with complaints about their opponents' ads.

Then, the group had trouble getting their public-service radio and newspaper ads, announcing the project's goals and methods, placed in the local media. The sponsors had asked the media to run these announcements free of charge, during a political season in which air time and ad space was at a premium. The ads were produced for the group by Wunderman Worldwide; the print ads featured the Statue of Liberty holding a telephone.

Once they realized they could not get free advertising, the groups tried to attract media attention. They got some coverage, but according to Ms. Culpepper, "Not enough people heard the word."[15]

The program was a failure, and not just because of logistical problems. Project Run Fair attempted to establish commercial advertisers as the self-appointed arbiter of campaign advertising tactics, but without any prior dialogue with the political community. Rather, Project Run Fair thought that a public groundswell would come out of the mere announcement of their program and its prohibitively expensive phone lines, and they would assume their rightful position, dispensing a seal of approval to ads that met their standards, while forcing unpalatable ads off the air. They had no regulatory power. no presence within the political community, no legal or even moral leverage. Project Run Fair was, in the end, merely a group of freelance media critics with no authority and, ultimately, no impact.

Project Run Fair was an attempt at social censorship. They hoped to encourage enough public pressure against negative ads that campaigns would drop the ones they found offensive. Now, there was a lot of harsh, negative advertising in the New Hampshire primary, particularly by the campaigns of Pat Buchanan and Tom Harkin. But the way to counteract bad ads is to respond to and expose them, not ignore them or shout them down. Project Run Fair should have realized this from the start.

John Phillips, former publisher of *Campaign* magazine, said of the effort: "The best safeguard against misleading advertising is not efforts at self-policing, but more comparative advertising and greater scrutiny of the records of incumbents and challengers."[16]

The League of Women Voters has a long and proud tradition of working to improve American politics by making it more democratic and giving voters more pertinent information on which to make their decisions. And the Markle Foundation has been involved in campaign reform for a long time. They are two outstanding organizations, whose involvement in elections stems from their dedication to, and great understanding of, the political system. The AAAA, however, had no business getting involved in the New Hampshire primaries. The project was a pet of Y&R's Alex Kroll, at the time, chairman of the AAAA. His agency, one of the largest in the country, handles several R. J. Reynolds accounts and was responsible for the infamous Joe Camel campaign until it was taken over by Y&R veterans Mezzina/Brown.

Why are the folks responsible for Joe Camel all of a sudden concerned about the content of political advertising? If they suddenly developed a conscience, why is their moral scorn directed at political advertising and not their own? At a speech before the American Association of Political Consultants, James Carville said, "The people who brought us the Marlboro Man and the [Ford] Pinto gas tank cover-up ought to crawl back under the rocks that they came from. Before they try to clean up someone else's house, they should take care of their own."

Commercial advertisers only want to increase their market share. Political advertisers may want the same thing, but they are also trying to help decide how the nation is to be governed. And while corporate sponsors can put up with a few disappointed customers who are fooled by misleading advertising, in politics, it is a lot tougher to get away with broken promises, as George Bush learned in 1992. As the old Hebrew National hot dog ad put it: "We have to answer to a higher authority." Carville notes that political consultants are "regulated by the most awesome regulatory force on the Earth, the American voters."

JERRY, WHAT'S THE STORY?

More recently, noted adman Jerry Della Femina tried to get in on the act. In a full-page newspaper ad published in the *New York Times* and the *Wall Street Journal* the day after the 1994 election, Ketchum Advertising, Della Femina's new agency, came out with an attack on political advertising headlined "Don't Call It Advertising." The ad read, in part:

> Let those of us in advertising, broadcasting, publishing and business stand up together and say: "Stop."
> Stop the character assassination.
> Stop the lies.
> Stop the ugliness.
> And, above all, stop calling what you're doing advertising.

Why did Della Femina enter, or more accurately, create, this controversy? He had recently joined the foundering Ketchum, a firm based in Pittsburgh that had just lost several accounts. Della Femina had been out of the business for a while. After a series of lucrative yet nasty mergers and buyouts, he opened several restaurants in the Hamptons, but soon grew tired of catering to the tanned and tony, and went back into advertising.

Della Femina is an indefatigable self-promoter. He is the author of several books, including the classic *From the Folks Who Brought You Pearl Harbor*, a memoir from the go-go years of advertising in the 1960s. His byline is often found in the general press, and recently he wrote a paean to the three-martini lunch in the *New York Times Magazine*. Among his many successful campaigns was the commercial for "Meow Mix" in which kittens lip-synched to a rather irksome little jingle. The spot was inspired when one of the kittens actually choked on the pet food, and to create a chorus line of singing kittens, the advertisers had to choke several more. Della Femina also did the Joe Isuzu "He's lying" campaign.

But how deep is his political commitment? Who knows? The fax number provided in his newspaper ad has been disconnected. It seems Jerry and Ketchum do not want to talk about negative political advertising anymore, at least not until such talk can get them more publicity and, they hope, more accounts.

FRAUD, SLEAZE, AND DECEPTION

Madison Avenue is in no position to criticize the standards of political advertising. First of all, political advertising is not any more negative than its commercial counterpart. About one-third of the 25,000 ads shown on network television each year are, in industry parlance, "comparative," which is to say, they contrast their product to their competitor, just like most negative political ads do. That is about the same proportion as political ads, although the negative spots do seem to be more prominent, because they are more easily remembered than positive messages.

Much of the negative campaigning in commercial advertising is either mean-spirited or simply idiotic. Coke is always battling Pepsi. Maxwell House attacks Folgers. MCI and AT&T

engage in a tedious exchange of attack spots that even further obscure the almost-insignificant and always-confusing differences between the two long-distance carriers. Sports figures in British Knights ads insult each other by saying, "Your mother wears Nikes." Few of these "comparative ads" are informational; they do not teach the consumer anything but cynicism and insults. Instead of pointing out what few real differences do exist between products, all they do is attack their competitors with spurious claims and ridiculous hype, attempting to move their market share a few points. Often, these ads are responded to by more negative ads, creating a dynamic of hysteria that makes the 1992 New Hampshire primaries look like a debate at the Oxford Union. Who profits? Besides broadcasters, just the advertising agencies, as they keep on making new ads and collecting their percentage on media buys for the old ones.

False claims have plagued advertising almost from its inception, and several government agencies and public-interest groups have worked hard to hold Madison Avenue accountable for what it says about the products it is flogging. In the 1980s, standards were relaxed, and false or misleading advertising claims often went unpunished. Now the Federal Trade Commission is cracking down on companies that make promises their products do not deliver. Still, the problem is immense.

"Soft-core nutrition pornography has ripped off the public for $10 billion a year," according to Victor Herbert, professor of medicine at Mount Sinai, and a lawyer who specializes in health fraud. "Few cases are effectively prosecuted. Laws don't protect us against deception by omission."[17]

Kellogg's All Bran was said to fight cancer. Ralston-Purina claimed its dog food prevented hip disease. Four different companies, General Mills, Mazola, Nabisco, and Quaker Oats, have been fined for falsely stating that their food products reduce cholesterol levels. And these are just the companies that have been caught and punished for making false claims in their advertisements. Countless other bogus promises—usually having nothing to do with the product (e.g., this car will make you a "babe magnet")—remain on the air, because the standard of truth and accuracy in commercial advertising is almost non-existent.

THE MERCHANTS OF DEATH

Let us not forget that in 1994, the latest year for which figures are available, the tobacco industry spent close to $5 billion advertising and promoting a product that kills more than 400,000 Americans each year (and that is without being able to advertise on television).[18] The following advertising agencies handle tobacco accounts:

- Leo Burnett (Alpine, Benson & Hedges, Bucks, Cambridge, Marlboro, Merit, Virginia Slims)
- Young and Rubicam (Dave's, Parliament)
- Bates USA (Lucky Strike)
- Grey Advertising (Kool, Carlton, Kent, Lucky Strike, Pall Mall, Viceroy)
- Saatchi and Saatchi (Benson & Hedges)
- Mezzina/Brown (Camel, Winston, Winston Select)
- Trune Advertising (Salem, More, Now)
- Coyne Beahm (Doral, Magna, Sterling, Century)
- Tatham RSCG (Barclay, Richland, Capri, Misty, Montclair)
- Avrett, Free & Ginsberg (All Lorillard accounts—True, Kent, Newport, Old Gold, etc.)

POLITICS AND COMMERCE

Politics is a higher calling than commerce, or, at least, it should be treated that way. And voting is not simply another consumer choice. Unfortunately, in the consumer culture that we now live, everything and everybody is judged by the bottom line, and a great deal of the blame for that lies at the feet of Madison Avenue.

Chapter 12

The Rise of Consultants

Political consultants are often blamed for the increasingly poisonous tenor of our political campaigns. After all, they are the ones who come up with negative advertisements. But it is not that simple. First of all, such criticism lets the candidate off the hook. Ultimately, candidates have to be responsible for their campaign messages. That is not to say political consultants are guiltless creatures merely doing the bidding of their nefarious clients. Indeed, consultants often convince their candidates to go negative early and often. They will attempt to explain the necessity of scorched-earth tactics by saying that if they do not do it, their opponent will. They will say they are getting paid to win an election—in other words, to influence people and not make friends. They will say that politics is a dirty business, and you cannot win fighting fair.

I believe they are wrong. Politics does not have to be poisonous, and you can fight hard and still fight fair. But the problem is not just going negative. It is how those attacks on your opponent are performed, and whether there is any positive information delivered by the campaign.

"What's deplorable about negative TV advertising isn't that one candidate criticizes another," political consultants Dan Payne and Todd Domke write in the *Boston Globe*. "Differences on issues are useful, fair and legitimate. But when differences are trivial, dishonest, misleading and overwhelmingly personal, the quality of debate is demeaned and elections lose meaning as expressions of public will."[1]

Although critical ads about your opponent are an integral part of a campaign strategy, they should not be the only message. The pressures to go nuclear often come, not from a sober assessment of the long-term goals of the campaign, but from the quick bumps in polling numbers that a new negative spot often provides. These bumps are seen as necessary, particularly in the early stages of the campaign, to prove a candidate's viability and attract fund-raisers, so the campaign can afford to buy more spots. Although the financial and competitive pressures are great, this doctrine of necessity that supposedly forces campaigners to go negative is not so much a cause as an excuse, an easy way to rationalize a decision based on expediency rather than ethical judgment or long-term perspective. In the end, negative spots used in the absence of positive messages simply add to the increasingly negative tenor in our debate and make voters disgusted with consultants, politicians, and even politics itself.

NEGATIVE TECHNIQUES

Negative ads have become the nuclear arsenal of the political consultant. Unfortunately, what once was a strategy of deterrence has become all-out ballistic warfare as campaigns are striking harder and faster than ever. Ken Swope put it this way: "Presidential politics is like nuclear war: he who strikes first wins."[2] That strategy has become prevalent in lower ballot elections as well, where candidates go ballistic as soon as the campaign is joined.

Some candidates are initially unwilling to go negative, yet their consultants advise that if they do not, in the words of Democratic pollster Mark Mellman, "You'll get creamed."[3]

Other candidates want to go negative hard, fast, early, and exclusively, and hire consultants who will do the job for them.

Even while they are using little else but negative ads, consultants may try to spin the other way. In the middle of the Punch-and-Judy Show that was the 1994 Virginia senatorial race, Republican challenger Oliver North's media guru Mike Murphy claimed,

> Oliver North has moved up in the poll with an issues campaign. Earlier this week, the Robb campaign went up with an inaccurate ad attacking Col. North; we counter-attacked. I think we'll mix it up for a couple of days and then I think the Robb forces will regret what they started. And we'll get back to the issues, which is where we've tried to keep the campaign all along.[4]

Democratic Senator Chuck Robb's consultant David Doak was not much better:

> [T]his campaign's probably been more positive than any-one thought it would be. The truth is that Senator Robb's been criticized by a number of people—including people in the press who've talked to me privately—and other Democrats for not getting tougher with Ollie North sooner.[5]

Who could possibly have wanted a more negative campaign than Robb–North? Machiavelli himself would have been disgusted by the level of nasty rhetoric and the lack of issues-based argument in that race. But in the murky world of spin, there is little worry if one's words do not correspond to reality. All that matters is the effect they have on people's perceptions.

Some consultants admit they are running negative campaigns, but say that it is not their fault; they're just giving the voters the only messages they will believe. "[T]he public's cynicism about politics and politicians is such that whatever you assert positively about your candidate, it's almost impos-sible to get beyond the cynicism," said Bill Carrick, who ran Democratic Senator Dianne Feinstein's campaign against Michael Huffington (R). "The reaction is, 'Who can believe any-thing that a politician says about themselves?'"[6]

Carrick has a point. But that rationalization also conveniently leaves out the role that such ads play in fomenting public cynicism about politicians. It is a curious dynamic. Does public cynicism create the market for negative spots, or do negative spots create cynicism? The answer to this classic chicken-or-egg question is "yes" to both. What we have is a vicious circle in which both phenomena feed on each other. The consultants, candidates, and even the voters play a part in this ugly course of events.

Consultants have an obligation to their candidates, to be sure. They are paid to win elections. But they also have an obligation to the public at large, and running a campaign based only on negative spots, exploiting the cynical tendencies that already exist, may win elections in the short term but will eventually create a poisonous political atmosphere in which cynicism is not merely the dominant mood but the only one. Imagine if Coca-Cola's advertising agency did nothing but say how awful Pepsi was, and Pepsi did nothing but disparage Coke. After a while, nobody would drink either. But we can live without cola. Outside of a handful of radical libertarians, no one wants to live without government and the protections it provides for our safety and physical health, and against financial destitution. We boycott elections at our own peril.

Ralph Murphine, chairman of the American Association of Political Consultants, says that "a full-time diet of negative personal attack for political gain is a strategy, like all strategies, of limited nutritive value for the body politic." Unless candidates and consultants realize that the short-term gains of attack ads and the tactics of polarization are wreaking serious and possibly permanent damage on the very political system they inhabit, nothing is going to change. It is in the best interest of everyone involved in politics that our debate be honest, substantive, inclusive, lively, and inspiring.

"Just as those who hold public office hold a public trust, so do those who manage the machinery by which social interests are translated into political power,"[7] says Christopher Arterton, dean of the Graduate School of Political Management at George Washington University. Unfortunately, a commitment to public trust often gets ignored in an increasingly competitive, lucrative, and ego-driven profession.

THE ROOT OF ALL EVIL

Every consultant will tell you that half the money spent on advertising is wasted. Trouble is, they can never figure out which half. So they spend as much as they can get. Money is a profoundly corrupting force in politics, and political consultants are certainly not immune to its seductive power. Although what consultants do for money is seldom illegal, it is sometimes unethical or, at least, highly questionable.

Consultants have a vested interest in media rather than traditional campaigns. The more ads they produce, and the more often those ads get shown on the air, the more money they make. Generally, a consultant will get a flat fee for creative work or general consultation, and then the standard 15 percent agency commission on the cost of paid media, the same as any commercial ad agency. As might be imagined, there is a lot more to be made from the markup than the flat fee itself, particularly in campaigns where tens of millions of dollars are spent in media buys.

After their candidates win election, some consultants parlay their close ties with their former clients into lucrative lobbying deals. The Republican consulting firm of Black, Manafort, Atwater, and Stone turned the connections they established during the Reagan campaigns into access at the Reagan White House for their lobbying clients. But most media consultants do not lobby, and those who do represent certain interests stick to making the case for their client through the media, not by influence peddling or direct lobbying.

Money corrupts the electoral process; it makes the whole system less competitive and less fair. The need for an expensive television campaign, normally comprising predominantly negative ads, has made elections prohibitively expensive and therefore less open to real competition. Television campaigns require consultants, and reliance on high-priced media talent often freezes out underfunded competitors, making political contests a domain of the rich and well connected.

Consultant Frank Luntz points out: "Today, well-funded challengers, using paid political advertising, can compete with the incumbent on a more equal footing than was possible a decade ago." The operative term is *well-funded*. Candidates who do not have great sources of ready money to draw upon often do not have the ability to effectively challenge incumbents. Therefore, we see more and more independently wealthy candidates, many of whose political experience is negligible, and their background woefully inadequate for the challenges of public life. The only qualification they have is the financial wherewithal to mount a television campaign. Although the public often sees through the transparent insubstantiality of a Michael Huffington, or the eccentricity bordering on derangement of an Abe Hirschfeld, what is scary is that these candidates were taken seriously, simply because they could afford to spend millions on spots. Would Ross Perot have garnered 19 percent of the national vote—or even run for office in the first place—if he did not have billions of dollars at his disposal? In the early days of the 1996 presidential campaign, millionaire Steve Forbes spent $1.5 million of his own money in less than a month and briefly bought his way into competition for the Republican nomination. In today's political marketplace, who you are and what you stand for is not so important as how much money you have, and how willing you are to spend it. As a *Washington Post* editorial noted, "In modern campaigning, capital—in the form of campaign cash—definitely has primacy over labor."[8]

CONSULTANTS AS CELEBRITIES

Recent campaigns have seen the rise of political consultants to a new form of celebrity. In 1988, the GOP's diabolic duo of Ailes and Atwater was more feared than their candidate George Bush, and got more credit than he did for the victory. Two rival tacticians in the 1992 presidential race, James Carville and Mary Matalin, were often a greater focus of media scrutiny than their candidates. Part of this had to do with the fact that the backstage competitors were romantically involved and later married, creating a Tracy–Hepburn love story that was indeed interesting, if not terribly germane to the selection of a president. But it was not just the romance. D. A. Pennebaker's documentary *The War Room* made James Carville and George Stephanopoulos into movie stars. Following the spectator-sport and insider models of journalism, countless newspaper, magazine, and television features endlessly examine the inner workings of political campaigns, often reporting with breathless awe the media mastery of the Spin Doctors. Many of these reporters are too superficial to realize that as they document the effects of spin, they are themselves the victims of it.

The cult of the consultant started back with Joe McGinniss's *The Selling of the President 1968*, which featured the young Roger Ailes as an ornery perfectionist, a veteran of the *Mike Douglas Show* who gave political messages Hollywood production values. Ailes's reputation only grew, until, after the 1988 Bush campaign, he was seen as both the king of negative advertising and a formidable presence in his own right, comparable to either Darth Vader or Vince Lombardi, depending on one's political perspective. In 1990, after his opponent hired Ailes as an adviser, Senator Paul Simon (D–Ill.) said he was "running against Roger Ailes as much as I am against Lynn Martin."[9] The

Republican aspirant had to send her media advisor around to meet with newspaper editors—just like a candidate—to prove that he was not evil incarnate.

This was not just fear talking. In many cases, pronouncements against a political consultant are a form of inoculation—an attack on the opponent's media consultant as soon as he was hired. In virtually every campaign in which Ailes consulted since 1988, his candidate's Democratic opponent—before a single ad was produced—predicted that Ailes was going to run a dirty campaign. This served two purposes: (1) to damage in advance the credibility of the GOP candidate's advertising, and (2) to provide a justification for the Democratic candidate's attacks ("You have to fight fire with fire"). Perhaps these attacks are one reason Ailes has retreated to the relative anonymity of running a television network, first CNBC, and now the Fox News Channel. Republicans also used this tactic against Democratic consultants such as Robert Squier and, in 1994, against the team of James Carville and Paul Begala.

But the deification of political consultants is not just the result of campaign strategy. As Fred Barnes wrote in *The New Republic*, "Political reporters, including me, are suckers for tales of consultants' legerdemain. By ascribing election victories to consultants, they explain the secret, behind-the-scenes reality of politics."[10] This has created a condition the *Washington Post* calls "consultantitis." In an editorial discussing Ed Rollins's claims that he paid black ministers to keep voter turnout down in the New Jersey gubernatorial campaign, the *Post* said that "the obsession with consultants is part of a series of obsessions: with technique over content, image over truth, the game over its purpose."[11]

CONSULTANTS AND REPUTATION

With fame comes both adulation and disgust. Public opinion surveys frequently rank political operatives below used-car salesmen and televangelists in terms of reliability and trust-worthiness. It is ironic that political consultants are seen this way by the general public, because within the business, re-liability and trustworthiness are essential to success. A political consultant has little more to trade on than his or her reputation. Matt Reese calls a good reputation "the hardest thing to earn and the hardest thing to lose." Indeed, many consultants have been cruising on their reputations for years. The more Roger Ailes was criticized, the more work he got, mostly from candi-dates who wanted strong negative campaigns like the ones for which he was being criticized. Bob Squier has been involved in many campaigns in which the advertisements his firm pro-duced were of dubious effectiveness or even questionable ethics, including the doctored headline ad for Ann Richards and the infamous "crying farmer" spot for Harriett Woods in her 1986 bid for a Missouri Senate seat. Yet, he continues to be considered one of the best in the business and handled the television advertising for the 1996 Clinton–Gore reelection campaign. After helping Clinton win the White House, James Carville lost several high-profile races, and his reputation has not suffered. Some consultants cannot lose for winning.

If the primary sales feature of political consultants is their reputation, then it would stand to reason that they would do anything to maintain a good one. Some measure their reputa-tion strictly in terms of win–loss records. They take on incum-bents, who are virtually assured of reelection, and then claim credit and only work for challengers who either stand a very good chance of winning or are so far behind that a respectable loss is as good as a win, so far as the consultant is concerned. Why then can a consultant's reputation not also be judged on ethical issues? Why should consultants not be held accountable for not just whether they win or lose, but how they play the game?

Consultants and candidates together should be held re-sponsible for the ads that they produce. That does not happen now. Consultants hide behind the candidates, saying that they are just giving them what they want. And the candidates hide behind the consultants, claiming that their media advisers insisted on fighting dirty. Sometimes the candidates even claim ignorance, saying that nasty attack ads were done without their knowledge. In the 1994 campaign, a radio ad in support of Representative David Mann (D–Ohio) made the following charges about his opponent:

> Steve Chabot wants to destroy families of the poor only because they are black and poor. Steve Chabot wants the death penalty to apply unequally to African-Americans. Chabot wants more African-Americans given the death penalty than white Americans. But you shouldn't be surprised, Chabot's a Republican.[12]

After the ad had been aired for several days, the Mann campaign claimed that the candidate had not been aware of it, and had it taken off the air. Mann found himself in an Iran–Contra conundrum: If he did know about the ad, he is in trouble, and if he did not know about the ad, he is in trouble as well. The two possibilities show either irresponsibility and dishonesty or fecklessness and lack of control over his organization.

Ultimately, candidates have to be responsible for the messages of their campaigns. It is their campaign after all. It is not the consultant's job to tell the candidate what to say, but to suggest how to say it. Still, the consultant should not be let off the hook. If a consultant cooks up a nasty, unfair ad, and it is approved by a candidate and winds up on the air, both of them should be roundly castigated, not just by the media and the public, but by their peers as well. And by the political parties themselves.

THE NEW BOSSES

Political consultants have taken over many of the functions of the old party bosses. As Lawrence Grossman points out,

> Professional pollsters have displaced precinct party chair-
> men as the principal source of information about what the
> public is thinking. Politics has turned from "labor inten-
> sive work," requiring lots of shoe leather and handshak-
> ing, to "capital intensive work," requiring lots of money
> for advertising and direct mail. Money and media have
> replaced personal contact as the chief energizing source of
> politics.[13]

He might have added that when a candidate signs up a top consultant, that is often considered as much a measure of via-bility as a party endorsement once did.

Political consultants have replaced the party hierarchy as the apparatus of campaign organization. But despite the occa-sional independent candidate, all other political aspirants run in primaries or seek nomination from one of the two parties.

Most consultants are loyal to one party. They are either Democrats or Republicans, and so are most of their clients. A small handful (Dick Morris, David Garth) might cross party lines, but they are the exceptions. And back when there was such a thing as a liberal Republican, Democratic consultants occasionally signed on to their campaigns.

With a weakened party system, candidates are entrepre-neurs, affiliated with a party and often looking for its nomina-tion, but basically autonomous. Even once they achieve nomi-nation, get the endorsement of the party, and enjoy the support of the party apparatus, they are still fairly independent. Politi-cal consultants may have party loyalties, but they are primarily loose associations of freelancers who often compete directly against each other. Consultants on the same side compete for billings and then campaign against each other in the primaries. Consultants on opposite sides often find themselves fighting each other not only year after year, but even in different cam-paigns during the same election cycle. And sometimes that competition can be fierce. Electoral politics is a zero-sum game that one person must win and at least one other must lose.

This is endemic to democratic politics, and it should not be any other way. Direct competition is the best method of giving voters a clear choice between candidates, and it also makes elections vital and exciting events. But politics is not merely a game. Even the most cynical political operative believes, at some level, that he or she is making the country a better place. Even the most high-minded idealist enjoys the thrill of the chase. And both of them are being corrupted by the win-at-any-cost philosophy now dominant among political professionals.

HOW CONSULTANTS CAN ELEVATE THE DEBATE AND SAVE THE PARTY SYSTEM

Now that political consultants stand in many ways as the new kingmakers of American politics, they should assume some of the responsibility that goes along with their power. One aspect of this responsibility would be to recognize that instead of completely replacing the political parties, they have risen to their current position of influence only as adjuncts to the parties. Without the parties, consultants would have very few candidates to represent, and those they did represent would be increasingly marginal and eccentric.

The Democratic and Republican parties are not accidents of history. They represent two separate and opposing tendencies in American politics. Even when one party often sounds pretty much like the other, as the Republicans did in the liberal 1960s and the Democrats do now, there are still profound philosophical differences that are represented in divergent approaches to politics and policy.

The Republicans have been much more successful in using both the techniques of political consultants and the consultants themselves in their party apparatus. The Democrats would be well advised to integrate more fully the talents of their top consultants not only to support single candidates, but also to advise and organize partywide campaigns and operations. More importantly, the Democrats need to articulate a single, partywide message about who they are and what they stand for. Right now, they offer little more than echoes or qualifications of the Republican platform. And they wonder why voters are abandoning them.

Until the Democratic Party goes back to its roots and develops a clear and consistent message that is a necessary counterpart to the Republicans' agenda, then they are going to continue to lose too many elections. Democratic consultants could help the party reestablish its credentials as the true representative of the American working man and woman and in doing so help shift the political alignment back in the party's favor.

In 1994 and early 1995, the Republicans had a clear agenda and were much better organized. There was—and still is—no Democratic equivalent of Newt Gingrich's GOPAC, which was as instrumental to Republican victories in the 1994 elections as the "Contract with America." In a way, that is to the Democrats' credit, as GOPAC's abuses exceed those the Democratic Party may have been guilty of in 1996. But Democrats should try—ethically—to replicate the function of GOPAC. GOPAC helped congressional candidates raise money and formulate a consistent message. As a result, the Republicans assumed congressional leadership with a degree of organizational coherence that the Democrats will need to emulate whenever they recapture Congress—if they want to hold power for a long time again. GOPAC also, not accidentally, elected a class of Congress with high, sometimes rabid, loyalty to its new Speaker, and given Gingrich's plummeting popularity, it took an unusually long time before there were many vocal defectors.

But many of the campaigns financed by GOPAC and the National Republican Congressional Committee (NRCC) were unrelentingly negative. If political consultants are to revive the party system in a way that will increase participation and give voters someone to vote for, rather than against, they are going to have to start injecting more positive messages into their media strategies, devoting more of their argument to substantial discussion of the issues rather than trash talk and scandal, and using more traditional techniques of campaigning. They also have to keep in mind who they are working for.

IT'S THE CANDIDATE, STUPID

Consultants, and their fans in the media, should realize that without the candidate, they do not have a campaign. And all the sophisticated polling technology, media manipulation, and tactical maneuvering that money can buy will not elect a candidate who is unsuitable. They can run negative spots from the primary to election day, but if they do not give voters a reason for supporting their candidate, then they will not—or at least should not—win the election.

Some candidates hire high-profile consultants to bolster their own viability—a necessity for raising the enormous sums of money needed to run a competitive race. "No serious candidate for statewide office would not have a political consultant," says Ed Mahe. "[I]f they don't have one, they are not seen as a serious contender by the press, the PACs, and the national party organization."[14]

Andrew O'Rourke, a Republican running against New York's then-indomitable Governor Mario Cuomo, hired members of Reagan's phenomenally successful Tuesday Team. "I think that when people see the panache of the Tuesday Team, they will say, 'Maybe O'Rourke has a fighting chance and we should help him.' "[15] Even with such high-priced talent, O'Rourke never really threatened the incumbent, and Cuomo took it in a walk.

While they are certainly influential, the various powers of political consultants are consistently exaggerated. People, even political pros, often forget that politics is an art, not a science.

The techniques that help win one election may not work in another. Michael Schudson quotes one consultant as saying, "We are still artists, trying to develop a dramatic way of capturing the attention and then inspiring resolve…. But we really don't know a great deal. If we knew more we would be dangerous."[16]

My Career as a Political Consultant

In case you could not tell already, I'm a liberal Democrat. But I started out as a liberal Republican, back when there was such a species.

When I was a kid in Chicago, my next-door neighbor Mr. Stoltz was the Republican precinct captain, an often difficult task in that overwhelmingly Democratic city. Because of Mr. Stoltz, I became a Republican, helping campaign for city GOP candidates, and often taking a lot of heat from my friends and neighbors for it. From those early days, and into college, my intellectual side kept trying to justify my party loyalty. Many of my political heroes were Democrats, like Illinois Senator Paul Douglas. Of course, I had Republican heroes as well, like New York Governor Nelson Rockefeller, Senator Jacob Javits of New York, and Senator Ed Brooke of Massachusetts. My kind of Republican was socially progressive while being fiscally responsible. But the GOP was moving farther to the right, and liberals like Rockefeller were losing ground to conservatives like Goldwater.

I found myself growing uncomfortable with the right-wing ideology many in the party were adopting. In 1964, I worked for Youth for Scranton when the Pennsylvania governor challenged Goldwater for the Republican nomination. After the Goldwater debacle, I earned a master's degree in rhetoric from the University of New Mexico (where I also worked on political campaigns). Then I moved to Washington, D.C., to go to law school and continue my involvement in politics.

continued

While attending law school, I also taught full time and was active in National Young Republicans. I backed the more liberal candidates, and all my candidates lost. Then, in 1967, Nelson Rockefeller announced that he would run for president. By the time I decided to leave law school to work on his campaign, he was already almost out of the race. So I signed on to the Nixon campaign as one of the Rockefeller people. At first, I served as head of educators for Nixon–Agnew. Then, I went on to become overall director of administration and assistant to the chair of Citizens for Nixon–Agnew.

One of the reasons I supported Nixon was that I truly believed he had a plan to end the Vietnam War, whereas Hubert Humphrey (who I thought was a great leader) was still supporting the failed policy of President Lyndon Johnson.

When Nixon was elected in 1968, I served as head of administration for the inaugural. But I did not work in the Nixon Administration. From what I had seen of many of the Nixon people, they were ideologues and loyalists, and in hindsight the Watergate scandals were not that surprising, considering both the character of the president and the people he had working for him. I did, however, serve as administrative assistant to the late Representative Seymour Halpern (R–N.Y.), a liberal in the Rockefeller–Javitz tradition.

Eventually—and for many of the reasons stated in previous discussions of Nixon in this book—I became turned off to the GOP. In 1972, I voted as a Democrat for the first time, casting a ballot for George McGovern.

I later went to work as assistant to Bob Georgine, president of the Building and Construction Trades Department, AFL-CIO, an umbrella for the 15 construction unions representing four million members. There, I worked on press and public relations, events and politics, including advertising, telecommunications, and polling. I was only planning to be there for six months before going on to work for then-Vice-President Rockefeller. Instead, I stayed at Building Trades for 9 years.

In 1977, AFL-CIO President George Meany asked me to head up the special task force on labor law reform, lobbying for six pieces of legislation designed to level the playing field between labor and management, and give more workers the right to choose whether they want to bargain collectively with their employers. Four of the six laws were passed. But the most important legislation, labor law reform, was defeated by a Senate filibuster.

Out of that experience, I saw the need for the causes that I cared about to have the same tools available to them that their opponents did. Labor unions and their natural political allies (the Democratic Party and liberal groups) needed the same sophisticated methods and technologies that the Republicans and conservative groups were using. The techniques and technology of political media were changing rapidly, and, for the moment, the Republicans were using television, radio, direct mail, polling, and coalition outreach much more effectively than our side.

This realization led me to pursue a career as communications consultant. In 1980, I hung out a shingle, and with the help of one full-time office manager and one part-time writer, I started The Kamber Group (TKG). At first, we worked almost exclusively with labor organizations, but soon the firm became more diversified, working on public interest issues and political campaigns, and even taking on some corporate work, as long as that did not conflict with our natural base of labor and liberal issues. Soon, the firm was employing 100 people and working on a wide range of political and public-interest campaigns.

In the first elective campaigns we worked on, TKG represented six candidates: three Democrats and three Republicans. Although all six of our candidates won, we realized that we could not work both sides, so we decided to commit ourselves to Democratic candidates. Soon after that, we conducted a poll of our leading people and asked them whom they would like to see as president in 1984. Of 15 responses, 14 voted for Alan Cranston (the one vote for Walter Mondale came from Frank Greer, who eventually left the firm to work for Mondale). The firm was hired by Cranston to consult and provide overall strategy, and also

continued

was responsible for direct mail and earned media, but not paid media.

After the Cranston effort, we realized that TKG would have to establish a separate entity for political campaign consulting, with its own talent and staff that could draw upon the larger resources of TKG itself when necessary, but would also be able to operate independently. So we set up Politics, Inc., which has been enormously successful in individual candidate races, as well as some referenda and public interest campaigns. Among the firm's recent achievements was the election of one of only four Democrats to capture a Republican House seat in 1994, Representative John Baldacci (Me.), and three Democratic newcomers in 1996, Representatives Dennis Kucinich (Ohio), Alan Boyd (Fla.), and Mike McIntyre (N.C.).

In just 16 years, TKG has grown from three employees to more than 100. In addition to our headquarters in Washington, we have offices in New York and Los Angeles, and we work with clients all over the world. Although TKG's work is wide and varied, we remain committed to our core beliefs — social justice, a government that looks out for working men and women, and an economy that is both prosperous and fair — those same beliefs that animated my first forays into politics.

Chapter 13

The Lost Art of (Small-d) Democratic Rhetoric

As pathetic as it may be, television advertising is our dominant form of political rhetoric. It is the way most candidates communicate with the public and argue with their opponents. It is the primary method, along with television news, by which most voters are politically educated. Almost all of our political debate is now conducted on or for television. When a candidate for national office does venture outside the friendly walls of the advertising studio, it is usually for a rally that he or she hopes will be televised, and the speech, along with other theatrical elements, is geared toward getting on the news.

Democracy is founded on rhetoric. We elect our leaders based on what they say, and we reelect them, or not, based on how well they lived up to those promises. As Theodore Windt writes, "In a democratic society, words establish the compact between the governor and the governed, a secular trust not to be taken lightly."[1] Despite the fact that the term is now in disrepute, *rhetoric* can not only be a positive force in politics, but it is also an essential component of politics. Rhetoric is not merely a technique used by politicians; it informs the very soul of democracy. And if our rhetoric, to use common parlance, sucks, so then will our politics.

CLASSICAL RHETORIC AND ATTACK ADS

Rhetoric was profoundly important in Ancient Greece, and Aristotle made the first comprehensive study of it. He broke down political argument into three basic appeals: *logos*, an appeal to reason; *ethos*, an appeal based on the character of the speaker; and *pathos*, an appeal to the emotions. An effective political speaker would use all three appeals in measure, not forsaking one for the others. Today, we have little else but pathos—appeals to the emotions, particularly fear—and attacks on a candidate's ethos.

Ethos was further divided by Aristotle into personal morality, good sense, and goodwill. Irresponsible attack ads do not address a candidate's performance; instead, they attempt to paint him or her as an evil person. This demonization is profoundly destructive not only to the candidate who is attacked, but also to the political system as a whole. By pushing the terms of debate outside that which is arguable and into the realm of absolutes, irresponsible attack ads reduce rhetoric to irreconcilable claims of certitude. Everyone is either absolutely right or totally wrong, and there is no room for compromise or conciliation, for nuance, or even for argument itself. This mutual vilification is not only counterproductive but also contradictory to the very premise of democratic politics.

Rhetoric has been defined as "public persuasion on significant public issues."[2] And those issues about which we argue are debatable because they are, well, debatable. According to Aristotle, "Deliberation is about matters that appear to admit of being one way or another."[3] In other words, we debate issues about which the answers are not self-evidently clear. How do we fix the economy? Are we better off now than we were four years ago? The answers to these questions are not subject to easy definitive answer. This allows for a vigorous and continuing debate so long as each side argues in good faith. But we seem to have lost our ability to argue in good faith, because argument is no longer seen as an expression of self, but merely as a means to an end.

According to classic rhetorical theory, the development of an individual's rhetoric was more than just learning the skills of argument. Instead, a speaker sought to cultivate an ethos, what historian Kenneth Cmiel describes as "a character that pervaded one's whole self."[4] Rhetoric was a means of expression and development of what Aristotle called a "unified soul." Cmiel notes: "If successful, one's ethos, or character, defined his or her every action."[5]

Opposed to the notion of ethos was persona, the tendency toward role playing and arguing from expediency. If someone could adopt any persona, then his or her character was not consistent, and he or she could not be trusted. Socrates had ethos coming out his ears, whereas the sophists were merely talented personas. Agree with him or not, Jesse Jackson has ethos, a clear and consistent public stand on the issues that has helped shape his unique personal style. On the other hand, Bob Dole is mere persona: "I'll be Ronald Reagan if you want me to be," he told Republican activists early in his 1996 presidential campaign. And by shifting from decades of being a deficit hawk in Congress to a born-again tax cutter on the campaign trail, Dole was following through on this promise.

Today's political debate is basically a cast of aggressive personas tearing each other down instead of telling us who they are. But it was not always that way.

AMERICA'S FOUNDING RHETORIC

The Federalist Papers is a brilliant work, laying out the challenges of democracy in general, and examining the particular circumstances of America, a large country with autonomous states, and finally, arguing for a system of federal government that has resulted in the most successful democracy the world has ever known. *The Federalist Papers* may be a profound treatise of political philosophy, but hardly bedtime reading, unless you want to go to sleep right away. Here is a selection, picked not quite at random, for it addresses the subject at hand.

> The use of words is to express ideas. Perspicuity, there-
> fore, requires not only that the ideas should be distinctly
> formed, but that they should be expressed by words dis-
> tinctly and exclusively appropriate to them. But no lan-
> guage is so copious as to supply words and phrases for
> every complex idea, or so correct as not to include many
> equivocally denoting different ideas. Hence it must hap-
> pen that however accurately objects may be discriminated
> in themselves, and however accurately the discrimination
> may be considered, the definition of them may be ren-
> dered inaccurate by the inaccuracy of the terms in which
> it is delivered.[6]

Huh? The writing style is so elegant as to be almost incomprehensible. And that is the way our Founders spoke as well.
Here is the opening of Jefferson's Inaugural Address:

> Called upon to undertake the duties of the first executive
> office of our country, I avail myself to the presence of that
> portion of my fellow citizens which is here assembled, to
> express my grateful thanks for the favor with which they
> have been pleased to look toward me, to declare a sincere
> consciousness that the task is above my talent, and that I
> approach it with those anxious and awful presentiments
> which the greatness of the charge and the weakness of my
> powers so justly inspire.[7]

Enlightenment rhetoric certainly had a high style; it was
elaborate to the point of being orotund; at least, that is how
it sounds to us unenlightened postmoderns. But many of the
Founders' fellow citizens also found such rhetoric hard to follow. *The Federalist Papers* was written by gentlemen for gentlemen; their assumption of a gentleman's classical education is
indicated by the writers' common pseudonym, Publius. Jefferson's speech was addressed to his "fellow republicans." But
the classically educated gentlemen of the aristocracy were not
the only voices in America. Some low forms of expression were
also heard, and by many more than read Publius. In his preface
to *Common Sense*, Tom Paine promised to "avoid every literary
ornament and put it in language as plain as the alphabet."[8] The

work's enormous popular success and widespread political impact was the direct result of a style that "was central to the explosion of political argument and involvement beyond the confines of a narrow elite to 'all ranks' of Americans."[9]

Tom Paine was merely the first in a long line of rhetorical democrats. Classical elitism could not last long in America, and soon the lofty rhetoric of Jefferson and Hamilton was successfully challenged by the plain speech of Jacksonian democracy. The conflict between high and low expression formed the history of 19th-century American rhetoric, as the educated elites battled the plain-speaking masses for control over the language of democracy. The result was a "middling" style that attempted to accommodate both cultural tendencies and speak in a combination of high and low style. Middling style was plain, often blunt speech, but it still had rhetorical flourishes and dramatic power. It was a characteristically American compromise.

Rhetoric both mirrors and embodies a political system. The conflict between genteel eloquence and democratic simplicity was not only a debate over language but also an expression of the political struggle between the elites and the masses. It is a fight we will never conclude so long as there are wide disparities of wealth and power in our nation—disparities that the politics of attack and division seem only to be exacerbating. But rhetoric does not have to divide us, even when it states our political differences in stark and honest terms. The Lincoln–Douglas debates are an example of how democratic rhetoric can bring us together, even as we disagree.

THE LINCOLN–DOUGLAS DEBATES

It is difficult to imagine a political event inspiring such enthusiasm as did the series of debates between Abraham Lincoln and Stephen Douglas. The two candidates were running for senator from Illinois. Douglas had recently broken with

President James Buchanan and was desperately seeking to maintain the Democratic coalition. Lincoln represented the newly formed Republican Party, which had risen from the disintegration of the Whigs. Although there were many other issues facing the nation, none was as important, or as divisive, as slavery, and that was all the two debaters discussed.

The two men differed in party, ideology, temperament, and appearance. "Two men presenting wider contrasts," wrote one New York journalist, "could hardly be found as the representatives of the two great parties." Douglas was "a short, thick-set, burly man, with large round head, heavy hair, dark complexion, and fierce bull-dog bark ... proud, defiant, arrogant, audacious," whereas Lincoln was "the opposite ... tall, slender, and angular, awkward even, in gait and attitude.... In repose, I must confess that 'Long Abe's' appearance is not comely. But stir him up and the fire of his genius plays on every feature."[10]

Both candidates spoke extemporaneously, although Lincoln had a small notebook of newspaper clippings, quotes, and speeches to which he sometimes referred. The debate format called for an initial hour-long speech by one candidate, followed by a response from the other that ran for an hour and a half. Then, the first candidate returned for a half-hour closing statement. There were seven debates in all, and each took turns, as the first candidate had a clear advantage by both opening and closing the debate.

While the debates were long, substantive, and often inspiring, they were not free from invective. One of the main strategies of both candidates was to persuade the audience that their opponent was part of a conspiracy. Lincoln argued that his opponent wanted to extend slavery beyond just the territories, whereas Douglas tried to prove that Lincoln was fomenting abolition. Douglas frequently referred to Lincoln and his allies as "Black republicans," and often called slaves "niggers." Lincoln used the word a few times himself. Their records as politicians were given fierce partisan scrutiny. Lincoln was attacked for not supporting the Mexican War, whereas Douglas got pasted for his support of the Dred Scott decision.

But the debate was not just an argument on the issues. Lincoln scholar Henry Holzer describes it thus: "The speakers attacked each other and defended themselves with biting humor, bitter sarcasm, and hellish fury ... replete with personal insults and name-calling."[11] At one point, they slung more than just mud: Lincoln supporters smeared Douglas's carriage with what one journalist called "loathsome dirt," which we can assume was excrement. There were also frequent interruptions from the audience. One heckler broke in during a Lincoln speech to call the Republican a fool. Lincoln responded: "I guess there are two of us."

Despite the bitter and often ugly attacks on each other, the issues were clearly, even exhaustively, discussed, and there were times when the rhetoric just shone. Lincoln stated his objection to slavery, saying that the Founders had known slavery to be immoral and hoped that it would not last. By extending it into the territories, they would be strengthening and perpetuating that loathsome institution. Douglas countered by arguing that it was up to the states to decide, and that the federal government had no authority in such local matters. The crux of the argument, federal power versus states rights, is one of the primal conflicts in American politics, an issue that has been debated extensively at various points in our history, from the ratification of the Constitution to the Civil Rights Era, and today has been put at the forefront of political debate once again by the Republican Congress.

Lincoln saved his greatest rhetorical volleys for the last debate, perhaps knowing that the argument could not be stated in bold moral terms at the outset. He restated the Republican position as looking "upon slavery as a moral, social and political wrong,"[12] and argued that the Democrats "did not believe it to be wrong." This difference between the two parties, and the two candidates, was to Lincoln, essential:

> This is the real issue! An issue that will continue in this
> country when these poor tongues of Douglas and myself
> shall be silent. These are the two principles that are made
> the eternal struggle between right and wrong. They are
> the two principles that have stood face to face, one of them
> asserting the divine right of kings, the same principle that
> says you work, you toil, you earn bread, and I will eat it.
> It is the same old serpent, whether it come from the mouth
> of a king who seeks to bestride the people of his nation,
> and to live upon the fat of his neighbor, or, whether it
> comes from one race of men as an apology for the enslav-
> ing of another race of men.[13]

Although Lincoln and Douglas certainly both deserved
credit for the relatively high standard of political discussion,
one writer commented: "The real heroes of the occasion were
the common people of Illinois who demonstrated by their pro-
digiously patient attendance their capacity to digest this heavy
political fare."[14] As David Zarefsky noted,

> The debates were both a serious discussion of the issues
> and a form of communal entertainment. People arrived
> early, held picnics and parades, greeted the arrival of their
> candidate with frenzied enthusiasm.[15]

The Lincoln–Douglas debates were historic not just in their
discussion of the issue that would eventually lead the country
to Civil War and their introduction of a great new leader onto
the political scene. As a political event they showed how our
democratic debate could enthuse, inspire, educate, and motivate the electorate to a higher level of understanding and participation. They were the high-water mark of middling style
and a sterling example of how the American language can be
used not merely to convince people to vote a certain way, but
also to encourage them to think and deliberate, carrying on the
discussion themselves in their homes and public places. The
Lincoln–Douglas debates proved that democratic rhetoric
could empower citizens to use the language of democracy
themselves, thereby creating a political environment in which
issues were debated not merely by leaders and experts, but also

by those whose lives were shaped by the decisions that they themselves would make together.

The Lincoln–Douglas debates show what American politics could be: informative and important, but also lively and entertaining, a great public celebration that helped decide a great issue. Importantly, the debates were public events, bringing partisans of both sides together, face to face, so each side could see that the other did not have horns, and perhaps they could exist together in competitive amity. Today, our political debates are creations of the media, with our candidates presented as living deities or else demonized and slandered; either way, they exist beyond human recognition. Democratic participation has been reduced to simply watching attack ads on the television and then voting on election day—or not. One cannot imagine a more lonely or dispiriting form of citizenship.

THE RISE AND FALL OF AMERICAN RHETORIC

The Lincoln–Douglas debates, and the subsequent speeches and writings of Lincoln himself, marked a new era in American rhetoric, in which moral vision was expressed in speech that was clear and comprehensible without sacrificing the power of articulate form. Around that same time, American letters came into their own, not as an imitation of European literature, but with a true and resonant national voice. Walt Whitman's poetry and the novels, stories, and satires of Mark Twain made great art out of the American vernacular. Later, the fiction of Dos Passos and Hemingway showed that idiomatic speech had a place even in modern art.

The political legacy of Lincolnian rhetoric was to last well into the next century. William Jennings Bryan, an obscure 36-year-old Midwestern lawyer with just a short term of service in Congress (a résumé startlingly similar to Lincoln's), rose to national prominence with a single speech attacking the gold standard. "You shall not press down upon the brow of labor this crown of thorns," Bryan ended his oration at the 1896 Democratic convention. "You shall not crucify mankind upon a cross of gold." Bryan's speech was so effective that not only was the gold-standard plank dropped from the Democratic platform, but also the party nominated him to run for president.

Teddy Roosevelt turned the presidency into an office of moral leadership, a "bully pulpit" from which the nation's chief executive used rhetoric as a means to inspire the nation toward positive action merely by the force of his own persuasive powers. He gave many important speeches to the public, hoping that they in turn would let their wishes be known to their representatives. Using this technique, which was later perfected by his fifth cousin, Franklin Delano Roosevelt, Teddy Roosevelt was the first president to go over the heads of Congress. And he initiated the presidential press conference, a forum which, when properly and honestly used, both communicates the executive's message and holds him accountable to the voters through the media.

Woodrow Wilson further enhanced the power of the presidency using his own style of scholarly egalitarianism to appeal to both high-born progressives and the common man. Some 100,000 people attended his first inaugural, in which he reviewed the changes of the recent past and stated the need for the country to reappraise its common goals. In this speech, the echoes of Lincoln resonate:

> The Nation has been deeply stirred, stirred by a solemn passion, stirred by the knowledge of wrong, of ideals lost, of government too often debauched and made an instrument of evil. The feelings with which we face this new age of right and opportunity sweep across our heartstrings like some air out of God's own presence, where justice and mercy are reconciled and the judge and the brother are one.[16]

FDR changed the language of democratic rhetoric by adapting it to the conversational simplicity of radio. In December 1940, as war was erupting over Europe, FDR knew that many Americans were still clinging to the desperate comfort of isolationism. So, he devoted one of his fireside chats to a call for a national effort against Nazi aggression:

> The experience of the past two years has proven beyond doubt no nation can appease the Nazis. No man can tame a tiger into a kitten by stroking it. There can be no appeasement with ruthlessness. There can be no reasoning with an incendiary bomb. We know now that a nation can have peace with the Nazis only at the price of total surrender.

To the arguments of American isolationists that the United States should seek a "negotiated peace," FDR responded: "Nonsense! Is it a negotiated peace if a gang of outlaws surrounds your community and on the threat of extermination makes you pay tribute to save your own skins?"

While calling for a greater national effort to help our European allies and also protect ourselves, FDR also restated his commitment to a democratic America that represented and protected all of its people:

> I would ask no one to defend a democracy which in turn would not defend every one in the nation against want and privation. The strength of this nation shall not be diluted by the failure of the government to protect the economic well-being of its citizens.[17]

Since FDR's fireside chats, there have been other high points in democratic rhetoric, many of them specifically fashioned for delivery over the new technologies of mass media. But there have been many low points as well. And in the last few years, there has been a quick descent into ignominy.

The crash of democratic rhetoric has been hard and fast. The rhetoric of the 1960s combined plain speech and high aspirations in such a way that might possibly never be equaled again. John F. Kennedy may have been a competitive campaigner and not above kicking Dick Nixon around, but he also inspired a nation to meet the future with hope and great expectations. Yes, Lyndon Johnson ran attack ads against Barry Goldwater, but he also spoke of the "Great Society." In the nonelectoral arena, Martin Luther King led a movement of righteous anger to seek justice in nonviolent confrontation—a movement that sought to make society more moral by itself acting according to the highest moral standards.

Then something happened. Americans ceased believing *in* their leaders and then stopped believing them altogether. Those leaders returned the favor; they no longer tried to inspire, but merely attempted to gain advantage though attacks upon some Other, be it their direct opponents or some unnamed enemies in the society at large. The rhetoric of uplift was replaced by the politics of degradation, which created an atmosphere of distrust and antagonism that has made a virtue out of animosity and turned hope into a futile delusion.

THE LOSS OF A LANGUAGE

"Why should people expect politics to be any different from the rest of the culture?" Representative Barney Frank (D–Mass.) asks. "It's not as if politics is deteriorating but everybody's watching Shakespeare."[18]

He is right. The decline of democratic rhetoric is part of a greater entropy of articulation and literacy. The American language is being diminished by laziness, vulgarity, and the forces of lowest-common-denominator marketing and mass-media homogeneity. We are losing not only the eloquence of high rhetoric but also the vital poetry of common speech as people from various walks of life, from different geographic regions and ethnic backgrounds, all try to sound like television personalities. The vapid cliches of the media, the jargon of the academy, the soulless technospeak of science, and the irresponsible vitriol of political candidates in attack ads are all laying waste to what was once a vivid and robust language. But it is not just television's fault. The Gettysburg Address could be made into a 30-second spot if only somebody would write another one.

It is apropos that Frank should hold Shakespeare as the standard, for the Bard had a profound influence on the literary and speaking style of the great master of democratic rhetoric, Abraham Lincoln. His contribution will forever stand as a model of high ideals and intellectual sophistication spoken in plain, comprehensible, yet stirring language. And Shakespeare himself knew how to bridge the gap between high eloquence and earthy expression, for he was not only a great artist but also a popular one, equally at home in the Queen's court and the local tavern.

America's genius has always been to merge the high and the low, the elite and the popular, the genteel and the idiomatic. This talent has extended from culture—the uniquely American art forms of blues, jazz, and movies—to politics, where FDR, an aristocrat, spoke the language of the people, whereas Lincoln, a commoner, crafted a rhetoric of lofty inspiration that echoes to this day. Dr. Martin Luther King, Jr. rose above the bitter invective of racial antagonism and spoke the truth to power, his moral suasion matched only by his eloquence, and his message one of inclusion, forgiveness, even love. Now we have only attacks and slanders traded over television spots, with each candidate trying to prove who can be more effective at polarizing, terrifying, and ultimately repulsing the electorate. Political rhetoric is almost completely given over to the vulgar, and as a result, we have a crude, irresponsible politics and a diminished public life.

We have come a long way down from the ennobling rhetoric and high aspirations of the civil rights era to the gutter politics of attack ads, from Dr. Martin Luther King, Jr. to George Herbert Walker Bush. The man who wrote "Letter from a Birmingham Jail" had ethos. The man who gave us Willie Horton and "a kinder, gentler America" at the same time was a mere persona. King was arrested, beaten, and ultimately murdered for his commitment to justice. Bush was little more than an empty suit wrapped around ambition. King led his people out of bondage, while Bush exploited the nation's fears and hatred. A little more than 20 years separate "I have a dream" from "Read my lips, no new taxes." And yet, in that short time, we have lost so much.

Chapter 14

Fighting Fair

Negative ads do not have to be nasty. You can make an effective attack on your opponent, one that is relevant and even vital to the debate, without slinging mud.

The key to an effective and honest attack is to speak to the issues. Even if you call a candidate's character or personality into question, it should be done within the context of how he or she would govern. For example, voters in Louisiana deserved to know the details of David Duke's Nazi past—details that Duke tried to hide. And if Bob Packwood had stayed in office and run for reelection, then his sexual harassment would most certainly have been fair game.

There have been a great many negative ads that were disgusting, insipid, and, let us hope, easily forgotten. However, there also have been many that were fair, pertinent, and effective. And there is no reason why these should be ignored or lumped in with all the other trashy negative spots, because these ads actually contributed to the debate by clarifying the issues and stating a candidate's weaknesses or mistakes in stark, though honest, terms.

STRONG ATTACKS

An opponent's own words can be used against him or her. This is perfectly legitimate so long as the statements are accurate and not taken out of context. Barry Goldwater was prone to shooting from the lip, and that habit got him in trouble when he ran for president. The Johnson campaign used Goldwater's gaffes and irresponsible remarks in a series of radio and television ads to emphasize the Republican's extremist views. Using Goldwater's quote that "the country would be better off if we could just saw off the Eastern Seaboard and let it float out to sea," the Democrats produced an ad showing just that. His statement about the space program, "I don't want to hit the moon, I just want to lob one into the men's room of the Kremlin," was made into a Johnson radio ad. All these attacks reinforced voters' opinions that he was a reckless radical, a charge that Goldwater only encouraged by saying, "Extremism in pursuit of liberty is no vice." The "Daisy" ad was only one component of an overall campaign to paint Goldwater as a dangerous man, one who should not be trusted with the office of the presidency. While today, Goldwater's views paint him more as a mainstream conservative—a sad commentary on the extremism of the Newt Gingrich wing of the party—in 1964, his positions, especially on use of the military, were out of step with most Americans.

Experienced politicians usually have a long public record that opponents can use to beat them over the head. However, some neophyte challengers also have significant public records, especially now that media personalities and businesspeople are becoming more prominent in politics. For example, when Barbara Boxer (D) ran against Bruce Herschensohn (R) for an open seat in the U.S. Senate in 1992, she used her opponent's own words against him. Herschensohn, a shoot-from-the-lip conservative commentator, had made a number of irresponsible or impolitic remarks during his long media career. Boxer ran spots featuring clips from Herschensohn's public pronouncements, which reinforced voter suspicions that this was not the kind of person they wanted representing them in the world's greatest deliberative body.

In a 1980 Oregon Congressional race, challenger Denny Smith (R) showed that incumbent Al Ullman (D), then chair of the House Ways and Means Committee, was so out of touch with his constituency that he did not even have a home in Oregon. The spot opened on a shot of the challenger's home in Salem, then quickly cut to a post office box. "This is the Oregon address of Al Ullman, until last year." Show another post office box. "Then Al moved here—down the block so to speak." The ad went on to show Ullman's Virginia residence, his Maryland beach home, and three rental properties that he owned. "Too bad Al Ullman doesn't want a home in Oregon," the ad said in closing. "It would be nice to have a Congressman who likes to live here."[1] I believe that whether a member of Congress actually lives in a district is fair game. But it should not become the dominant point of debate in the campaign—that should be the candidates' voting records and agendas.

RESPONDING TO NEGATIVE ADS

Negative attacks and responses used to be relegated to surrogates. But all that has changed. Now, candidates attack directly and respond directly, creating the often-ridiculous volleys of charges and countercharges that make a playground dispute between a couple of eight-year-olds look mature and responsible by comparison. However, there are ways to effectively respond to a negative attack and sometimes turn an opponent's argument against him or her.

Many attack responses start with the candidate turning off the radio or television that is playing the original attack ad. This technique was used by Michael Dukakis in 1988 against George Bush, and it has since been repeated by New York Governor George Pataki (R) and countless others. Perhaps the

most ingenious use of the media turnoff was Republican Don
Young's campaign for reelection to his Alaska House seat in
1986. His daughter Dawn turned off the radio and then sat
down to set the voters straight about her dad's attendance and
voting records.

The most famous response to attacks on a politician's family came in the pretelevision age. In the 1944 election, Thomas
Dewey ran a harsh negative campaign against FDR, claiming,
among other things, that the president dispatched a destroyer
to bring back his dog, which he had left behind in Alaska. The
Republicans hoped to draw the president out into a series of
attacks and counterattacks that would certainly hurt the incumbent more than the challenger. But FDR responded with characteristic charm, saying, "Republican leaders have not been content with attacks on me, or my wife, or my son. No, not content
with that, they now include my little dog, Fala."[2] The Republicans were rebutted, and FDR maintained both his dignity and
his office.

When the late Senator John Tower (R) of Texas was castigated for not shaking the hands of his opponent, Tower replied
in a spot that his opponent had slurred his wife and daughters.
"My kind of Texan doesn't shake hands with that kind of man."
Tower said. He then promised viewers that "integrity is one
Texas tradition you can count on me to uphold." Still, the
question remains, why were the candidates arguing over
whether Tower should have shaken his opponent's hand, instead of focusing on the issues?

Another Texas tornado blew up when Lloyd Doggett (D)
ran against Phil Gramm (R) for Senate in 1984. Doggett ran a
spot quoting his opponent as saying the following about the
elderly: "They're 80 years old. Most people don't have the
luxury of living to be 80. So it's hard for me to feel sorry for
them." Then Doggett claimed that Gramm would cut Social
Security and Medicare. "Can Texas take pride in that kind of
Senator?" Phil Gramm shot back. Sitting at his desk, cool as a
bottle of Lone Star, Gramm held up a check for viewers to see.

"My mama worked 39 years as a practical nurse carrying bed-pans to earn this $333 a month from Social Security. And I'm never gonna let anybody take this check away from my momma." Then he went on to promise that he would never let anyone take benefits away from the voters, either. On one level, this is a fair interplay. But on another level, the voters would have been better served by a review of Gramm's actual voting record on Social Security than a mere war of emotionally charged words.

After the successful NCPAC independent expenditure campaigns of the late 1970s and 1980, the Democrats fought back hard. The party ran a series of generic spots against the Republicans, including one ad that had an elephant rampaging through a china shop, knocking over whole shelves of glass and flatware. Another ad described "trickle-down economics," showing champagne flutes catching an endless stream of bub-bly, while a hand holding a tin cup beneath them got only a single drop. The tag line for these spots went "It's not fair, it's Republican."

The party was also more organized to fight back. The Democratic Congressional Campaign Committee issued the following response strategy to its candidates:

> Anticipate what the New Right targets are going to use against you and hit back quickly. Don't let the candidate respond personally to the attack; find someone else—a staff member, a friendly group leader, or an elected official—to do it for you. Keep the targets on the defensive; expose their tactics, question their credibility, denounce their motives.[3]

Sometimes the best response is to simply ignore the charge. Once, Ralph Nader circulated a publication that called Senator Bill Scott of Virginia the dumbest person in the Senate. Scott immediately called a press conference denying the charge. Case closed.

The problem with responses to negative ads is that they often do not stop at just that. The response is then responded to and that itself is answered, until all the positive messages are crowded out, and the voters only remember the back and forth of nasty charges and even nastier rebuttals. It is difficult, not to mention politically dangerous, to let a charge go unanswered. But campaigners should try not to let things degenerate into a bout of yelling and name calling that even a five-year-old would be ashamed of. Because then there are no winners.

"I'VE MADE MISTAKES"

Sometimes the best offense is a good defense. When the criticisms of incumbents are accurate and fair, the most they can do is admit mistakes and promise to do better, or use the admission as a launching-off point to promote some of the positive aspects of their careers.

David Garth pioneered this genre, called the "mistakes" ad, in New York Mayor John Lindsay's 1969 reelection campaign. The patrician Lindsay had been criticized by blue-collar voters for neglecting the problems of the outer boroughs. This was most evidenced by the sluggish response of the city's snow-plow crews in clearing the streets of Queens and Brooklyn after a heavy snowfall. Using a technique that his then-associate Jeff Greenfield called "political jiujitsu," Garth produced a spot in which Lindsay admitted that he had made mistakes and then went on to point out how he had built more police and fire stations than any other mayor, something that went over well in the outer boroughs, where many of New York's finest and bravest lived. Although Lindsay, first elected as a Republican, was only nominated on the Liberal Party ticket, he won reelection, defeating both the GOP and Democratic nominees.

The "mistakes" tactic was also used quite profitably, at least in the short run, by Illinois Senator Chuck Percy (R). In 1978, Democratic challenger Alex Seith came from virtually nowhere to pull ahead of Percy, running a strong negative campaign that included a radio spot linking Percy with former secretary of agriculture Earl Butz, who had resigned in the midst of controversy over racist remarks. Percy was in trouble, and his media adviser Doug Bailey counseled him to give a public *mea culpa*. The result was a spot called "I Got the Message," in which Percy appears in his living room, surrounded by his family, speaking directly to the camera in sincere and contrite tones. He mentioned not only his mistakes, but the possibility of his losing the election.

> The polls say that many of you want to send me a message. But after Tuesday, I may not be in the Senate to receive it. Believe me, I've gotten the message: and you're right. Washington has gone overboard. And I'm sure I've made my share of mistakes. But in truth, your priorities are mine too. Stop the waste. Cut the spending. Cut the taxes. I've worked as hard as I know for you. I'm not ready to quit now. And I don't want to be fired. I want to keep working for you. And I'm asking for your vote.[4]

The confession was coupled with a series of hard-hitting attacks on his opponent. Percy was 18 points behind before his campaign unveiled these new spots. Soon, he had pulled even with Seith, and he wound up winning by a seven-point margin. But the *mea culpa* came back to haunt him in his next campaign, as opponent Paul Simon (D) used the confession in a spot asking whether Percy had indeed gotten the message. "Paul Simon means never having to say you're sorry," ran the tag line. Simon won the election, and Percy was finally sent home.

TWO PROMISING CAMPAIGNS

The television campaigns of Senator Paul Wellstone (D–Minn.) and Russ Feingold (D–Wis.) are both examples of how the medium can be used to discuss issues of substance with both a seriousness and a sense of humor that is sadly absent from too many races.

The two candidates were in some ways very similar. Both were traditional liberals from the northern Midwest. Both were young, bright, and Jewish. Both of them had great senses of humor and, though Wellstone's Wallace Shawn looks are hardly out of central casting, both were comfortable with the medium of television. They were both underfunded challengers fighting against powerful incumbents. And they both won.

Wellstone ran in 1990 against Rudy Boschwitz (R–Minn.) and again, just as successfully, in 1996—see the Epilogue for more details. In one of his 1990 spots, Wellstone used the format of the documentary *Roger and Me*, in which filmmaker Michael Moore tries to get an interview with General Motors Chairman Roger Smith. Wellstone visited the offices of his opponent, asking Boschwitz's aides about the issues when he could not get the candidate to comment on them. In another spot, he drew simple pictures in the dust collected on the window of his campaign bus to make a point about the environment.

Feingold ran an innovative campaign. He wrote a campaign contract on the garage doors of his home, promising voters that if elected he would (1) maintain residence in Wisconsin, (2) rely primarily on Wisconsin citizens, rather than outsiders, for campaign contributions, and (3) accept no pay raises. One of his spots was called "Home Movies," in which we see his house, with the contract boldly displayed on the garage doors. Then he takes us inside his modest home and shows us around. "Here's my closet, look, no skeletons," he says, opening up a hall closet.

In other spots, Feingold introduced himself as "the underdog running for United States Senate." During the primaries, he obliquely mentioned the scandals concerning his opponents, saying that Senator Bob Kasten (R) would rather face either one of them than Feingold himself, who did not carry any such baggage.

Feingold traveled across Wisconsin, shooting a series of "person in the street" ads in towns such as LaCrosse and Janesville. These spots were called "Back of My Hand," for Feingold said that was how well he knew the state. And in planning his next trip, Feingold would use, like any good Wisconsiner, the back of his hand as a map resembling the state. The ads were spirited, yet also quite informative. Feingold himself addressed the voters on the street, and instead of talking at the people, he asked them questions and listened when they spoke. He asked the elderly what they thought about Social Security and Medicare. He asked construction workers what they thought about the budget. He asked a Velcro jumper plastered to the side of a wall what he should do if he gets to the Senate. As the candidate himself put it, "You've got to listen, not just talk."

Another Feingold spot showed a broken Statue of Liberty being repaired with bubble gum and Band-Aids. While Feingold argues against "quick fixes" such as the balanced budget amendments, Lady Liberty quickly falls back into its original state of disrepair.

But all of this fun and games did not detract from serious discussion of the issues. In fact, it only enhanced it. At the end of Feingold's ad campaign he says, "Sure we've had a lot of fun with the ads. But take a look at the issues from my point of view and my opponent's." Feingold was able to run an inspiring race, using his honesty and sense of humor to project his own character onto the television screen. He was a candidate, not an actor, and yet his candidacy provided some of the more entertaining moments of the 1994 elections.

Neither one of these television campaigns relied on misleading video techniques, distorted claims, cheap rumors, or demagoguery. Instead, they showed us the candidates in a personal, even intimate light. This is what television can do best, when it is used responsibly. The medium can foster an intimacy that is sorely lacking in contemporary campaigns. After watching the Feingold and Wellstone spots, you really get a sense of who they are, not just as candidates, but as people. We can hope that Feingold and Wellstone are part of a new generation of political leaders, baby boomers who grew up with the tube and are comfortable with the medium, yet use it to reveal their personalities and discuss the issues rather than hiding behind the camera. Bill Clinton, in some of his 1992 appearances, especially those on the television talk shows, revealed that he, too, had that talent, but once he assumed office, he became the equivocator in chief. If we are going to reinvigorate our political rhetoric, there is little choice but to do it, at least in part, through the medium of television. Feingold and Wellstone have shown us that a television rhetoric that is substantive, informative, inspiring, and entertaining is not only possible, but it can also win elections.

UNFAIR ADS

Throughout this book, we have seen examples of harsh and hateful ads, but they are not the only forms of bad negative spots. Some spots distort the truth or engage in defamatory and irrelevant personal attacks. Others use manipulative or contrived techniques. Former New York State Comptroller Edward Regan described the staging on one of his ads, which, although not negative, was certainly misleading:

> Let me tell you [about the] best commercial we ran. We're standing in Union Square Park. This commercial had to do with the soft side of the comptroller's office. So there's this group of actors standing in kind of a semicircle, and the camera's running around panning them. And at one point, the camera just caught these marvelous looks just coming out of these faces, old and young, well dressed and, you know, and they were just radiating up to me, and there was a voice-over saying what we were talking about. It was the best single shot of any commercial that year. You know what this was about? I told them, to break the ice, to start the conversation, who my nephew was. My nephew is the hottest casting director in New York City. And they went wild with me.[5]

Although people-on-the-street ads are commonly assumed to be documentary, in fact, they usually involve trained and scripted actors. (And here, I must admit using this device in some of my firm's work.) Regan's admission is troubling not so much in itself, but in its broader implications. If voters are being led to believe that the candidate is talking to real constituents in the ad, should we not mandate an on-screen disclaimer that these folks are paid actors pretending to be constituents?

Another example of a contrived ad was the spot used by Howard Baker's (R) 1980 presidential campaign, in which the then-Senator was filmed addressing a college audience during a campaign appearance, and an Iranian student started heckling him about U.S. support of the Shah, asking, "Why weren't you concerned about international law?" Baker responded sharply, "Cause my friend, I'm interested in 50 Americans. That's why. And when those 50 Americans are released, I'm perfectly willing to talk about that."[6] After Baker apparently silenced the heckler, the crowd erupted in applause. However, the applause had actually occurred at the end of Baker's speech, not directly following his exchange with the Iranian. But through the tricks of film editing, it was made to seem as if the crowd was spontaneously reacting to Baker's riposte.

Some ads make claims that are transparently false or vulgar. In the 1982 Senate race between Jerry Brown (D) and Pete Wilson (R), Brown came out in favor of a nuclear freeze and tried to use techniques of the "Daisy" ad to paint the then-moderate Wilson as a warmonger. A television spot showed a nuclear explosion, then quickly switched to the face of a young boy who said, "I want to go on living." A female announcer gave the tag line: "Jerry Brown supports a nuclear freeze. Pet Wilson doesn't. Vote for Jerry Brown, as if you life depends on it."[7] Brown's support dropped precipitously right after this ad was aired, and the spot was soon taken out of circulation. He fell behind Wilson in the polls and was eventually defeated.

In the 1990 Texas gubernatorial campaign, Ann Richards's

media consultant Bob Squier produced an ad using a news-paper headline that apparently supported his candidate's claims. However, journalists soon protested that the headline was missing the two crucial words "Richards Alleges." Squier said that the words were inadvertently dropped during the making of the ad. He apologized, and the spot was taken off the air.

With increasingly sophisticated video techniques now available to candidates at all levels of office, the amount of distortion and slick manipulation has reached unprecedented heights. Although there have always been some elements of distortion in political spots, the last few elections have seen more than their share.

Sometimes candidates will distort opponents' images or voices to make them sound worse. We have already seen how Jesse Helms did that to Harvey Gantt in a way that played on racial stereotypes. But sometimes a media team can alter its own candidate's voice to make him or her sound better. In some of Jimmy Carter's 1976 spots, the audio was speeded up to make the slow-talking Southerner seem to be more decisive and have less of a drawl. In 1992, George Bush's voice was slowed, to make him sound less whiny, deeper, and stronger. Meanwhile, his primary opponent Pat Buchanan speeded up the president's voice to make him sound high-pitched and wimpy.

The question is not so much whether special effects tech-niques are used—they are used in almost every spot—but whether they are being used to manipulate or deceive. Accord-ing to a study done by Lynda Kaid of the University of Okla-homa, some 15 percent of presidential campaign spots from 1952 to 1992 "contained ethically suspect uses of technology in their production and presentation."[8] But looking at the history of these spots, we see a troubling development: As the technol-ogy became more sophisticated, its abuse became more preva-lent. According to Kaid and her research team, 70 percent of the ads coded as using "technological techniques to create ethically suspect messages" appeared in the last 12 years. Negative ads are much more likely to contain distortions than positive ads. Somewhat surprisingly, issue ads are more likely than image ads to contain distortions. And, interestingly enough, Democrats are more likely to use ethically suspect techniques in their ads than Republicans, perhaps due to the fact that, until 1996, they were more often than not presidential challengers—with more candidates in competitive primaries—rather than incumbents.

Some distortions are obvious, such as Senator Ernest "Fritz" Hollings (D–S.C.) being dolled up with a turban or beret in the "Lifestyles of the Rich and Famous Spoof." Other distortions are not so clearly apparent. A 1992 George Bush spot attacking Bill Clinton's record as governor of Arkansas showed Clinton surrounded by state officials, all of whom applauded each time the announcer mentioned a tax increase. Clearly, the speeded-up pixilation of the officials was an attempt at slapstick humor. But hidden in all the commotion was the implied message that Clinton and his cronies enjoyed raising taxes.

It should always be clear when special effects are being used, and whenever the use of a special effect is not visibly apparent to the average viewer, then it ought to be labeled as such.

The Soul of Wit

Humor is a highly effective and often overlooked campaign technique, particularly in negative advertising. Democratic pollster Mark Mellman says, "Once you start laughing at somebody, they don't have much of a chance."[9] Politicians with good senses of humor have been able to go far. Great leaders such as Lincoln, Franklin D. Roosevelt, and John F. Kennedy often used self-deprecating humor to deflate their enemies' attacks. Other politicians such as Calvin Coolidge and Adlai Stevenson showed a dry and mordant

continued

wit. Bob Dole, now that he has left politics, could have a successful second career as a stand-up comic if he wants one — his timing is that good. (If he had shown more of it in the campaign, he surely would have done better.) Humor is a necessary lubricant to the often-grinding gears of politics and a welcome ingredient to any politician's message.

Some candidates even had the temerity to laugh at political advertising itself. In his first race for the Senate in 1990, Paul Wellstone (D–Minn.) did an ad poking fun at the standard political bio spot. "We've only got thirty seconds," Wellstone told the camera, "so I've got to talk quickly." At an increasingly frantic pace, the candidate shows us his home, his neighborhood, and goes quickly through the various high points of his public life.

In his 1992 presidential bid, former California Governor Jerry Brown (D) turned the celebrity endorsement on its ear. Brown supporters Carroll O'Connor and Rob Reiner reprised their television roles as Archie and Meathead. Although the two actors had aged a bit since *All in the Family* was originally aired, they slipped easily into character. They discussed Brown's candidacy and his proposal of a flat tax, then coming out of character, made a sincere endorsement.

Politicians can deflect negative charges or even preempt them entirely by using humor. If a challenger is going to attack a candidate for spending cuts, he or she might try to characterize him- or herself as a cheapskate. Or the other way around. Senator Pat Leahy (D–Ver.) was charged by his opponent Richard Snelling as being a big spender, until Leahy was able to come up with witnesses testifying to his frugality, if not downright cheapness. If age is an issue, the candidate may do what elder statesman Ronald Reagan did in 1984, when he said that Walter Mondale's "youth and inexperience shouldn't be held against him." In 1996, the 73-year-old Dole poked enough fun at himself that it largely defused a similar age issue — he lost for other reasons.

Candidates running against well-known incumbents can often use their opponents' prominence against them, especially if it seems the office has gone to their heads. Republican challenger Don Bain ran an ad criticizing then–Denver Mayor Federico Pena as being inaccessible. As we follow the mayor through his busy day, we do not actually see him, because he is surrounded by a cluster of body-guards. He goes shopping, plays baseball, jogs, and walks down the street, but we only see the bodyguards swarm around him, in dark suits and sunglasses, acting as body shields for the candidate.

In 1992, Russ Feingold visited a joke shop, because he felt it would be "a good place to ask what you think about (incumbent Senator) Bob Kasten's latest ads." Inside the joke shop, he inquired about an advertised "personal attack alarm." "Does that fend off personal attacks from your polit-ical opponents?" When Feingold announced that he had secured Elvis's endorsement, Kasten shot an ad using an Elvis impersonator, but the jokes fell flat.

John Kerry (D) ran against his opponent without men-tioning him in his race for Lieutenant Governor of Massa-chusetts in 1982. "Ever wonder what lieutenant governors do?" the ad asked, while the video showed a man sitting at a desk, playing with a stuffed goose. Then we see this man, presumably the lieutenant governor, presiding over a meet-ing that includes only himself, slicing his tie in half while cutting a ceremonial ribbon, and talking again to his stuffed goose. Kerry's work experience is contrasted to the ceremo-nial laziness of the current officeholder in a manner that is humorous, oblique, and effective. (Ironically, the ad also contrasted with Kerry's earnest-to-a-fault and usually hu-morless manner.)

In his 1990 Senate reelection, Kerry skewered his oppo-nent, Republican James Rappaport, in a series of mock soap operas called "The Life of James Rappaport." Differ-ent episodes included "We Squeeze Vermont Taxpayers," "We Buy a Cow from Ourselves," and "We Make Millions on an S&L Deal."

Humor is not all fun and games; it can be also used to make a serious point. Tony Schwartz produced an ad in 1968 calling into question the abilities of Republican vice-presidential-candidate Spiro Agnew. The ad simply showed "Agnew for Vice President" on a television set for 30 sec-onds, while the offscreen viewer laughed hysterically. The

continued

tag line at the end was "This would be funny if it weren't so serious."

During David Duke's infamous run for the Louisiana governor's seat, the opposition produced a series of ads focusing on the former Klansman's racist and Nazi past. One of the most effective, and most amusing, was a spoof of the *Jeopardy* game show format called "Jabberwocky" (produced by Politics, Inc.).

Video

A game show set with three seated contestants (Bill, Debbie, and Alan) and a host. The host enters the set, talking into his microphone. "Jabberwocky" in large letters behind the contestants. The game board is set up like *Jeopardy*, with dollar amounts on each box for the following categories: "False Patriots, Tax Cheats, Good Buddies, Basement Booksellers, Crazy Ideas."

Audio

ANNOUNCER (reading voice-over): "He was kicked out of ROTC, lied about serving his country, and never spent a single day in the military."
DEBBIE: "Who is David Duke?"
ANNOUNCER: "Correct."
DEBBIE: "Good buddies for 300."
ANNOUNCER (reading voice-over): "He hired ex-Nazis to work on his political campaigns. Bill?"
BILL: "Who is David Duke?"
ANNOUNCER: "Yes."
BILL: "Paul, I'll try tax cheats for 200."
ANNOUNCER (reading voice-over): "He failed to file state income taxes from 1984 to 1987. Alan?"
ALAN: "Who is David Duke?"
ANNOUNCER: "Right."
ALAN: "Crazy ideas for 400, Paul."
ANNOUNCER (reading voice-over): "He has advocated that America be divided into separate race nations. Debbie, again."
DEBBIE: "Who is David Duke?"

ANNOUNCER: "Correct."

DEBBIE: "Basement booksellers for 300."

ANNOUNCER (reading voice-over): "He say's he's changed his ways, but just last year he was caught selling Nazi books and tapes from the basement of his legislative office. Alan?"

ALAN: "Who is David Duke?"

There is not enough humor in our politics and, certainly, not enough of it in our negative ads. That is because comedy is a tricky art, and it is tough to walk that fine line between satire and slander, between lampooning someone and insulting them. Some of the ads we have just examined are perhaps a bit undignified, even sophomoric. But they also bring liveliness and entertainment value to the political debate, and remind us that even our most serious endeavors can sometimes be fun or, at least, amusing, and that we should always be able to laugh, particularly at ourselves.

Chapter 15

Reforming Our Political Debate

Almost everyone agrees that political advertising is dreadful and only getting worse, but no one agrees on what to do about it. Legal measures concerning political speech often run up against the First Amendment. Still, there are several ways that we can address the insidious spread of irresponsible attack ads without doing damage to the Constitution.

Speech, particularly political speech, is given special protection by the First Amendment and subsequent court rulings interpreting it and enlarging its scope. The reason that the framers wrote the Bill of Rights to begin with was to protect citizens' ability to participate in our democracy. They knew that without the right to free speech, a free press, and peaceful assembly, you cannot have a democracy. However, they also believed that these protections would promote deliberative democracy, something that we have very little of these days.

Still, as we consider possible legal measures to restore deliberative democracy, we should be very careful, always making sure that any new laws allow for a diversity of voices and do not shut anyone out of the process.

OTHER COUNTRIES

Television is an American invention that has spread throughout the world, and we often think of it as our own. But television, particularly political television, is vastly different in other countries. And it is well worthwhile to explore others' experience for possible lessons of our own.

Most European nations have a mixed broadcasting industry of public and private stations, as the established public, largely noncommercial monopolies are increasingly being challenged by private enterprises. There is still a greater tradition of television being seen as a public service, rather than simply another private, profit-oriented industry. Following this approach, other Western countries have much stricter controls on political advertising. In Germany, spots have to be 2.5 minutes long. In Great Britain, the major political parties are given free air time in 5- and 10-minute chunks. Denmark gives its parties 10-minute spots. Finland has tough restrictions on negative ads, allowing no attacks on individuals. France has detailed codes regulating the content and form of political spots. In Israel, ads have to be approved by an Election Commission before they are allowed to air.

Paid direct advertising of the type seen in U.S. campaigns is not permitted at all in France, West Germany, and the United Kingdom. Italy allows it only at the local level. Canada puts strict limits on the total amount of time that may be purchased. Only in Venezuela is paid, direct political advertising of major importance. There, it is even more influential—and expensive—than in the United States. (Not coincidentally, it has attracted a number of American political consultants to work for candidates in that country.)

The differences in political systems are also quite substantial. American candidates pay for their own advertisements, whereas in most parliamentary countries, free spots are allocated in proportion to electoral strength gauged by either representation in the national Parliament or popular votes in the preceding general election. The only exception is in France's presidential election, where free time is awarded to all candidates equally. The campaign seasons are different as well. A parliamentary government can call for an election at any point during its term, and the campaign cycle is usually much shorter than it is here in the United States. England, for example, has a campaign of only a few weeks.

Of course, cultural differences, not to mention legal obstacles, would make it impossible to simply transplant a great many of these practices and restrictions into American politics. Some of them we would not want, and others we do not need. However, it is important to highlight these different approaches to political advertising in order to show that there are viable options out there, and that the free-market, anything-goes system of political advertising that has debased and trivialized our politics is a choice and not a necessity.

REFORM PROPOSALS

Here follows a series of reform proposals that seek to make our elections more substantive, more fair, and more competitive—in other words, more democratic.

Media and the Public Interest

The media, particularly television, enjoy protections unlike any other industry. As *The New Republic* describes it, "Broadcast stations are granted a big piece of a limited resource—the broadcast spectrum—for free. Cable stations share in a government-protected oligopoly."[1] And very little is asked of them in return. There are some content-driven regulations requiring public-interest shows, and a few form-driven regulations, for example, the laws limiting the amount of commercial time in children's television shows. But for the most part, television is one of our least regulated industries. And it is probably the one with the greatest political impact.

There is no reason why the price for admission in this enormously profitable industry cannot be a greater and more responsible involvement in our political life. The proposals described here will probably cause television executives to cry that their First Amendment rights are being abridged. But what they are really concerned about is loss of profits. Television executives should stop hiding behind the Constitution and quit pretending that they are in this business as a public service—a ruse that no longer has any credibility with the networks, now owned by the profit-driven General Electric, Disney, Westinghouse, Rupert Murdoch's News Corporation and now, with the Turner merger, Time/Warner. Television stations make truckloads of money. And the telecommunications bill that passed the 104th Congress means that ownership will become increasingly monopolistic as virtually all restrictions on the number of outlets that can be owned by a single entity have been eliminated.

Television stations and the executives who operate them are profoundly influential agents in our political life. With all the power they have, they ought to assume more responsibility. Unfortunately, it is not just profit-conscious broadcasting executives who are in the way. The Federal Election Committee (FEC) itself ruled against a North Carolina television station's plan to give candidates free 30-second spots, saying free airtime represents an "impermissible in-kind campaign contribution from a corporate-owned entity."[2] This, despite the fact that the station was willing to give equal time for all candidates.

The news media, particularly broadcast television, should make a more concerted effort not to give neutral or positive publicity to irresponsible attack ads, and to give their truth boxes and ad watches real teeth. Instead of treating political commercials like just another story, they should be allowed to freely critique them for truth and relevance—but *not* effectiveness—and come to independent conclusions rather than using objectivity as an excuse for their lack of critical faculties. Above all, news operations need to be reoriented so that information, and not entertainment, is their primary objective. That is unlikely to occur without countervailing power from the federal government to curb corporate greed.

Media Reforms

The following reforms should be instituted to make our media more responsible and our public debate more positive and substantive.

• Establish more stringent public-service requirements for television and radio stations. Each broadcast and cable channel should be required to set aside a certain amount of time, during prime hours, for political policy debate. Allow them to be somewhat creative in the programming. For instance, let MTV do something like "Rock the Vote," while BET does a documentary about affirmative action, and a local cable channel sponsors a debate among city council candidates. But the requirements have to be strict, clearly articulated, and enforceable.

• Pass federal legislation regulating the cable industry. Rigorous federal standards must be established concerning the public-service requirements of cable television. Right now, franchises negotiate with their host communities for public access and public-service requirements. All too often, these franchises quickly ignore such requirements, or renegotiate their contracts to lessen their responsibilities. Once they have started digging up the streets, it is awfully hard to get rid of a cable company. But if public service requirements were standard and nationwide, enforced by the FCC, then cable companies would be forced to live up to them.

These requirements could include having all cable markets offer full and unmediated coverage of open, public assemblies such as city council and school-board meetings, sessions of the state legislatures, and addresses by major public officials. In areas that are not served by cable, require that the coverage be broadcast on UHF channels.

• Require that the national networks give six hours of prime airtime during the major parties political conventions in a presidential election year. Even though the conventions almost never decide who the candidates will be and have become television shows, with delegates reduced to the role of a studio audience, they are still virtually the only opportunity for the parties to show who they are and what they stand for. And our politics would benefit by becoming more party, rather than personality, driven. With television coverage mandated and planned, the parties can put their most important speakers in the time slots, guaranteeing them the national spotlight, while relegating much of the procedural maneuvers and minor speeches—in other words, all the boring stuff—to CNN and C-SPAN.

• Require the networks to sponsor debates during presidential years. We need to make them a permanent and consistent part of the campaign process. Now, too much time is given over to tactical negotiations about the time, place, and manner of the debates. Allow the networks and the parties to come up with a standard format and stick to it, so the candidates and their campaigns can spend more time discussing the issues, rather than talking about lighting, podiums, and makeup.

• Require every television and radio station to give free airtime to the parties—ideally "roadblocked" in prime time so the entire nation's attention is turned to the campaign. Former *Washington Post* reporter Paul Taylor made invaluable progress toward this goal in 1996.

Because some television markets contain several different political constituencies, it is not feasible to require that broadcasters give airtime to individual candidates. A New York television station might have to turn over all its ad space to the literally hundreds of candidates running for office within its market. Instead, give the parties the airtime and let them decide which candidates, or issues, to focus on. This will restore to the parties a measure of needed power, with a concomitant—and highly desirable—reduction in the power of special interests and campaign consultants. The airtime should be significant and prominent, say, a minimum of five minutes during prime time per day, seven days per week for the 30 days leading up to the election. This should not be restricted just to the major parties. If third parties qualify for federal matching funds, or get a percentage of the last election's vote equal to that required for matching funds, they should be allowed in the debate as well.

• Reimplement and enforce the Fairness Doctrine. When television was first developed, the FCC realized the enormous potential for enhancing democratic debate. They also understood the risks of using the public airwaves for partisan political messages. So they instituted the Fairness Doctrine, which required equal time for political speech, so one party or cause did not unfairly dominate the airwaves. During the 1980s, and as part of the overall communication deregulation frenzy, the Reagan Administration decided to ignore the Fairness Doctrine and generally allowed broadcast and cable operators to set their own standards for public service programming. Reagan himself may have borne a special animus to the Fairness Doctrine, as it kept his Hollywood movies from appearing on late-night television during his campaign. In 1984, Reagan's FCC chair Mark Fowler expressed the administration's feeling that public interest should be determined by "the public interest." This free-market approach has created what Fred Friendly calls "an electronic midway." And it has not been any good for democracy. As a result of this tacit rescinding of the Fairness Doctrine, some radio stations air *Rush Limbaugh* as their public-service requirement, while others relegate community talk shows to the wee hours. We need to rewrite the Fairness Doctrine so that it clearly establishes what is partisan speech and how it should be answered.

If the Republicans really believe, as they so often charge, that the media are dominated by liberals and (in Newt Gingrich's words) "socialists," then they should welcome the Doctrine's return. Their opposition proves they are fully aware that between the Rush Limbaughs and G. Gordon Liddys of radio, the George Wills and John McLaughlins of television, and the Robert Novaks and Fred Barneses of print, right-wing views are not only well represented, but they also *dominate* the media.

• Enforce "lowest unit charge" regulations. Since 1972, television and radio stations have been required to sell airtime to federal-level political candidates at the lowest price offered to commercial advertisers during the 45 days before a primary election and 60 days before the general election. This provision has been constantly violated and ignored by greedy stations eager to gouge campaigners who simply have to get their messages on the air, and have no option and little legal recourse. The lowest unit charge law should be enforced, with strict penalties for stations that violate it.

• Give the FCC more regulatory power. Mark Fowler once referred to television as "a toaster with pictures." And House Speaker Newt Gingrich has said that he would like to "phase out the FCC in three to five years at most."[3] Both of them ignore the immeasurable impact that television and other communication technologies have on our public life. The mass communication industry does not need to be deregulated; it needs to be reregulated. The free-market orgy of the Reagan–Bush years has resulted in mass media predominantly owned and controlled by a few very large, very rich corporations, and a corresponding, and sadly predictable, lack of public responsibility in pursuit of higher profits. The current megamonopolies of the mass-communications corporations will, if unchecked, result in a concentration of power in the hands of a few corporate executives who, in Representative Ed Markey's words, would "make Citizen Kane look like an underacheiver."[4]

The FCC should be used to maintain diversity and balance, and make sure that "competition" does not result in oligopoly. The agency should be given broader powers controlling media ownership, cable franchising and rate-setting, licensing requirements and, yes, even content control. The successful battle over children's programming requirements should now be extended to a debate over the content of all television. When framers of the Constitution wrote the First Amendment, they were talking about protecting political and religious expression, not the confessions of demented transvestites on afternoon tabloid talk shows.

In 1929, the Federal Radio Commission, which later became the FCC, said that broadcast stations were "licensed to serve the public and not for the purpose of furthering the private or selfish interests of individuals or groups of individuals. The standard of public interest, convenience, or necessity means nothing if it does not mean this."[5] The agency should be given the power, and the responsibility, to enforce this initial charter and guarantee that the media of mass communications be used with more of a focus on the public interest than private gain.

Regulations on Political Spots

Political speech is, of course, protected by the First Amendment. And it is distinguished from commercial speech, which is subject to legal controls and sanctions. But federal legislation can, to a certain degree, dictate the form, if not the content, of political spots.

• Require that all independent expenditure campaign ads have disclaimers that clearly distinguish them from candidates and party campaigns, both through audio and printed words that can easily be read from the television screen. One such disclaimer could have said, at the end of the Willie Horton ad: "This announcement was produced by Citizens for Bush, an independent group that is not associated with the Republican or Democratic Parties, or with either presidential campaign."

• Increase the disclaimer notification on regular campaign ads. There should be a five-second, full-screen photo of the candidate at the end of each ad, announcing that he or she paid for it and is responsible for its content. If George Bush's face was plastered at the end of his campaign's infamous "Revolving Door" ad, would it have been as effective? Would it even have aired?

• Allow no new ads or literature to be produced or disseminated in the last week of the campaign. All too often, the last days of a political campaign are filled with late-minute attacks, many of which are slanderous or irresponsible. And the victim of these attacks has little or no time to respond. If a candidate has something to say during that time, he or she can make a speech or give a press conference. If the new message is of any relevance and significance, it will get aired.

A Step toward Public Financing

We should have full public financing of political campaigns. It is the only way we are ever going to have fair and competitive elections. However, the political tenor is such that any proposals for public financing are fantastical at best. But perhaps we can give the proposal a low-risk trial, to measure public support and willingness to participate voluntarily. If it works, then we might explore the possibility of fully public-financed campaigns.

• Increase the check-off tax donation for political campaigns from $3 to an unlimited amount, and make that money available to lower ballot federal elections. Distribute that money to the qualified candidates in each state, commensurate to money donated in that state, for paid political advertising on television and radio, subject to strict content control by the FEC.

Of course, if taxpayers check off a significant amount to go toward the campaign fund, there might be a revenue shortfall. But how much would it actually amount to? Even if we have full public financing of all federal elections, the total cost would be $1 billion annually. This may seem a lot, but, in fact, it only amounts to 0.06 percent of the total federal budget—six 100ths of 1 percent.[6] That is a small price to pay for democracy.

The increased check-off proposal would be a trial balloon for public financing. It would gauge voter enthusiasm for the project and show taxpayers how little it would actually cost to have publicly financed, and therefore non-special-interest-group-dependent, and publicly regulated, federal elections. Public financing would seriously diminish the corrupting influence of big money and make our elections cleaner, more competitive, and more fair.

Money and Advertising

In contemporary politics, money has a profoundly anti-democratic effect. Big money has a disproportionate advantage in access and influence, and candidates spend far too much time raising funds and genuflecting to contributors, many of them special interests whose narrow agendas often conflicts with the greater common good. We need to change the way money operates in our political system, and the following are a few items of campaign reform.

• Level contribution limits. We should keep the personal contribution limit at $1,000 for a primary and another $1,000 for the general election (for a total of $2,000; $3,000 when a runoff election is also involved), and apply the same level to PAC contributions, lowering them from the present limits of $5,000 per primary and $5,000 per general election. Soft-money contributions should also be limited to the $1,000 per election standard.

• Mandate full and regular disclosure. There should be full disclosure on all political contributions, including soft money and independent expenditures. This disclosure should not just be a few pieces of paper buried in a courthouse or federal agency, but a matter of open, public record available on the Internet to anyone who wants to know. Campaigns should be required to publish lists of their contributors and the amount donated in the form of legal notices in newspapers serving their constituencies. Such publication should be required regularly throughout the campaign, say, once a month, starting a year before the election, or once campaign contributions have reached a certain level. If we cannot control the amount that billionaires and millionaires spend on their own campaigns, at least, we should make their spending a matter of open public record.

• Reduce incumbent perks. Either eliminate free-mail privileges for incumbents during the six months before an election, or give qualified challengers the power to frank, sending mail at no cost to constituents. Have stricter enforcement of prohibitions on Congressional staff from working on campaigns and as fund-raisers.

• Get rid of free incumbent media. Members of Congress should be banned from hosting or being featured on radio and television shows produced by the House and Senate broadcasting galleries. And if they host a television or radio show produced by a local station or cable operator, that show should be taken off the air during the nine months prior to the election, unless their opponents are offered equal and comparable time.

The Fair Campaign Practices Committee

At the height of the McCarthy era in 1954, a private, nonpartisan organization was established to monitor political campaigns. The Fair Campaign Practices Committee (FCPC) investigated charges of unfair campaign tactics for more than 20 years. FCPC actions centered around a code, which candidates for federal office signed voluntarily. The code required that candidates conduct their campaigns in the "best American tradition." Those who signed agreed to condemn character defamation; false, distorted, or unsubstantiated campaign material; prejudice based on race, creed, or national origin; and election fraud.

The FCPC covered more than 500 races for state and federal elective office each year. Of the 63 complaints on congressional elections handled each election year between 1966 and 1976, the vast majority were settled without binding arbitration.

In 1976, the Internal Revenue Service ruled that FCPC

disclosure of the names of candidates who signed its code constituted an attempt to influence the outcome of elections and violated IRS provisions for nonprofit organizations. Voluntary contributions subsequently declined, and the Committee became largely inactive.

We should bring back the FCPC, but, this time, give it teeth. Make it a part of the FEC, and give it power to punish violators of fair campaign practices. The FCPC could act as a campaign tribunal, being a clearinghouse for all political messages and a watchdog against dirty tricks, both rhetorical and tactical. Make the FCPC the court of first resort for libel and defamation of character claims, so that the legal system is not clogged with charges and countercharges by disgruntled candidates. And give the FCPC power to recall elected officials who have seriously transgressed its code, and to mandate new elections that have been tainted by libel or fraud.

• Get the parties involved. Both major political parties have a stake in clean and fair elections. Give representatives of the parties nonvoting seats on the FCPC, so that they are involved in the deliberation, if not the ultimate judgments, of that commission. If the FCPC is to be the clearinghouse of political ads and literature, then the parties will have to have full-time message monitors, who scrutinize the other party's campaigns for false, misleading, or inflammatory content.

Libel

Political candidates who are unfairly or inaccurately attacked by their opponents should have greater legal recourse. Under current libel laws, based on the *Times vs. Sullivan* decision, as public figures, candidates have to prove intentional malice in order to successfully sue for libel. But what can be more intentionally malicious than some of the nasty attacks that are being aired today?

Several states have enacted tough prohibitions against false statements in political advertising. But while such legislation is well-intentioned, there is as yet no evidence that the quality of political discourse in those states is significantly better than in the rest of the nation. In fact, states with such laws, including California, Massachusetts, Michigan, North Carolina, and Ohio, were the scenes of some of the most negative campaigns in recent memory.

We need federal-level libel laws that are clear, strong, and enforceable. In 1964, Ralph Ginzberg, publisher of *Fact* magazine, commissioned a poll asking psychiatrists, "Is Barry Goldwater psychologically fit to be president of the United States." The psychiatrists overwhelmingly answered "no." Goldwater sued Ginzberg and won, becoming one of the first public figures to successfully sue for libel. Since then, very few public figures have brought their cases to court. More candidates should take legal action against their accusers. If nothing else, this would create a positive chilling effect, and campaigns would think twice about running a questionable ad. If the FCPC were used as a preliminary court to decide the validity of libel and defamation charges before going on to courts of law, that might reduce many of the spurious and troublesome challenges of campaign claims.

DUBIOUS PROPOSALS

Although the disgust and revulsion that many feel toward attack ads is certainly understandable, some of the proposals offered to counter or control them are dubious at best. Former Senator Warren Rudman (R–N.H.) and Senator Daniel Inouye (D–Hi.) proposed a "talking heads rule," in which all political advertising on television would consist only of a full-face shot of the candidate talking to the camera. This rule would do two things: First, it would create a bias against untelegenic candidates or those without well-developed acting skills. We would end up represented by a bunch of newscasters and spokesmodels like Ronald Reagan. Second, like many other suggested reforms, the "talking-heads rule" assumes that politics can only be serious, and that to be substantive, debate must also be boring. The Lincoln–Douglas debates and the 1992 elections prove that democracy does not have to be dull. But a political season of talking heads, droning on about arcane issues of public policy, could drive even more voters away than the slugfests we are seeing today.

Robert Bellah and his colleagues would go even further: "To cut to the heart of this corrupting institution, the antithesis of real politics, we suggest radical surgery: outlaw campaign advertising on radio and television."[7] Eugene McCarthy has also argued that "the most direct way of avoiding the socially corrupting effects of political advertising is by banning it altogether."[8]

Although the prospect of an airwaves free of mudslinging may be a pleasant thought, we certainly do not want to eliminate political advertising altogether. If often misleading and detestable, it is still a vital form of voter information, and campaigns should be encouraged to communicate with voters as much as possible, albeit in longer, more substantive form than 30-second spots. For better and for worse, we are stuck with a system of mass-media advertising to inform the electorate of its choices. How else are candidates supposed to get their messages across to voters, if not through commercial advertising? True, there has been an overemphasis on television and radio spots in contemporary campaigns, and their tone and content have become increasingly negative, but the solution is not to eliminate them entirely. Instead, we need to modify the system that we have, putting reasonable restraints on political advertising, while having strict and enforceable legal penalties to punish those who misuse it, and adding incentives for longer form communications.

CAMPAIGN REFORM AT THE PERSONAL LEVEL

Here is something you can do: Do not vote for a candidate who uses the techniques and language of poison politics. If it did not work, candidates would not do it anymore.

Chapter 16

The Power of
Positive Participation

We have seen through the course of this book how politicians and their operatives have used the technologies of the mass media to exploit our baser emotions, exaggerate our differences, ignore our commonalities, and divide rather than unite us. America has always been a fragile corporation, the tenuous bonds of patriotism and unity often threatened by ethnic tensions, regional and religious separatism, and class division. Our politics should be a means of bridging those differences, and joining our country together in common endeavor.

In a democracy, how we speak to each other determines how we are governed. When we allow campaigns to degenerate into shouting matches and scandal frenzies, we suffer from a politics that is not only mean-spirited but also counterproductive. Instead of bringing us together, political rhetoric is driving us apart. It is only going to get worse unless we work to make it better. And to do that, we need to change the very manner in which we engage in political argument.

POLITICS AND THE AMERICAN LANGUAGE

"Political corruption begins with the corruption of language," said George Orwell. There is a powerful dynamic of corruption that destroys both rhetoric and politics. Our language "becomes ugly and inaccurate because our thoughts are foolish, but the slovenliness of our language makes it easier for us to have foolish thoughts."[1]

Orwell was writing before sophisticated manipulation of the technology of mass communication was brought to bear upon public opinion. By present-day standards, Goebbels was a crude propagandist. Now instead of the Big Lie, you get the Big Spin.

"Spin is the weaving of basic truth into the fabric of a lie, the production of a cover garment that protects, or obscures, or deflects public examination," according to Marlin Fitzwater, former press secretary to Reagan and Bush, and no mean practitioner of spin himself.[2] One recent example of the big spin is the Republicans' manipulation of words in their fight to cut Medicare.

Republican pollster Linda DiVall had conducted a series of focus groups with both seniors and younger voters, and found that the Republicans needed to soften their rhetoric in order for their assault on Medicare to succeed. Words such as *cut*, *cap*, and *freeze* made people scared. Instead, DiVall counseled, the Republicans should use words such as *preserve*, which evoked stability and made their proposals seems less, well, revolutionary. Their strategy of cutting Medicare would remain unchanged; only their rhetorical tactics, meant to create support among voters, would change. "Our job," DiVall said, "is to get them to choose the option we want them to choose."[3]

The rhetorical tactic not only created a consistent and effective message for the Republicans, but it also increased Gingrich's personal power and control over the agenda. Gingrich has risen to the leadership of the GOP in part by putting words in his colleagues' mouths. As the *Washington Post* described it, the Medicare war of words

was all part of Gingrich's unified approach to communications, honed since he was a backbencher in the late 1970s
and used now to give him tighter control of the message
and make it possible for him to maintain discipline within
the ranks.[4]

Gingrich's cadre of House colleagues, pollsters, and communications specialists was named CommStrat. They met once
a week in Gingrich's conference room to plan their assault on
Medicare, focusing mostly on the language they would use.
The came up with a series of words such as *restructure, modern-
ize, transform, change, save, improve, protect,* and *preserve.* These
words were market-tested among a group of 400 adults 50
years of age and older. *Improve, protect,* and *preserve* got the most
favorable ratings.

Then–Republican National Committee Chair Haley Barbour, who had initially urged the party to stay away from
Medicare until after the 1996 elections, eagerly endorsed the
rhetorical trinity. "This is the last time we're using the old
phrases." Barbour said. "Starting today we're going to say the
new stuff."[5] Gingrich rearranged the order so that the line now
was "preserve, protect and improve," making it sound like the
oath of office.

The Republican leadership went out into battle, armed
with these new rhetorical weapons. But Frank Luntz found that
improve created unrealistic expectations among some seniors.
They thought they would be getting better services or lower
prices. His suggestion that *improve* be replaced by *strengthen*
was quickly adopted by the party.

Republican leadership worked hard to keep the message
consistent. Budget Committee Chair John Kasich fined members one dollar for using the word *cut* in discussions—he was
the first one to pony up a fine. Haley Barbour promised to raise
"unshirted hell" with any members of the media who used the
term. But that is just what the Republicans were doing, trying to
cut Medicare, raise fees, and limit choices. No amount of rhetorical disingenuity would cover that fact. Many of them had
learned from the Reagan Administration's failed attempts to

gut Social Security and other programs that harsh policy proposals have to be couched in warm and fuzzy language. Reagan himself learned that lesson quickly. Nicaraguan thugs became "Freedom Fighters." An unprecedented (and unnecessary)
arms buildup became "Peace through Strength," and the crackpot Star Wars weapon system became, or tried to become, "The
Strategic Defense Initiative," or, more simply, "The Space
Shield."

Of course, this kind of obfuscation did not start with Reagan. As White House Aide George Stephanopoulos said about
the Republicans' Medicare rhetoric: "It sounds like the old
Vietnam argument that they had to destroy the village in order
to save it."[6] The problem is that, these days, the use of such
language is not an obvious act of desperation by a distressed
Pentagon press office, but a well-organized, well-financed, and
often successful public relations campaign. Words are market-
tested for their effectiveness rather than used for their accuracy.
In the end, we get a political language that is both manipulative
and empty, for if words can mean anything, they wind up
meaning nothing at all.

Soon, political terms become modular words that can be
arranged in any random manner to say whatever the speaker
wants them to mean, much like the modular furniture that can
be arranged according to different floor plans. In 1994, anyone
who had ever voted for a budget could be characterized as a
"big-spending liberal." Anyone who had ever been in office
while a violent crime was committed could be tarred with being
"soft on crime." Every incumbent was a "career politician." In
the private sector, companies "renegotiate," "streamline," and
"downsize"—Orwellian euphemisms for cutting wages and
workforces in order to increase short-term corporate profits.

"When words are used merely as instruments of publicity
or propaganda, they lose their power to persuade," the late
social critic Christopher Lasch wrote. "Soon they cease to mean
anything at all. People lose the capacity to use language precisely and expressly or even to distinguish one word from
another."[7] In the end, what we have is not rhetoric, but noise.

But one can still look for the rhetorical intent behind even the emptiest phrases. The Republicans repeat their mantra of "family values" until the term becomes meaningless by repetition. Meanwhile, their policies seem to indicate that it is just another way of saying, "I'm all right, Jack." According to a *Time*/CNN poll taken soon after the 1994 elections, 61 percent of those surveyed agreed with the statement, "The way things are today, people have to worry more about themselves and their families and less about helping others."[8]

When Dan Quayle invoked the family, he spoke of exclusion, protecting the family from outsiders, and looking after one's own. His message was one of fear and greed. When Mario Cuomo spoke of the family, his vision was more inclusive; he meant the national, not just the nuclear, family. He wanted to extend the commitment to each other that characterizes the family beyond the bonds of blood to the nation itself, to show that our commonalities are greater than our differences, that we are all in this together.

Unfortunately, the right-wing vision of family has, for the moment, prevailed. So, the nuclear family nestles into the sterile confines of the suburbs, living in high-security communities protected by armed response, interacting with others only through the media or the marketplace, and watching the world on television rather than living in it. Our national family has become atomized, selfish, and exclusive, forever subdividing into smaller and more antagonistic tribes, until our common life has been reduced to shouting at each other on television, talk radio, and the Internet. Civil society has become a nostalgic abstraction that many claim to want but no one knows how to recapture.

Closely linked to the loss of meaning, in our words and in our lives, is the crisis of belief. "Genuine belief seems to have left us," Walt Whitman wrote in *Democratic Vistas* over 100 years ago, and since then, we have become a much more skeptical, cynical nation.[9] In the absence of faith in our fellow citizens and the institutions that hold us together, politics becomes not a search for remedy but merely a scramble for advantage.

"The American people are cynical and turned off about all the institutions, and politics is only one of them," said the late Lee Atwater. "Bull permeates everything."[10] Of course, Atwater himself was partly to blame for this. Toward the end of his life, Atwater realized what he had done and sent letters of apology to some of those he had excoriated on the campaign trail. But the damage was already done, and Atwater's legacy of hatred and division lives on, while his pleas for forgiveness have been unheard by his successors.

The politics of fear and greed has created a realignment that has allowed the Republicans to lay claim to being the majority party. Unless the Democrats return to their egalitarian roots and recapture their traditional constituents, that realignment is only going to become more lasting in 1998 and 2000, when history says the incumbent presidential party will suffer losses. And if things do not change, then our rhetoric, our politics, and our people, will continue to suffer.

THE DREAM AND THE LIE
OF RULING-CLASS POPULISM

In 1877, a young Woodrow Wilson described what he saw as the problem with American politics, "No leaders, no principles; no principles, no parties."[11] The Gilded Age had placed a primacy on industrial development, imperial expansion, and crude economic power. Corruption reached the highest offices in Washington, and powerful business interests wielded disproportionate influence through their newly formed "lobbies." Workers and farmers rose in anger against the unjust policies that allowed corporate and robber-baron interests to run over the common man. But the Populist movement never really went beyond the politics of protest. It was not until the ruling class itself took on the cause of good government that the Progressive movement was able to effect some changes in the way America was run. Teddy Roosevelt, the New York aristocrat, stirred populist rage with his fiery speeches against the "malefactors of great wealth." Progressive legislation such as the Sherman Anti-Trust Act helped break up powerful monopolies. Meanwhile, the press began exercising its newfound independence from party loyalty, publishing muckraking exposés of greedy businessmen and corrupt politicians.

For most of the 19th century, Americans had gotten by with limited government. There was no income tax and very little regulation. But the rise of powerful business interests, with the ability to literally transform the nation, brought with it a need for countervailing power. No longer would the federal government be strong only in emergency. Now, it would have to operate as a negative force to control the ambitions of the new ruling class that the Industrial Age had created.

Some years later, when Wilson himself became the standard-bearer of Progressivism and Democratic presidential candidate, he enunciated his vision of government's role in a capitalist democracy. "The business of government is to organize the common interest against the special interests."[12] As Richard Hofstadter describes it, "What has happened in America, Wilson told the voters, is that industry has ceased to be free because the laws do not prevent the strong from crushing the weak."[13] Wilson was a champion of that new social entity, the American middle class, which he saw being crushed by the economic and political power of big business. In Wilson's own words, "The middle class is being more and more squeezed out by the processes which we have been taught to call the processes of prosperity."[14]

Sound familiar?

In the Gilded Age, the lords of industry were allowed to expand and conglomerate without the government requiring them to pay their workers a decent wage, respect the environment, or fulfill any long-term responsibilities to the healthy functioning of the economy or the nation as a whole. The result was a series of economic catastrophes, not to mention the persistent subjugation of America's workers, who were often kept from organizing by violent repression. The Progressives did much good, but when they were defeated by the Republicans of Harding, Coolidge, and Hoover, *laissez-faire* economics once again prevailed, and we got the Great Depression. FDR's New Deal was not a socialist plot. Instead, it was designed to save capitalism, a system that his labor secretary Frances Perkins said she took as much for granted as her own family. FDR's policies not only saved our economic system, but they also created a new role for government. No longer was it merely a negative force, controlling, regulating, collecting taxes. FDR turned it into a positive force, able to ameliorate some of the harsher aspects of life and act as an agent for vital and necessary change.

During World War II and the boom that followed, the federal government was an immensely positive force, not only in the lives of American citizens but also throughout the world. We won the war and then helped rebuild Japan and Germany, the very people we had just defeated, as industrialized, capitalist democracies. The Marshall Plan was crucial in the recovery, even the survival, of a civilized and democratic Western Europe. At home, recently discharged veterans attended college under the GI Bill or got low-interest loans for new houses. Their children went to affordable state universities, often financed by federally guaranteed student loans, government aid, and scholarships. With Social Security, their grandparents enjoyed financial stability in what, for previous generations, had been a time of fear and destitution. Later, when Medicare was passed, they were given the kind of medical attention that had previously only been available to the rich. Through these programs and countless others, the federal government helped create a strong, healthy, and prosperous middle class. Each generation enjoyed a higher standard of living. Until this one.

Between 1945 and 1973, or roughly between the end of World War II and the end of the New Deal coalition, real income rose steadily for all economic classes. As New Deal and Great Society programs kicked in, we dramatically reduced life-threatening poverty. A rising tide was indeed lifting all boats. But over that same period, we had historically unprecedented dominance over the world economy. In the years immediately following World War II, America's gross national product (GNP) accounted for more than half of the world's total output. Of course that would not last, as emerging and recovering nations began to compete in the global market. In the 1970s, rising energy costs, foreign competition, inflation, and stagnation caught up to us, and we began to see the limits of our economic miracle. In some ways, retrenchment was inevitable, but government policies have made the middle class suffer while the wealthy got even more rich. Inflation rose higher than wages and helped devalue savings, the tax rate became regressive, and real earnings for working Americans fell for the first time since the Great Depression.

Meanwhile, by standard abstract measurements, the American economy is apparently healthy. Productivity and profits are up, the Dow–Jones average topped the once-unthinkable 7,000 mark in early 1997. Why, then, is there pervasive economic insecurity and even despair? Because this prosperity is not being shared equally, particularly among the American workers who are most responsible for it. Forty years ago, some 35 percent of the American workforce belonged to unions. Now, just a little over 10 percent of private-sector workers are unionized, and increasingly, they belong to lower-wage service industries rather than well-paying industrial jobs. Organized labor was able "to take wages out of competition," so that companies would compete not by lowering wages and benefits, but by being more innovative and productive. Now, they compete by laying off employees, shipping jobs to low-wage countries, or hiring part-time or temporary workers, so they do not have to pay for benefits. The much-vaunted "American Industrial Renaissance" has come at the direct expense of the workers who built America the first time around.

The economic and social policies of a dozen years of conservative Republican presidents and more than two years of an even more conservative GOP Congress—aided and abetted by business-oriented Democratic lawmakers—have laid waste to the middle class, giving more advantages to those who own rather than those who work. The almost surreal budget deficits initiated by Reagan's patently bogus supply-side delusions have burdened future generations of Americans with trillions of dollars of debt and made it almost impossible for government programs to be initiated or expanded to meet new challenges or solve existing problems. Reagan created a successful coalition of ruling-class populism, in which, by blaming the poor for economic troubles, the middle class found common cause with the rich. There is nothing wrong with a little class warfare; without it, you can never achieve social or economic justice. But Reagan turned class warfare upside down, using the slick demagoguery of capitalist *kitsch* to convince the middle class that the culprits behind their economic decline were the poor who suffered even more than they, and not the rich who were profiting off their decline.

But Reagan would not have succeeded in creating this misalliance without some help from the Democrats. For 175 years, the people had a party that spoke for their interests. That was the party of Andrew Jackson, Woodrow Wilson, Franklin Roosevelt, and Lyndon Johnson. Now, the party rarely speaks for them, and often will not even listen.

Starting in the 1980s, the Democrats turned from the party of the people to the party of the powerful. Former House Majority Whip Tony Coelho (D–Calif.) created a fund-raising mechanism by which the Democrats got millions of dollars from traditionally Republican benefactors—corporate PACs and CEOs—and sold the soul of the party in the process. The rise of the largely corporate-funded Democratic Leadership Council further removed the party from its roots. Soon, George Wallace's slogan as candidate for the American Independent Party was proved accurate: "There ain't a nickel's worth of difference between the Republicans and the Democrats."

Though, of course, neither party would recognize coin of such small denomination.

Politics is a zero-sum game, and when one side wins, another loses. The Republicans made substantial gains in the South and among the white middle class at the expense of the Democrats' traditional New Deal constituency. But realignment did not just occur because the Republicans sold working Americans on ruling-class populism. The Democrats lost those voters, because they had neglected them and were no longer seen as their allies and protectors. The New Deal coalition fell apart, because the Democrats stopped making the case for positive government action on behalf of working Americans.

WHO ARE THE DEMOCRATS?

The last time the Republicans controlled Congress while a Democrat sat in the Oval Office, Harry Truman explained the GOP's electoral success in Congress by saying, "Why vote for a pseudo-Republican when you can have the real thing?" The party that had recently enjoyed the leadership of the greatest president of the 20th century was now simply mimicking the "do-nothing" Republicans. But at least its president was not afraid to call a spade a spade.

Our present Democratic occupant of the White House is in no position—nor does he seem to have the inclination—to criticize his party for being ideological invertebrates. Except for an initial few stabs at enacting liberal policies such as health-care reform and allowing openly gay men and women to serve in the military, Clinton has, in words attributed to him, governed like an Eisenhower Republican. David Broder described what he thought the presidential class of 1996, including the incumbent, sorely lacked: "An inner conviction that you are where you belong, that you know yourself, that you trust your abilities and instincts, and that you are clear about your goals."[15] In other words, leadership.

Clinton had a chance to lead, to dealign ruling-class populism and reestablish the Democrats as the party of working men and women. But he did not take advantage of it—perhaps because at heart, he is more a pragmatic Southern governor than a figure for the history books. In the 1992 campaign, he often spoke like an economic populist. "For more than a decade our government has been rigged in favor of the rich and special interests," argued a Clinton–Gore campaign pamphlet. "While the wealthiest Americans get richer, middle-class Americans work harder and earn less while paying higher taxes to a government that fails to produce what we need."[16] But outside of his initial jobs bill, his expansion of the Earned Income Tax Credit, and his signing of the minimum-wage increase, he rarely acted on that rhetoric. Much of Clinton's appeal was to traditional Democratic voters, but if he garnered their votes for his reelection, he also failed to inspire them or galvanize partywide support precisely because voters had a hard time figuring out which side he was on.

If the Democrats were to nominate a strong liberal and run hard on traditional liberal issues geared toward helping working Americans, he or she might lose the election (though I would bet not) but eventually win the war. Some 40 percent or so of the electorate are loyal Democrats. If the party made a more active effort to register voters, particularly minority voters, and then turn them out to vote, it could go a long way toward building a majority. As the GOP plays grinch economics and maintains an extremist stance on abortion and other social issues, the gender gap keeps widening. Young voters turned off by the greedy puritanism of the Republicans voted for Clinton in droves. Seniors who want Social Security and Medicare protected could also serve as a more significant, and active, part of the coalition.

Political victory often sprouts from seedbeds of failure. Remember that the present-day Republican coalition was fashioned from the wreckage of the Goldwater campaign in 1964 and survived the Watergate scandal to reemerge only six years later in Reagan's election. But the Democrats will not be able to recover from their present defeats if they do not offer an entirely different vision of America's future than the Republicans already do.

In the absence of a clear choice, many voters are agitating for a third party. But we do not need a third party; we need a second party. Most of the disillusioned third-party supporters would be satisfied if we simply had two parties that stood for clearly different things. And unless the Democrats present themselves as the polar opposite to the Republicans' policies of greed, hatred, and opportunism, they will continue to be threatened by defections and calls for a new party.

THE "L" WORD

It is yet another indicator of how our political language has degenerated that you cannot even use the word *liberal* anymore, except as an insult. This, of course, ignores the proud liberal tradition in American politics, and the enormous liberal achievements enjoyed by conservatives, middle-of-the-roaders, and liberals alike.

Right now, American politics resembles a one-winged turkey trying desperately to fly. E. J. Dionne, in his book *Why Americans Hate Politics*, argues that we have lost a vital center. But in order to have a center, you need corresponding edges. We already have a right-wing fringe so extreme that its most radical elements have actually resorted to terrorism. Where is even the nonradical left wing, outside of organized labor?

There are plenty of liberal and left-wing intellectuals in the academy, but their discourse is increasingly abstruse and irrelevant. They have marginalized themselves in a ghetto of trendy theory and incomprehensible jargon. The media, which conservatives still insist on characterizing as liberal, keep creeping farther and farther to the right. To take just one example, Rush Limbaugh's audience is estimated at somewhere around 20 million, whereas liberals have to fight to keep National Public Radio on the air. In social arenas out beyond the Beltway, the debate is consistently framed by the conservative agenda. As economist Jeff Faux points out in *American Prospect*:

> It is no accident that the same phrases can be heard within days on right-wing talk radio, Christian political TV, and in the speeches of Republican candidates—and then in bars and at church suppers.[17]

One of the reasons our political debate is so impoverished is that the left does not have anything near the intellectual infrastructure that the right now enjoys. Ten years ago, the Cato Institute was a marginal libertarian think tank headquartered in a town house on Capitol Hill. Now it inhabits a towering glass box on Massachusetts Avenue. The Heritage Foundation provided the Reagan administration with people and ideas, and the American Enterprise Institute became the place for conservatives to lick their wounds after public defeat or scandal forced them from office. All these think tanks enjoy lavish funding from corporate and entrepreneurial America, in other words, wealthy business interests, who want lower taxes and less regulation. The Brookings Institution (which is not all that liberal), the Economic Policy Institute (which is doing great work), the further-left Institute for Policy Studies, and other liberal think tanks simply cannot match their right-wing counterparts in fundraising acumen, in large part because their ideas often restrict or criticize corporate power.

And corporate America also exerts direct influence on the debate. Mobil buys a regular column on the *New York Times* op-ed page through its "advertorials." Could the Natural Resources Defense Council ever afford the same? The lobby against healthcare reform was well financed, well organized, and geared toward one specific objective (and, by the way, poisoned the debate through the infamous "Harry and Louise" spot). The lobby for healthcare reform was not very well funded, not very well organized, and often sought divergent goals. Is it any surprise which side won? As the news media get gobbled up by smaller concentrations of corporate power, their coverage of events increasingly reflects corporate values and interests.

How can the left develop an intellectual infrastructure able to combat the right in the war of ideas? The Democratic Party could provide funding and organization—after the 1994 defeats and 1996 elections, the remaining Democrats are proportionately more liberal—if it were not too busy trying to outdo Republicans at raising money from special interests. To some degree, we can try to defund the Right. How happy would corporate shareholders be if they knew that money donated to the Cato Institute helped finance a paper endorsing the legalization of drugs? But we still have to come up with our own agenda.

For the last 100 years, socialism and Marxism provided liberals with an extreme model of economic reorganization and a critical language that they were able to modify and defang into a program that eventually made the world safe for capitalism. The welfare state may not be popular in the GOP Congress, but it is a fact of life, not only in America, but all over the world. Governments have realized that, left to its own devices, the capitalist free market is a cruel and destructive force that requires controls not just to ameliorate its injustices but also to keep it from self-destructing. The intellectual underpinnings of the welfare state came from the more radical programs of state socialism, which have proved to be unworkable, and which most liberals did not want in the first place. With the fall of communism and the general discrediting of socialism, we no longer have that radical model to adapt, and mainstream liberals are left out on the fringe, with no ideological extreme beyond them. Capitalist ideology is so predominant that even Fidel Castro has doffed his combat fatigues, addressing the United Nations wearing a business suit. And the party of Mao

Zedong embraces *laissez-faire* economics, keeping only the to-
talitarianism and repression of Communism.

Market values have pervaded our political, social, and
even our personal lives. Much of our social contact is mediated
through the market; we know each other more as consumers or
producers, colleagues or competitors, and less as human be-
ings. People meet through personal ads, selling themselves like
automobiles. And everybody is saying that government should
be run like a business. Much of Ross Perot's popularity was
based on the notion that he could take the United States over
and turn it around, just like any other enterprise. A hundred
years ago, the Progressives and Populists argued that business
had corrupted politics. Today, people argue that politics has
corrupted business. That shows how deep our devotion to the
market is, and how blind we are to the significant differences
between business and governance. Sure, government should be
more efficient, less wasteful, more accountable. But it is a
wholly different enterprise than private-sector business. It is
a matter of joined endeavor and public trust, in many ways
above the tawdry pursuit of profits.

Liberals never said that capitalism was not efficient, only
that it was not always fair, just, or ennobling. Now, as the world
is being rapidly transformed into the global market, the critics
of capitalism have been silenced. But, in fact, we need them
more than ever.

With no countervailing political power to curb the rapa-
cious nature of the free market, workers are left undefended
against the mighty power of organized capital. As even the
barest securities of the social safety net are unwound by the
Republican Congress and some "me-too" Democratic partners,
working Americans are faced once again with the prospect of
destitution and physical risk, dangers we thought we had eliminated generations ago.

Despite the fact that the two largest federal welfare programs, Aid for Dependent Children and food stamps, took up

only 2.7 percent of the federal budget, ruling-class populists have campaigned as if "welfare reform" (eliminating the guarantee of assistance, without guaranteeing that jobs would be available to those thrown off the rolls) would both balance the budget and force the underclass to assume the proper duties of late-capitalist serfs—in other words, work harder for less money and not complain about it. This is the worst form of class warfare, blaming those least responsible for our decline, as if the poor, rather than the rich, controlled the economy. And this heartless politics is now being reflected in the larger society as well. Instead of private-sector charities stepping in to assume the responsibilities that the government is trying to back down from, as social Darwinists from Reagan to Gingrich have predicted, voluntary charity has decreased, particularly those charities that directly help the poor. Food banks and soup kitchens find it increasingly difficult to get financial support and even food donations. Damaged canned goods that once were given to charity are now sold at discount warehouses to financially strapped middle-class consumers.

The Republicans have been waging a class war against working and poor Americans, a war that all too many members of the diminishing middle class have been eager to join, thinking that by allying themselves with the forces of corporate power, some of the riches will trickle down to them. Of course, the Democrats have been unable or unwilling to make the case for positive government action on behalf of wage earners and the poor. One exception among the Democratic leadership has been House Minority Leader Richard Gephardt (D–Mo.), who defended the minimum wage increase by saying, "The difference between us and [the Republicans] is that they think of low pay as part of the solution, while we think of it as part of the problem."[18]

The Democrats have to decide where their loyalties lie. Are they on the side of corporate America? Or are they on the side of America's working people? If they are on the side of working people, then they ought to start talking like it. As Jeff Faux writes, "Democrats cannot be the party of both the little people and the big money."[19]

If the Democrats are going to talk like Republicans, then they ought to talk like the greatest Republican, Abraham Lincoln, who said,

> I hold that if the Almighty had ever made a set of men that should do all the eating and none of the work, He would have made them with mouths only and no hands; and if He had ever made another class that He intended should do all the work and no eating, He would have made them with hands only and no mouths.[20]

AVOIDING THE ISSUES

Without a vigorous two-party system in which the parties actually stand for different and opposing values, it is no wonder that our democratic debate has become scandalized and trivialized. Since there is not much difference between the Republicans and the "me-too" Democrats, they have little else to argue over than whether one candidate is a liar and the other an adulterer. Negative campaigning has moved into the vacuum created by an absence of substantive debate over important issues. If we began a national conversation over which direction the country should take, and that conversation involved real and divergent choices, we would go a long way toward exiling poison politics to the fringes, where it belongs.

After 25 years of ruling-class populism, this country has become a more greedy and less tolerant place. This pervasive lack of compassion shows that politics is more than just policy, that a nation's moral attitude is influenced by its political leadership. In more generous times, we not only had more beneficent social programs but also leaders who instilled in us the virtues of faith, hope, and charity. Often, their rhetoric was as influential, and as lasting, as their policies.

The New Deal succeeded, according to one writer, "in no small part because Franklin Delano Roosevelt spoke to citizens, about citizens." FDR's policies "succeeded in capturing the American imagination because it promised to be a great act of civic inclusion."[21] In the same way that FDR adapted democratic rhetoric to the new technology of radio to give us the informative and inspiring Fireside Chats, we need to fashion a new rhetoric for television, one that is substantive without being dull, fair without being equivocal, strong without being harsh, and inspirational without being sappy. Using the advanced technology of television, we have been able to develop highly sophisticated methods of insult and attack, while neglecting our tradition of hortatory rhetoric, delivered in a plain yet intelligible, and often stirring, style. Our technological expertise has grown faster than our moral maturity.

But more important than media savvy is political leadership. FDR would not have been the great president that he was if he had merely been a radio personality. He was bold, often brash, always willing to take risks in his policies. He believed in positive action, and if those actions proved to be mistaken, he was not above changing course and trying something different. Rather than weighing in his mind the various options and then finally coming to a cautious and qualified decision, FDR simply led, for he understood that the office of the presidency was to a great degree symbolic and inspirational, and that the people wanted action, not holding a finger to the wind.

Such leadership is not without its price. Roosevelt created great antipathies at the same time that he developed strong loyalties. For every few farmers or factory workers who had a photo of FDR in their parlors, there was an industrialist who cursed him in the warm, smoke-filled comfort of his private club. FDR understood the personal nature of his presidency. In the 1936 election, he said, "There's one issue in this campaign. It's myself, and people must be either for me or against me."[22] During that same campaign, FDR compared himself to Andrew Jackson and his special bond with the common people, saying that "they loved him for the enemies he made." Chief among those enemies were the forces of capitalist royalism, what FDR called "the resplendent economic autocracy." And despite a few catcalls from his well-heeled critics, many of whom felt the effects of his policies in their own pocketbooks, FDR was no dictator. As he himself remarked, "History proves that dictatorships do not grow out of strong and successful governments, but out of weak and helpless ones."[23] One need only look at the French and Russian Revolutions, and the collapse of the Weimar Republic, for chilling examples.

Despite all the antigovernment rhetoric of both the Republicans and the Democrats, the federal government is going to remain a strong presence in our lives. The question remains whether that strength will be used to favor the already powerful, or whether it will be exerted to protect, sustain, and defend those people whose only power lies in their representative government.

That question will be answered only by a national conversation that we must begin now, eschewing poison politics, and instead arguing in honesty and good faith about the direction in which our country will be led.

Epilogue
The 1996 Campaign

After the relatively positive (if scandal-ridden) 1992 presidential campaign, and the Gingrich Gang's successful coup of Congress in the 1994 races, political observers looked to the 1996 elections to answer a host of important questions.

Would Clinton retain the presidency, or would the Republicans control both the White House and Congress? Could the Democrats recapture the House or Senate? How would new media (television and radio talk shows, cable television) and new technology (advanced video imaging, the Internet) be used in the campaigns? But most important to this discussion: Now that voters were more aware of negative advertising, and apparently disgusted by it, how would attack ads play in 1996?

By taking a look at three separate races, we can see how poison politics fared in the latest election.

WELLSTONE–BOSCHWITZ

As discussed previously, in 1990, Democrat Paul Wellstone (D) defeated incumbent Rudy Boschwitz (R–Minn.) for the U.S. Senate. The victory of an unrepentant liberal in the days of "me-too" conservatism was seen as a fluke by some, who ignored

the fact that Wellstone was a strong candidate, ran an innovative campaign, and represented a state with a proud history of
progressive politics.

Still, the Republicans thought they could unseat the former
college professor, especially after conservative Republican Rod
Grams was elected to Minnesota's other Senate seat in 1994.
Even nonpartisan observers saw Wellstone as one of the most
vulnerable Senate incumbents. In Washington, the National
Republican Senatorial Committee (NRSC), which Boschwitz
once chaired, went after Wellstone in a big way. The NRSC
started attacking Wellstone in late 1995. And since the group's
consultant was Arthur Finkelstein—a Johnny one-note who
has his clients always call their opponents "liberal, liberal, liberal," as if the term was somehow akin to "murderer"—the ads
made much use of the "L" word.

The Finkelstein ads were true to his reputation and reaf-
firmed his status as one of America's foremost practitioners of
poison politics. They called Wellstone a "big-spending liberal,"
"embarrassingly liberal," "ultraliberal," "unbelievably liberal," and finally "too liberal." The NRSC also attacked Wellstone's "liberal record on crime," with a spot showing pictures
of a gang member and a stabbing victim. By September, the
NRSC had spent an estimated $1.3 million attacking Wellstone,
and Wellstone's lead had shrunk to a single point from a 47 to
39 point margin in July.[1]

Wellstone seemed to delight in the attack, calling himself
the target of the Republican's "national attack machine," far
removed from "Minnesota values." A billboard above Wellstone's campaign headquarters showed a target with the tag,
"Millions of Republican Dollars Aimed Here." And a poster
at the office had a picture of Theodore Roosevelt with the
caption, "Embarrassingly Liberal."

"It's true that the pharmaceutical companies and the tobacco companies and the big insurance companies don't like
me," Wellstone said in stump speeches, referring to generous
contributors to Boschwitz and the NRSC. "But they already

have good representation in Washington. My job is to stand up for working families in Minnesota, and that's what I do."[2]

Instead of running to the right, Wellstone stood his ground, defending his record, making his beliefs and priorities clear, and presenting positive, instead of just defensive, arguments in response to the attacks. And he also fought back—hard and substantively.

Tired of being called "embarrassingly liberal," Wellstone told Boschwitz in a debate:

> If you're going to use the word embarrassing, what is embarrassing … is that you want to devastate Medicare. It's embarrassing that you want to devastate environmental protection.… It's embarrassing that you wanted to make meat inspection voluntary. What families were you thinking about when you did that?[3]

Boschwitz continued attacking Wellstone. Without any evidence whatsoever, Boschwitz charged that Wellstone had burned an American flag in the 1960s. When Wellstone successfully refuted the charge, Boschwitz retreated to the television studios.

One Boschwitz attack ad was notably awful. Under a banner reading "1967 Liberal Hall of Fame," a group of burnt-out hippies gather in a convention hall. There are many empty seats in the hall, and the few attendees are not all there themselves. They slouch in their seats, with their eyes glazed over, holding signs that say "Raise Taxes" and "More Welfare." One of the hippies announces the purpose of the gathering:

> Ladies and gentlemen, Paul Wellstone has voted consistently for more taxes, more government, and more welfare. So today I'm proud to announce that Paul Wellstone is officially a member of the 1967 Liberal Hall of Fame.[4]

The spot closed with the now-familiar tag line "Paul Wellstone—Embarrassingly Liberal."

The ad itself was embarrassing. As E. J. Dionne of the *Washington Post* pointed out: "A perfectly good case could be made that Wellstone is, indeed, a 'tax-and-spend liberal.' The case cannot be made that he's an avatar of sex, drugs, and rock-and-roll."[5]

Even when Boschwitz stuck to the issues, he could not help but get personal. In reference to Wellstone's vote against the welfare reform bill, Boschwitz called Wellstone "Senator Welfare." Wellstone, the only Democrat Senator up for reelection in 1996 who voted against the welfare bill, defended his vote in an ad that said,

> And, yes, I voted against the welfare bill because it will put one million more children into poverty. That vote may hurt my chances for reelection. But my parents taught me to stand up for what I believe in, regardless of the consequences. And I will always do just that.[6]

Wellstone never ran a pure attack ad. About half of his spots were just positive statements on policy positions that did not even mention Boschwitz. And when he did attack Boschwitz directly, he spoke to the record and the issues, offering substantive differences between the two candidates.

"People want you to be honest and talk to issues that affect their lives," Wellstone said, explaining his campaign technique. "They don't want to see campaigns that are harsh or personal."[7]

When Wellstone fought back with moderately toned comparative ads, the GOP candidate accused him of mudslinging.

One Boschwitz ad whined,

> Wellstone can't defend his record, certainly not on spending, or crime, or welfare, or just about anything else. So now, Wellstone's attacking Boschwitz personally. That's wrong, it's demeaning, and yes, embarrassing. Paul Wellstone: Embarrassingly liberal and throwing mud.[8]

This over-the-top response to Wellstone's reasoned and substantive comparison ads only made Boschwitz and his campaign look hysterical.

Said Wellstone consultant Mandy Grunwald,

> For a long time, the conventional wisdom in the business was that negative advertising should be "hit and run," not connected with your candidate, a separate thing. But I believe that people want to understand in one ad the contrast between each candidate on an issue or a set of issues. With so many ads running, people like having the contrast in one place.[9]

Local newspaper reporters characterized the Wellstone ad campaign this way:

> The strategy had these elements: Stay mostly positive and very substantive; attack only in comparative ads and even then avoid the kind of visual special effects that characterize negative advertising, such as unflattering photos or caricatures of the opponent.[10]

He even engaged in a little political jiujitsu, turning his apparent negatives to his advantage. "No, Paul Wellstone's not like the other senators. What a relief,"[11] ran one ad.

Minneapolis reporters found that "[d]uring September and October, as Wellstone's favorable ratings rose and voters were asked why they feel more positive toward him, they often repeated the themes of Wellstone's ads."[12] Conversely, when voters complained about Boschwitz, they often cited his harsh negative ads.

Nonpartisan tracking polls taken just before the election showed:

> Twice as many voters considered the Boschwitz and NRSC ads attacks on Wellstone as considered Wellstone's ads attacks on Boschwitz.
> Seventy percent of those who thought Boschwitz' ads attacked Wellstone voted for Wellstone.
> When voters were asked whether the ads had made them more likely to vote for Wellstone or Boschwitz, Wellstone won by 46 to 20 percent.[13]

Overall, in the election itself, Wellstone prevailed by 50 to 41 percent.

And what about being "too liberal"? First of all, liberal is not a dirty word in progressive Minnesota, the home of Hubert Humphrey, Walter Mondale, and the Democratic Farmer–Labor Party.

As Hubert Humphrey III, son of HHH and now Minnesota's attorney general, said,

> This business of [Wellstone] being called too liberal is nonsense. If you think that being too liberal means raising the minimum wage, advocating health care for everyone, protecting the environment, taking on the tobacco industry, enacting campaign-finance reform, and putting more cops on the streets, then guess what? That's what Minnesotans want.[14]

When asked by a reporter why she was supporting Paul Wellstone, Cleona Welch of St. Cloud said, "Because he's an ultra-ultra liberal."[15]

But how much did Wellstone's victory have to do with Minnesota's being unfashionably progressive? According to one poll taken before the 1996 election, only 15 percent of Minnesotans describe themselves as liberal, and 30 percent call themselves conservatives.

Perhaps it was not that Wellstone is a liberal, but that he is a good candidate and a good senator—and a rarity: a public official who has the courage of his convictions. In the campaign, he argued the issues instead of resorting to name-calling. He told the voters who he was and what he believed in. The Wellstone–Boschwitz race was not just about television spots or the "L" word. As he did in 1990, Wellstone traveled throughout the state, talking about the issues directly to voters.

"You can't just run TV campaigns," Wellstone said. "Democrats have to go back to run labor-intensive neighborhood campaigns."

And Wellstone even went beyond the issues. He also sought to join Minnesotans together in a common endeavor—using the much maligned institution of politics.

"Politics is not about observations and predictions," Wellstone said. "Politics is what we create out of what we do, what we hope for, what we dare to imagine."[16]

Is the Wellstone victory a precursor of elections to come, with message-driven campaigns defeating nasty attack ads? Could it spell the death of poison politics? Let us hope so, although unfortunately, in 1996, it was more the exception than the rule—as the next example shows.

TORRICELLI-ZIMMER

When Bill Bradley stepped down from representing New Jersey in the Senate, he pronounced that "politics is broken." And in the subsequent campaign to replace him, neither candidate did much to help repair it. New Jersey voters had to choose between two veteran congressmen to replace Bradley: Representatives Dick Zimmer, a moderate-to-conservative Republican, and Robert Torricelli, a moderate-to-liberal Democrat. A tough, expensive, and nasty campaign was anticipated—and it more than lived up to expectations. This is how *National Journal* described the Senate contest in the Garden State: "A preoccupation with fund raising, 30-second ads, slash-and-burn tactics and only the most superficial discussion of issues."[17]

Both campaigns sought to portray their opponent as an extremist: Zimmer was painted as a right-wing zealot, while Torricelli got called "foolishly liberal." And when criticism came from all sides of the political spectrum, including Governor Christine Todd Whitman (R), both candidates apologized for the nasty tenor of the race and then blamed the other guy. Former Republican Governor Tom Kean blamed the political consultants Bob Shrum (Torricelli) and Arthur Finkelstein (Zimmer). "If you hire an ax murderer, you're going to get an ax murder."[18]

The race drew similarly gruesome comparisons from other observers. "The New Jersey Senate campaign is like a particularly grisly highway accident that you can't drive by without staring, but at the same time, you're revolted by it," said Rutgers University political scientist Ross Baker.[19]

Zimmer and Torricelli both blamed the press for negative portrayal of the race.

"The press doesn't cover substance," Zimmer said.

"There is an assumption by editors that people aren't interested in political news," Torricelli commented, saying that his speeches were not given much coverage, and he had to take to the airwaves to make his case to the voters.[20]

In part, this is true because of the peculiarities of New Jersey's geography. The Garden State has two media markets— New York and Philadelphia—that focus most of their attention on their home states, not the one across the river. New Jersey has no network affiliates and only one commercial television station, the independent WWOR. The four largest newspapers—the *New York Times* and the *Daily News*, and the *Philadelphia Inquirer* and the *Daily News*—give short shrift to New Jersey politics. The Newark *Star-Ledger* is the only New Jersey paper with its own Washington Bureau, and its reporters were often covering other stories. As a result, despite the fact that both candidates were veteran members of Congress, few voters knew who they were. According to a *Star-Ledger* poll in September 1996, some 40 percent of voters said they did not know who Zimmer was, and 33 percent did not recognize Torricelli.[21] So, to some degree, they had to ratchet up the volume to get noticed by the near-100 percent of New Jersey voters tuning in to New York and Philadelphia television stations.

"Ninety-five percent of the electorate didn't know who the hell this guy Zimmer was, or Torricelli either, so they don't know what to believe," said New Jersey GOP politico Ralph Mickey. "They both take tiny things and blow them into massive things. What do the voters know now? A lot of mud."[22]

Still, the blame for an unrelentingly negative campaign has to rest on the candidates themselves. The nastiness started early and was a significant feature of campaign strategy for both camps. Three days after Zimmer won the GOP primary, a Torricelli press release lobbed a preemptive strike: "Political observers have already warned that the election promises to be extremely negative and based on personal attacks."[23]

The Zimmer campaign fired back with a series of press clips labeled "Bob Torricelli—Ethically Challenged."

Many of the television spots were about—well, other spots themselves. The two candidates traded a series of charges and countercharges. Both camps claimed that the other got campaign funds from "mobsters." They traded arguments about the accuracy of their ads, as well as reports of sleazy campaign fund-raising, stories about evil genius political consultants, and the standard poison political fare.

Zimmer ran a commercial made to look like a newscast highlighting the "Torricelli Scandals." The actor/anchor "reported" that questions had been raised about the Democratic congressman's character and fitness for office, and accused him of being friendly with terrorists and taking contributions from mobsters.

While Zimmer called his opponent "too liberal" (remember, his consultant was Johnny-one-note Finkelstein), Torricelli fought back with spots portraying the Republican as "too extreme." His spots claimed that Zimmer voted to cut Medicare.

At one point radio shock-jock Howard Stern got into the race, promising to endorse whichever candidate called in to his show first. When both Torricelli and Zimmer called at virtually the same time, Stern moderated a debate between them but refused to endorse either candidate. Talk about politics descending into the gutter.

Of course all that television trash talk costs money. Of all Senate candidates, Torricelli was the fourth-highest spender, at $9.1 million, and Zimmer the fifth-highest, at $8.2 million.[24]

Statewide New Jersey races tend to be expensive. To reach voters in the southern half of the state, you have to buy spots on Philadelphia stations, the fourth-most-expensive media market in the country. And to reach voters in the northern half, you have to buy spots on New York stations, America's priciest media market. This is costly and wasteful, as the campaign message gets spread far beyond the constituency.

Of course, there are other ways of campaigning. New Jersey is a large state in terms of population, but it is not terribly big in terms of area. Indeed, it is the most densely populated state in the country. Several Jersey politicians have had successful ground-level campaigns, driving buses from one in-person appearance to another. After beating each other up in spots, both Torricelli and Zimmer tried to get out among the voters, but it was too little, and too late.

During the last days of the campaign, both candidates finally began running as many positive spots as negative ones. But that was not enough to change the nasty tenor of the campaign.

Up until the last weekend before the election, the race seemed dead even. Then the undecideds (who made up as much as 22 percent of the electorate) went heavily for Torricelli. In the end, the Democrat won by a 10 percent margin.

According to an exit poll, Zimmer was seen as the villain by three out of five voters. However, Torricelli was also criticized by two out of five voters.

Despite public disapproval, someone had to win the Jersey race, and there is the danger that candidates and consultants will look to the Torricelli–Zimmer slugfest as proof that you have to fight dirty to win. As former Governor Kean said, "I'm afraid whoever wins will put an arm around their campaign consultant and say, 'Thanks! It worked!' "[25]

It certainly did not work for Finkelstein. Out of five Senate races and one House campaign, Finkelstein's candidates lost all but one. His pathetic batting average sticks out like a sore thumb, given that overall the Republicans gained two seats in the Senate, winning 9 of 13 closely contested races.

"People have become either cynical enough or savvy enough about that kind of simplistic name-calling. They are draining the term 'liberal' of any meaning in our society." said

Mark Mellman, Democratic pollster who faced off against Finkelstein in two 1996 races.[26]

"He created a cookie-cutter ad, charged a lot of money, and it just didn't work," said Dennis Johnson, a former Democratic political consultant and now academic dean at George Washington University's Graduate School of Political Management. "If you do a side-by-side comparison of Finkelstein's ads for each candidate, they are practically the same word for word."[27]

By making blanket statements and personal attacks about candidates, not only did Finkelstein not offer his clients any kind of positive message, but he also did not give voters comparative issues by which to judge. As we have seen throughout this book, negative ads usually work best if they speak to something tangible and accurate. Mere name-calling will only backfire.

"We can only hope this is the end of Finkelsteinism," said Ross Baker.[28]

But is it the end of *liberal* being a dirty word? Let us hope so.

THE POISON POLITICS AD OF THE YEAR

There was a lot of competition, but the award for most poisonous attack ad of the year has to go to Tim LeFever's spot against Representative Vic Fazio (D) in a California Congressional race. Fazio is the third-ranking House Democrat, representing the Sacramento area and nearby rural counties. But in 1992, when reapportionment changed his district, he came under heavy fire from the GOP.

In 1994 he beat back a challenge from Republican hopeful Tim LeFever, defeating the upstart by only four points. But LeFever came back in 1996, fighting hard and nasty, and focusing on the volatile issue of crime.

One LeFever billboard screamed: "Vic Fazio—Extremely Liberal. Opposes the Death Penalty—Raised Our Taxes—Biggest Spender in History." One anti-Fazio flyer was put together by an antitax group organized by the John Birch Society.[29] The candidate himself told voters that Fazio "doesn't think like us, doesn't act like us and doesn't live like us."[30] Another ad (paid for by the National Rifle Association) claimed that Fazio was trying to disarm police officers.

LeFever ran an ad accusing Fazio of having built "his entire political career defending people like Richard Allen Davis from the death penalty." Davis was the convicted murderer of twelve-year-old Polly Klaas. "In the race for Congress," the ad said, "the issue is crystal clear; one candidate supports the death penalty, the other does not."

Roll Call said that the ad "amounts to a crude morph of the congressman and the convicted killer."[31]

Aside from being inflammatory, the ad is simply untrue. Fazio voted for the death penalty in Congress several times. And Davis was sentenced under state law, not federal law.

LeFever was not the only Californian to feature Davis in attack ads. The victim's father, Marc Klaas, called on Representative Frank Riggs (R–Calif.), who had used Davis in one of his ads, to "stop exploiting my daughter Polly's death to fulfill his own political ambitions.... We certainly want Polly to have a strong legacy, but we don't want that legacy to be based on getting Frank Riggs or anyone else elected to Congress."[32]

And the Polly Klaas Foundation, with which Mark Klaas is no longer associated, called on

> all candidates on all levels to refrain from taking advantage of the kidnaping and murder of a 12-year-old girl for political purposes. This behavior is beneath the level of concern and professionalism we expect from our political leaders.[33]

President Clinton himself was not above using the Polly Klaas killing as an issue. In one Clinton spot, Marc Klaas endorsed the president's anticrime bill: "I hear people question the president's character and integrity. It's just politics. When it came to protecting children, the president had the courage to make a difference."[34]

Which just goes to show that neither party has a monopoly on emotionally charged exploitation of crime—and people's personal tragedies—for political gain.

New Technologies of Political Attack

The election of 1996 saw further development in the area of high-tech politics. Some of these developments deliver on the promise of a greater direct involvement by the voters and more relevant information available in the public debate. But new technology can also be used to make the techniques of poison politics more devastating.

Here is a summary of some of these developments:

Polls and Focus Groups. These are becoming increasingly more popular and more sophisticated. Often attack ads, particularly ones that are expected to be controversial, are pretested by focus groups in order to predict the reaction in the public at large. This way, the campaign can almost guarantee a powerful and effective attack on its opponent and diminish backlash against its own candidate. Focus groups are used for ads of all kinds, negative and positive, political and commercial.

Although focus groups are an effective means of divining public opinion, they should be used to help shape a message, rather than creating one out of whole cloth. The reactions measured by focus groups are often visceral and emotional, instead of thoughtful and reasoned. What campaigns should be doing more of is contextual surveys, in which the issues under discussion are put in a wider context, with the audience given more choices than simple emotional responses.

Push Polls. One particularly troubling development, these are a form of voter persuasion masquerading as pub-

continued

lic survey. In a push poll, the interviewer starts out inno-cently enough, asking a question such as "Do you approve of candidate X?" But the follow-up question may be some-thing like this: "Would you still support candidate X if you knew that he was soft on crime?" Or sometimes the sugges-tion is a little more acrid: "Would you still support candidate X if you knew he was in favor of giving criminals furloughs like the one that freed Willie Horton?"

The purpose of these push polls is twofold. Pollsters who need to see a temporary boost in their opponent's negative rating can use them to massage the numbers. Es-pecially, when so baldly stated as many of them are, push polls can have a strong, though often short-lived, direct effect. But that initial impact can have lasting repercussions. The candidate can now go to potential supporters and ask for money based on rising poll figures among "informed voters." Of course, the only thing that voters are informed by in push polls is slander. Also, campaigns and single inter-est groups can use the apparently neutral apparatus of a poll to try to convince voters on an issue or a candidate.

Direct Mail. Survey research amassed by polling and focus groups is often linked with direct mail to target spe-cific groups pinpointed by "geodemography," which takes census data and divides a constituency into areas of com-mon political interest. Once a campaign finds out that its opposition candidate has high negatives on his or her per-sonal life among, say, white Catholic voters over age 35, the campaign can target those voters through their databases and send negative ads in the form of direct mail right to those voters' homes.

Even by today's debased standards, direct mail attacks are some of the sleaziest forms of negative campaigning. Often utilized during the final days of the election, so a candidate does not have time to respond, direct-mail pieces link outrageous charges with some of the most vituperative language, harsh attacks that would never make it past the broadcast media censors. And candidates rarely know when a direct-mail campaign is being launched against them, until the damage is already done.

Cable Television. While the majority of political ads are still broadcast on traditional television outlets, political campaigns are increasingly exploiting the targeted markets of cable and satellite television. This is of particular use to candidates in large and expensive media markets, seeking to get their messages out to constituents in a focused and relatively inexpensive fashion. For example, politicians running for Los Angeles City Council, who now have to spend a lot of money broadcasting all across the Los Angeles basin, will be able to use cable channels to reach specific constituencies, say, Latino voters on a Spanish-language station, or African Americans on BET. "Narrow-casting"—although a legitimate campaign communications technique—is not without its pitfalls, however, as voter groups can be divided and appealed to with differing messages, as politicians have been doing for years on radio.

Video Imaging. High-tech television wizardry can create convincing false images. Sleight-of-hand technology was used quite frequently in recent elections. The sophisticated techniques used in movies such as *Zelig* and *Forrest Gump* show how advanced technology can be used to manipulate images with a dangerous potential for abuse.

In the 1996 Virginia Senate race, Senator John Warner (R) was challenged by Mark Warner (D). The incumbent's campaign ran an ad featuring the upstart candidate posing at a campaign rally with Bill Clinton and former Virginia Governor Doug Wilder. Or was he? It turned out that the John Warner campaign had superimposed Mark Warner's head onto a photo of Chuck Robb, in order to make the Democrat seem as if he were closer to the president and former governor (neither one of whom is terribly popular with conservative Virginia voters) than he actually was. When Mark Warner's complaints were made public, John Warner's consultant Greg Stevens was fired.

What next? Could negative ads go the way of some of the sleazier television news shows and create "dramatizations" of certain events?

With advanced imaging tools, television technicians can

continued

literally create reality. The potential for abuse is great and frightening.

The Internet. The 1996 election was the first in which the Internet really became a vital part of many campaigns. It seemed as if every candidate had his or her own web page. Most notably, according to a postelection Pew Researchpoll, 10 percent of the voters claimed to have received most of their political information on-line.

Much of the information provided on political web sites was substantive, positive, and accurate. The potential for an informed, active, and involved electorate using on-line computer services is enormous. Indeed, one of the great promises of the Web is that the voters can get what they want—unlike television or radio, for example, they can ignore negative information and point-and-click on the positive only. Whether that promise is fulfilled may be one of the great questions of the next few years and have a significant, even historic, impact on the content and tenor of our public debate.

Since it is cheaper to maintain a web site than air television ads, the Internet may give underfunded candidates more of a chance. And instead of getting all their information through the distorted mirror of the mass media, voters can go straight to the source, looking up voting records and issue stances, accessing position papers, even getting their questions answered directly by the candidates. And the media can use the Net to get information about the candidates. This way, small-market newspapers and television stations that cannot afford Washington bureaus themselves can avoid the standard wire coverage and get primary source material on their own.

In the not too distant future, the Internet will be far more capable of video delivery. Some proponents believe that this development may change the entire system of political advertising. Instead of broadcasting on television to a wide and uncommitted audience, candidates can provide political spots and longer biographical or issue films free to plugged-in constituents.

If the parties use the Internet correctly, they can reconnect with voters. ''It's cutting out all the nonsense, and letting voters make up their own minds," says Lisa McCormack of the Republican National Committee. On the Internet, content is king, and candidates who fill their web sites with fluff or trash talk are going to find out that their messages are easily ignored or dismissed.

But that is not to say that all the political discourse on the Net will be pure and edifying. Many vicious and irresponsible attack campaigns have already been launched via computer networks. Political extremists are using the Net to get organized and spread their message of hate. Neo-Nazi groups in the United States have grown four times in size, in a great measure due to their activities on computer networks, according to the Southern Poverty Law Center.[40] Also, some of the most outrageous, reckless, and unfounded rumors about President and Hillary Rodham Clinton have been spread on the Net.

The problem with the Internet is not just extremists. The average person with on-line capability is white, male, highly educated, and relatively affluent. This is the same demographic profile of those who, already politically active, have contributed greatly to recent Republican victories. Unfortunately, the groups that are already marginalized, disenfranchised, and unengaged are not being reached through the Internet, simply because they cannot afford the hardware necessary to go on-line. About 15 percent of all American adults have used on-line services, and they are 80 percent male, with an average income of $50,000.[41]

Until the Internet is accessible by people of all economic, social and racial backgrounds, the promise of cyberdemocracy will remain unfulfilled.

But even if it lives up to its potential, the Net is not going to completely transform political contests. According to Ron Faucheux, editor and publisher of *Campaigns & Elections*, "Online communications, only in its infancy, isn't replacing other forms of campaigning. But it's about to take its place in a well-rounded media mix, along with TV, newspaper, radio, mail, and phones."[42]

Even in the age of the Internet, political campaigns are still about getting your message across to the voters. Traditional forms of campaigning are still vital not only to electoral success but also to a robust democracy.

THE PRESIDENTIAL RACE

Some of you might not have noticed, but we just had a presidential election. Yes, the 1996 presidential campaign was not terribly dramatic, and the race seemed to have been decided early—like July. But there were still some interesting developments in the campaign, particularly in the early Republican primaries.

They were filled with negativism, so much so that despite wrapping up the nomination very early in the process, Bob Dole hardly recovered from the attacks and the rancor generated in those internecine battles. Steve Forbes spent millions of his personal fortune on his failed bid for the presidency. And most of that money went into attack ads beating up on Bob Dole. As *Newsweek* characterized it:

> The Forbes campaign deserves little more than a footnote in the history of American politics. But it is worth examining as an object lesson in negative campaigning. It shows what money can do to tear down an opponent, and how negative campaigning can drag all sides into a survivalist struggle that, in the end, scars the winners as well as the losers.[35]

When Forbes attacked Dole, the man from Kansas fought back, criticizing Forbes's flat tax scheme. Dole also criticized columnist Pat Buchanan as being an extremist. Although those attacks (and right-wing defections to the Forbes camp) helped neutralize Buchanan's largely symbolic candidacy, in the long run, they angered many Republican conservatives, even those who did not vote for either of the upstarts. The primary battles had enormous fallout, as the Dole campaign spent nearly all its money before the end of the race and had to wait to get federal funding before it could begin the national campaign in earnest.

The effects of nasty negativism on the Dole campaign were not just financial or tactical. As early as March 1996, more people had a negative than a positive perception of Dole. Those negatives began to decrease as Dole had a successful (or at least well-orchestrated, ready-for-prime-time) convention and then began to run his own ads. But in the end, the challenge was too great for Dole, and his own weaknesses as a candidate revealed themselves in a variety of ways, from dissension within the campaign team to an inability to successfully focus on key issues or give a compelling reason why Americans should vote for him. So when Dole did go negative, his attacks did not have much impact—and they also reinforced perceptions of Dole as bitter and mean-spirited that lingered from his "attack dog" performance in his 1976 vice-presidential bid.

As Jack Germond and Jules Witcover observed, the Dole campaign ignored "one of the basic premises of negative campaigning—that a candidate can afford to attack his opponent only from a position of strength."[36] So attack ads about campaign financing and other insinuations about Clinton's purported ethical lapses were seen by both political professionals and the voters themselves as desperate maneuvers by a candidate who did not have a message himself.

The presidential campaign was—by a mile—the most expensive in history. And although it was not as rancorous as some of the lower ballot races—indeed, in debates and other forums, both candidates called for civility and spoke respectfully of the other—there was still a great deal of negativism and false charges, especially in the proliferation of television spots from the candidates and interest groups.

Dole kept repeating the erroneous claim that the American Association of Retired Persons (AARP) supported the GOP Medicare plan. The AARP, which did not support the plan, repeatedly asked the Dole campaign to quit using it for an endorsement. The Republican candidate tried to score points by painting Clinton as being "soft on drugs." Dole said that Clinton cut funding for the drug czar's office, while he himself voted against creating the office in the first place. And at one point in the campaign, Dole said we were suffering the "worst economy in the century." But the economic growth rate under Clinton's first term was twice that of George Bush.

Both sides were guilty of fudging the facts: Dole accused Clinton of raising taxes on the middle class, when, in fact, income taxes were only raised on the wealthy; the only Clinton tax hike applying to the middle class was the measly 4.3 cent per gallon increase in the gas tax. Clinton quoted Common Cause, describing Dole as the senator "most responsible for blocking any serious campaign finance reform," while neglecting to mention that the organization criticized the president as well. However, the Dole message, because it was predominantly negative in the absence of anything positive beyond his less than credible pledge to cut taxes and still balance the budget without completely emasculating government, was seen as more negative.

In the end, of course, Clinton went on to reelection. How his second term goes down in history—as four years of lame-duck, "me-too" conservatism or a return to Democratic, pro-working-family core values—is up to the president himself.

THE LESSONS OF 1996

There was good news and bad news in 1996. Voters seemed to be more aware, and more critical, of negative ads. Still, the various forms of video attack continued to poison the well of political debate—and some of them remained successful in terms of winning elections.

"There seems to be some wisening up of the electorate," said Ben Ginsberg, professor of political science at Johns Hopkins University. "The shock value of negative advertising and dirt-digging has worn off, and I think we're heading into an era of kinder, gentler consultants."[37]

But even if consultants, both Democrats and Republicans, decide to be kinder and gentler, unless those techniques pay off in the polling booth, do not expect to see a decrease in attack and abuse.

It is not so much a question of whether we will continue to see negative ads, but what form they will take. Will attack ads become increasingly personal and nasty, or will they become more substantive and comparative? The 1996 election seems to indicate that negativism is a necessary component of political messages, and that as long as they are done intelligently and fairly, they will have an impact on voters.

"There's a place for tough, hard-hitting advertisements, but you have to be imaginative about it and not take it too far. You have to use a saber, not a meat cleaver," said Ross Baker.[38]

Pollster Diane Feldman saw negative ad campaigns backfiring all across the country:

> Voters this year became more critical consumers. They want to hear what candidates stand for. And they are not interested in attacks outside the political arena…. Voters this year demanded more civility and demanded clarity on just where the candidates stood.[39]

If voters demand more civility and more clarity from their candidates, then we cannot help but have a more responsible political discourse, because, in a democracy, the voters get the leadership they deserve.

Notes

CHAPTER 1

1. Arterton, F. Christopher, "The Persuasive Art in Politics," in McCubbins, Mathew D. (ed.), *Under the Watchful Eye: Managing Presidential Campaigns in the Television Era*. CQ Press, Washington, DC, 1992, p. 105.

CHAPTER 2

1. Lacey, W. K., and Wilson, B. W., *Res Publica: Roman Politics and Society According to Cicero*, Oxford University Press, New York, 1970, p. 119.
2. Plutarch, *Fall of the Roman Republic*, Penguin Classics, Penguin, New York, 1972, p. 338.
3. Spector, Robert D., *Political Controversy: A Study in Eighteenth-Century Propaganda*. Greenwood Press, New York, 1992, p. vii.
4. Cook, Richard I., *Jonathan Swift as a Tory Pamphleteer*, University of Washington Press, Seattle, 1967, p. 58.
5. Cook, pp. 69–70.
6. Cook, pp. 69–70.
7. Schama, Simon, *Citizens*. Vintage, New York, 1990, p. 732.
8. Schama, p. 521.
9. Popkin, Jeremy, *Revolutionary News: The Press in France, 1789–1799*. Duke University Press, Durham, NC, 1990, p. 146.

10. Popkin, p. 149.
11. Popkin, p. 150.
12. Popkin, p. 150.
13. Schama, p. 738.
14. Boller, Paul Jr., *Presidential Campaigns.* Oxford University Press, New York, 1985, p. 8.
15. Boller, p. 11.
16. Boller, p. 12.
17. Boller, p. 46.
18. Boller, p. 50.
19. Boller, p. 50.
20. Boller, pp. 44–46.
21. Ross, Shelley, *Fall from Grace: Sex, Scandal and Corruption in American Politics from 1702 to the Present.* Ballantine, New York, 1988, p. 126.
22. Ross, p. 158.
23. Troy, Gil, *See How They Ran: The Changing Role of the Presidential Candidate.* The Free Press, New York, 1991, p. 141.
24. Troy, p. 142.
25. Troy, p. 142.
26. Troy, pp. 144–145.
27. Troy, p. 145.
28. Troy, p. 153.
29. Troy, p. 153.
30. Troy, p. 154.
31. Boller, p. 225.
32. Boller, p. 225.
33. Boller, p. 229.

CHAPTER 3

1. Underhill, Robert, *The Bully Pulpit: From Franklin Roosevelt to Ronald Reagan.* Vantage Press, New York, 1988, p. 11.
2. Boller, p. 233.
3. Troy, p. 163.
4. Underhill, p. 18.
5. Underhill, p. 25.
6. Underhill, p. 25.
7. Michelson, Charles, *The Ghost Talks.* G. P. Putnam's Sons, New York, 1944, p. 13.
8. Mitchell, Greg, *The Campaign of the Century: Upton Sinclair's Race for*

Governor of California and the Birth of Media Politics. Random House, New York, 1992, p. 561.

9. Bird, William L., Jr., "The Whistlestop: The Father of Political TV 'Spots.'" *Campaigns & Elections*, Winter 1986, p. 68.

10. Diamond, Edwin, and Bates, Stephen, *The Spot: The Rise of Political Advertising on Television* (3rd ed.). MIT Press, Cambridge, 1992, p. 59.

11. Diamond and Bates, p. 62.

12. Diamond and Bates, p. 46.

13. Diamond and Bates, pp. 62–63.

CHAPTER 4

1. Patterson, Thomas E., and McClure, Robert D., *The Unseeing Eye: The Myth of Television Power in National Politics*. Paragon, New York, 1976, p. 111.

2. Patterson and McClure, p. 115.

3. West, Darrell, *Air-Wars: Television Advertising in Election Campaigns, 1952–1992*. CQ Press, Washington, DC, 1993, p. 51.

4. West, p. 51.

5. West, p. 52.

6. Patterson and McClure, p. 117.

7. West, p. 51.

8. Salmore, Barbara G., and Salmore, Stephen A., *Candidates, Parties, and Campaigns: Electoral Politics in America*, 2nd edition. CQ Press, Washington, DC, 1989, p. 159.

9. Bates, Stephen, and Diamond, Edwin, "Damned Spots" *The New Republic*, September 7 and 14, 1992, p. 14.

10. Popkin, Samuel, "Campaigns That Matter," in McCubbins, Matthew D., *Under the Watchful Eye: Managing Presidential Campaigns in the Television Era*. CQ Press, Washington, DC, 1995, p. 163.

11. Common Cause, "95 Percent of Incumbents Win Reelection in 1996, Aided by Dramatic Fundraising Advantage over Challengers, According to Common Cause," News Release, November 7, 1996.

12. Popkin, p. 163.

13. Schwartz, Tony, *The Responsive Chord*. Anchor Press, Garden City, NY, 1973, p. 96.

14. Blumenthal, Sidney, *The Permanent Campaign: Inside the World of Elite Political Operatives*. Beacon Press, Boston, 1980, p. 124.

CHAPTER 5

1. All polling data quoted in Kerbel, Matthew Robert, *Remote and Controlled: Media Politics in a Cynical Age*. Westview Press, Boulder, 1995, p. 13.
2. Matthews, Christopher, *Hardball: How Politics Is Played—Told by One Who Knows the Game*. Harper Perennial, New York, 1989, p. 155.
3. Witcover, Jules, *Marathon: The Pursuit of the Presidency, 1972–1976*. Viking Press, New York, 1977, p. 109.
4. Matthews, p. 156.
5. Witcover, p. 522.
6. Carter, Dan T., *The Politics of Rage: George Wallace, the Origins of the New Conservativism, and the Transformation of American Politics*. Simon and Schuster, New York, 1995, p. 108.
7. Carter, p. 329.
8. Bruck, Connie, "The Politics of Perception," *The New Yorker*, October 9, 1995, p. 50.
9. Carter, pp. 466–467.
10. Bruck, p. 50.
11. Toner, Robin, "The 1994 Campaign: Advertising; Image of Capitol Maligned by Outsiders, and Insiders." *New York Times*, October 16, 1994, p. A1.
12. Toner, p. A1.
13. Kurtz, Howard, "Political Peddlers' Bitter Bromides; Television Ads Serve Mean Cuisine to Voters Fed Up with the System." *Washington Post*, October 11, 1994, p. A1.
14. Quoted in Will, George, "Fingernails across the Blackboard." *Newsweek*, October 31, 1994, p. 72.
15. Bunzel, John H., *Anti-Politics in America*. Knopf, New York, 1967, p. 30.
16. Bunzel, p. 3.

CHAPTER 6

1. Lichter, S. Robert, and Noyes, Richard E., *Good Intentions Make Bad News: Why Americans Hate Campaign Journalism*. Rowman and Littlefield, Lanham, MD, 1995, p. 2.
2. Lichter and Noyes, p. 2.
3. Schudson, Michael, *The Power of News*. Harvard University Press, Cambridge, MA, 1995, p. 141.

4. Galen, Rich, "The Best Defense Is a Good Offense." *Campaigns & Elections*, October/November 1988, p. 29.

5. Dworetzky, Tom, "Original Spin: Has Reality Been Entirely Banished from Politics?" *Omni*, May 1992, p. 18.

6. West, p. 62.

7. Runkel, David, Ed. *Campaign for President: The Managers Look at '88.* Auburn House, Dover, MA, 1989, p. 136.

8. West, p. 14.

9. Alter, Jonathan, "How the Media Blew It." *Newsweek*, November 21, 1988.

10. Berke, Richard L., "The 1992 Campaign: The Ad Campaign; Bush: A Risky Republican Attack." *New York Times*, October 12, 1992, p. A13.

11. Lichter and Noyes, p. xviii.

12. Ifill, Gwen, "The 1992 Campaign: The Ad Campaign; Clinton: Focusing on the Economy." *New York Times*, August 31, 1992, p. A12.

13. Purdum, Todd, "U.S. Senate Race in New York: Simple Assertion, Complicated Realities." *New York Times*, November 1, 1992, p. 58.

14. Purdum, p. 58.

15. Purdum, p. 58.

16. Diamond and Bates, p. 391.

17. Lichter and Noyes, p. 235.

18. Lichter and Noyes, p. 235.

19. Lichter and Noyes, p. 249.

20. Lichter and Noyes, p. 22.

21. Kerbel, p. 97.

22. Thurber, James A., and Nelson, Candice J., *Campaigns and Elections American Style.* Westview Press, Boulder, CO, 1995, p. 124.

23. Biskupic, Joan, "Has the Court Lost Its Appeal?" *Washington Post*, October 12, 1995, p. A23.

24. Lichter and Noyes, p. 8.

25. Matusow, Barbara, "Fear and Loathing '88." *Washingtonian*, April 1988.

26. Kolbert, Elizabeth, "Robert MacNeil Gives a Thoughtful Goodbye." *New York Times*, October 15, 1995, p. H39.

27. Epstein, Edward Jay, *News from Nowhere.* Vintage Books, New York, 1973, pp. 4–5.

28. Lichter and Noyes, p. 54.

29. Kurtz, Howard, "Don't Tread on Me." *Washington Post*, October 11, 1995.

30. Lichter and Noyes, p. 218.

31. Twitchell, James B., *Carnival Culture: The Trashing of Taste in America.* Columbia University Press, New York, 1992, p. 240.

32. Lichter and Noyes, p. 240.
33. Lichter and Noyes, p. 240.
34. Kerbel, p. 106.
35. Kerbel, p. 113.
36. Kerbel, p. 140.

CHAPTER 7

1. Sacks, Oliver, *The Man Who Mistook His Wife for a Hat*. Harper & Row, New York, 1987, p. 82.
2. Sacks, p. 83.
3. Sacks, p. 84.
4. Sacks, p. 84.
5. Neuman, W. Russell, *The Paradox of Mass Politics: Knowledge and Opinion in the American Electorate*. Harvard University Press, Cambridge, MA, 1986, p. 134.
6. Twitchell, p. 207.
7. Bagdikian, Ben H., *The Media Monopoly*, 4th edition. Beacon Press, Boston, 1992, p. 207.
8. Bagdikian, p. 207.
9. Neuman, pp. 134–135.
10. Bagdikian, p. xii.
11. Paul Farhi, "Pulling the Plug on Capitol Hill," *Washington Post*, February 13, 1997, p. C1.
12. The *Hotline*, interview with Brian Lamb, February 13, 1997.
13. Moore, Jonathan, Ed., *Campaign for President: The Managers Look at '84 Auburn House*, Dover, MA, 1986, p. 206.
14. Grossman, Lawrence, *The Electronic Republic: Reshaping Democracy in the Information Age*. Viking, New York, 1995, p. 103.
15. Cannon, Lou, *Reagan*. Putnam, New York, 1982, p. 376.

CHAPTER 8

1. Samuelson, Robert J., "Has Crime Peaked?" *Washington Post*, August 16, 1995, p. A24.
2. Edsall, Thomas Byrne and Chain, Mary D., *Reaction: The Impact of Race, Rights, and Taxes on American Politics*. W. W. Norton, New York, 1991, p. 10.
3. Edsall, Thomas and Mary, "Race," *The Atlantic Monthly*, May 1991.

4. Jamieson, Kathleen Hall, *Dirty Politics: Deception, Distraction, and Democracy.* Oxford University Press, New York, 1992, p. 41.

5. Kurtz, Howard, "In 1994 Political Ads, Crime Is the Weapon of Choice." *Washington Post*, September 9, 1995, p. A1.

6. Collins, Scott, "Check Forger Gets 25 Years to Life under '3 Strikes' Law," *Los Angeles Times*, December 8, 1994.

7. Kurtz, p. A1.

8. Kurtz, p. A1.

9. "The Phony Use of Genuine Grief." *New York Times*, October 28, 1994, p. A30.

10. *New York Times*, p. A30.

11. *New York Times*, p. A30.

12. *New York Times*, p. A30.

13. Kaminer, Wendy, *It's All the Rage: Crime and Culture.* Addison-Wesley, Reading, MA, 1995, p. 211.

14. Kaminer, pp. 218–219.

15. Kaminer, p. 200.

16. Kaminer, p. 225.

17. Anderson, David C., *Crime and the Politics of Hysteria: How the Willie Horton Story Changed American Justice.* Times Books, New York, 1995, p. 17.

18. Anderson, p. 215.

19. Schram, Martin, "The Making of Willie Horton." *The New Republic*, May 28, 1990, p. 17.

20. Schram, p. 17.

21. Anderson, p. 235.

22. Anderson, p. 235.

CHAPTER 9

1. Carter, p. 213.

2. Carter, p. 393.

3. Carter, illustration page.

4. Carter, p. 372.

5. Carter, p. 372.

6. Carter, p. 348.

7. Carter, p. 349.

8. Kazin, Michael, *The Populist Persuasion.* Basic Books, New York, 1995, p. 226.

9. Carter, p. 380.

10. Maginniss, John, *Cross to Bear*. Darkhorse Press, Baton Rouge, LA, 1992, p. 19.
11. Toner, Robin, "Duke Takes His Anger into 1992 Race." *New York Times*, December 5, 1991, p. B18.
12. Meacham, Jon, "Dukedumb." *Washington Monthly* July/August 1992, p. 49.
13. Applebome, Peter, "Duke: The Ex-Nazi Who Would Be Governor." *New York Times*, November 10, 1991, p. A1.
14. Jamieson, p. 96.
15. Rob Christensen, *Raleigh News & Observer*, October 24, 1990.
16. Jamieson, p. 97.
17. Osterman, Jim, "Open Seats, Close Calls." *Adweek*, November 4, 1996.
18. Associated Pess, "Helms Replays Race Card in Senate Campaign." Published in *San Diego Union-Tribune*, October 23, 1996.
19. Ahearn, Lorraine, "Gantt, Helms Trade Ethics Charges." *Greensboro News and Record*, November 3, 1996.
20. Ahearn, op cit.; Bullard, Anne, "Helms Accuses Gantt of 'Demagoguery' and 'Distortion.'" *News and Observer*, October 28, 1996.
21. Schneider, William, "The Suburban Century Begins." *The Atlantic Monthly*, July 1992, p. 33.
22. Berke, Richard L., "The 1994 Campaign: The Voters; Campaigns' Tenor Disappoints Black Voters." *New York Times*, October 30, 1994, p. A1.
23. Edsall, Thomas B., "March Could Cast a Vote on Democratic Party." *Washington Post*, October 12, 1995, p. A12.
24. Gibbs, Nancy, "Keep Out, You Tired, You Poor ..." *Time*, October 3, 1994, p. 46.
25. Claiborne, William, "Loser Huffington Seeks Voting Fraud Evidence: Hotline Solicits Informers in California." *Washington Post*, December 2, 1994, p. A10.

CHAPTER 10

1. Kaminer, Wendy, "Crashing the Locker Room." *The Atlantic Monthly* July 1992, p. 59.
2. Witt, Linda, Paget, Karen M., and Matthews, Glenna, *Running as a Woman: Gender and Power in American Politics*. Free Press, New York, 1994, p. 60.
3. Witt et al., p. 23.
4. Witt et al., p. 181.

5. Jamieson, p. 264.

6. Victory Fund news release, November 1, 1994.

7. von Sternberg, Bob, "Religious Right Shifting Attack from Abortion to Gay Rights." Minneapolis–St. Paul *Star-Tribune*, September 24, 1994, p. 1A.

8. *Hotline*, October 13, 1995.

9. Anti-Defamation League, *The Religious Right: The Assault on Tolerance and Pluralism in America*. Anti-Defamation League, New York, 1994, p. 5.

10. Anti-Defamation League, p. 25.

11. Anti-Defamation League, p. 1.

12. Anti-Defamation League, p. 1.

13. Anti-Defamation League, p. 4.

14. "Religious Right and Clinton." *Christian Century*, July 13–20, 1994, p. 675.

15. *Christian Century*, p. 675.

16. *Christian Century*, p. 675.

17. Wilkinson, Francis, "Election Post-Mortem: The Hate Squad." *Rolling Stone*, December 29, 1994, p. 157.

18. Anti-Defamation League, p. 116.

19. Anti-Defamation League, p. 6.

20. Anti-Defamation League, p. 7.

21. Matthew 22:21.

CHAPTER 11

1. Wicker, Tom, *One of Us: Richard Nixon and the American Dream*. Random House, New York, 1991, p. 21.

2. Oudes, Bruce, Ed., "Richard Nixon, By the Press Obsessed," *Columbia Journalism Review*, May/June 1989, pp. 48–51.

3. Fox, Stephen, *The Mirror-Makers: A History of American Advertising and Its Creators*. William Morrow, New York, 1984, p. 307.

4. Fox, p. 63.

5. Fox, p. 308.

6. Fox, pp. 308–309.

7. Fox, p. 188.

8. Fox, p. 187.

9. McGinniss, Joe, *The Selling of the President*. Pocket Books, New York, 1970, p. 42.

10. West, p. 17.

11. Patterson and McClure, p. 105.

12. "Different Reasons, Same Conclusions: Constituency Marketing and the Building of Dominant Brands." McCann-Erickson Worldwide, New York, 1992.
13. Blumenthal, pp. 122–123.
14. "Martin Purvis' Toughest Pitch." *Business Week*, October 5, 1992, p. 88.
15. Elliott, Stuart, "The Media Business: Sponsors to Review a Project on Fairness in Political Ads." *New York Times*, February 20, 1992, p. D10.
16. Elliott, Stuart, "The Media Business: Advertising; Four A's Effort Takes Aim at Negative Ads." *New York Times*, February 4, 1992, p. D21.
17. Kanner, Bernice, "To Tell the Truth." *New York*, October 15, 1990, p. 22.
18. Source: National Campaign for Tobacco Free Kids.

CHAPTER 12

1. Domke, Todd, and Payne, Dan, "Pull the Plug on Negative Political Ads?" Reprinted in *Politea*, April/May 1995, p. 7.
2. "30 Seconds to Victory" *Harper's*, July 1992, p. 33.
3. Weisskopf, Michael, "The Professionals' Touch: Role of Political Consultants Keeps Growing." *Washington Post*, November 8, 1994, p. A1.
4. CNN, "Inside Politics," October 14, 1994.
5. Ibid.
6. Toner, Robin, "The 1994 Election: Advertising; Bitter Tone of the '94 Campaign Elicits Worry on Public Debate." *New York Times*, November 13, 1994, p. A1.
7. Arterton, Dean Christopher, "Professional Responsibility in Campaign Politics." Paper delivered at the Conference on Professional Responsibility and Ethics in the Political Process, sponsored by the American Association of Political Consultants, Williamsburg, VA, March 24, 1991.
8. "Capital vs. Labor in Politics." *Washington Post*, October 21, 1996, p. A23.
9. Diamond and Bates, p. x.
10. Barnes, Fred, "The Myth of Political Consultants." *New Republic*, June 16, 1986, p. 16.
11. "Consultantitis." *Washington Post*, November 16, 1995, p. A30.

12. Berke, Richard L., "The 1994 Campaign: Political Memo; Close Races Are Turning More Jittery." *New York Times*, November 4, 1994, p. A1.
13. Grossman, p. 122.
14. Luntz, Frank, *Candidates, Consultants and Campaigns: The Style and Substance of American Electioneering*. Blackwell, New York, 1988, p. 45.
15. Luntz, p. 45.
16. Schudson, p. 22.

CHAPTER 13

1. Windt, Theodore, "Presidential Rhetoric: Definition of a Discipline of Study," in Windt, Theodore and Ingold, Beth, eds., *Essays in Presidential Rhetoric*, 2nd edition, Kendall/Hunt, Dubuque, IA, 1987, pp. xxxiii–xxxiv.
2. Windt, p. xvi.
3. Aristotle, *The Art of Rhetoric*. Penguin Classics, New York, 1991, p. 76.
4. Cmiel, Kenneth, *Democratic Eloquence: The Fight over Popular Speech in Nineteenth-Century America*. William Morrow, New York, 1990, p. 25.
5. Cmiel, p. 26.
6. *The Federalist Papers*, Mentor Books, New York, p. 229.
7. Reid, Ronald D., *Three Centuries of American Rhetorical Discourse: An Anthology and a Review*. Waveland Press, Prospect Heights, IL, 1988, p. 203.
8. Cmiel, p. 50.
9. Cmiel, p. 50.
10. Holzer, Henry, *The Lincoln Douglas Debates*, HarperPerennial, New York, 1993, p. 16.
11. Holzer, p. 20.
12. Holzer, p. 357.
13. Holzer, p. 359.
14. Zarefsky, David, *Lincoln Douglas and Slavery: In the Crucible of Public Debate*, University of Chicago Press, Chicago, 1990, p. 234.
15. Zarefsky, p. 51.
16. Reid, p. 638.
17. Reid, p. 689.
18. Toner, Robin, "The 1994 Elections."

CHAPTER 14

1. Johnson-Cartee and Copeland, p. 119.
2. Matthews, p. 125.
3. Hershey, M. R., *Running for Office: The Political Education of Campaigners*. Chatham House, Chatham, NJ, 1984, p. 248.
4. Jamieson, p. 118.
5. Regan, Edward, Address to New York's City Club, January 8, 1988. Quoted in Bogart, Leo, *Commercial Culture: The Media System and the Public Interest*. Oxford University Press, New York, 1995, p. 87.
6. Johnson-Cartee and Copeland, pp. 114–115.
7. Luntz, p. 102.
8. Kaid, Lynda Lee, "Ethics in Televised Political Advertising: Guidelines for Evaluating Technological Distortions." Paper submitted to the International Communication Association Convention, Washington, DC, May 1993.
9. Johnson-Cartee and Copeland, p. 123.

CHAPTER 15

1. "Talking Heads," *The New Republic*, August 20 and 27, 1990, p. 7.
2. Nugent, John F., "Postively Negative." *Campaigns and Elections*, March/April 1987, p. 47.
3. Hickey, Neil, "Revolution in Cyberia." *Columbia Journalism in Review*, July/August 1995, p. 40.
4. Hickey, p. 40.
5. Hickey, p. 40.
6. *Budget of the United States Government, Fiscal Year 1997: Summary Tables* (based on total outlays for fiscal year 1997 of $1.6 trillion), U.S. Government Printing Office, Washington, DC.
7. Bellah, Robert, Madsen, Richard, Sullivan, William M., Swidler, Ann, and Tipton, Steven M., *The Good Society*, Knopf, New York, 1991, p. 142.
8. Luntz, p. 230.

CHAPTER 16

1. Orwell, George, "Politics and the English Language." In *The Collected Essays, Journalism and Letters of George Orwell: Volume 4*. Penguin, Middlesex, UK, 1970, p. 157.

2. Walker, Martin, "The Master of Spin." *New York Times Book Review*, November 5, 1992, p. 12.

3. Weisskopf, Michael, and Maraniss, David, "Republican Leaders Win Battle by Defining Terms of Combat." *Washington Post*, October 29, 1995, p. A1.

4. Weisskopf and Maraniss, p. A26.

5. Weisskopf and Maraniss, p. A26.

6. Weisskopf and Maraniss, p. A26.

7. Lasch, Christopher, *The Revolt of the Elites and the Betrayal of Democracy*. W. W. Norton, New York, 1995, p. 175.

8. Lacayo, Richard, "Down on the Downtrodden." *Time*, December 19, 1995, p. 30.

9. Robertson, Andrew, *The Language of Democracy: Political Rhetoric in the United States and Britain 1790–1900*. Cornell University Press, Ithaca, NY, 1995, p. 146.

10. Toner, Robin, "The Nation: Taking Sausage; The Art of Reprocessing the Democratic Process." *New York Times*, September 4, 1994, p. D4.

11. Hofstadter, Richard, *The American Political Tradition*. Vintage Books, New York, 1948, p. 169.

12. Hofstadter, p. 255.

13. Hofstadter, p. 256.

14. Hofstadter, p. 256.

15. Broder, David, "The 'Look.'" *Washington Post*, October 29, 1995.

16. Kazin, Michael, *The Populist Persuasion*. Basic Books, New York, 1995, p. 273.

17. Faux, Jeff, "A New Conversation: How to Rebuild the Democratic Party." *American Prospect*, Spring 1995, p. 35.

18. Kuttner, Robert, "America Needs a Raise." *Washington Post*, October 29, 1995, p. C1.

19. Faux, p. 35.

20. Kazin, p. 9.

21. Dionne, E. J., *Why Americans Hate Politics*. Simon and Schuster, New York, 1991, p. 333.

22. Hofstadter, p. 336.

23. Schlesinger, Arthur Jr., *The Cycles of American History*. Houghton Mifflin, Boston, 1986, p. 248.

EPILOGUE

1. Hamburger, Tom, and Black, Eric, "The Refuge: Race for Senate: Minnesota." *The New Republic*, October 28, 1996.

2. Dionne, E. J., "Radical Realist." *Washington Post*, January 17, 1996, p. 8.

3. Hamburger and Black.

4. Dionne, p. 8.

5. Dionne, p. 8.

6. Dionne, p. 8.

7. "Wellstone Re-Elected in Minnesota." *Portland Oregonian*, November 6, 1996.

8. Grow, Doug, "Political Turnabout Makes for a Finkel." Minneapolis-St. Paul *Star-Tribune*, October 13, 1996.

9. Black, Eric, and Hamburger, Tom, "Minnesotans Decidedly Down on Negative Ads." Minneapolis-St. Paul *Star-Tribune*, November 10, 1996.

10. Black and Hamburger, "Minnesotans Decidedly Down."

11. Dionne, p. 8.

12. Black and Hamburger, "Minnesotans Decidedly Down."

13. Black and Hamburger, "Minnesotans Decidedly Down."

14. "Wellstone Re-Elected in Minnesota."

15. Dionne, p. 8.

16. Dionne, p. 8.

17. Cohen, Richard E., "Clueless in New Jersey." *National Journal*, September 28, 1996, p. 2063.

18. Russakoff, Dale, "Scorched Earth in the Garden State." *Washington Post*, November 2, 1996.

19. Russakoff, op cit.

20. Cohen, p. 2063.

21. Cohen, p. 2063.

22. Russakoff, op cit.

23. Cohen, p. 2063.

24. *The Hotline*, January 3, 1997.

25. Russakoff, op cit.

26. Orr, J. Scott, "Strategist May Have Gone to the 'L' Word Too Often." Newark *Star-Ledger*, November 7, 1996.

27. Fitzgerald, Nora, " 'L' Is Not for Loser." *Adweek*, November 18, 1996.

28. Orr, op cit.

29. Wildermuth, John, "Vic Fazio Being Branded with Liberal Label." *San Francisco Chronicle*, October 30, 1996.

30. Wildermuth, op cit.

31. Shapley, Thomas, "Election-Year Malarky Discredits Process." *Seattle Post-Intelligencer*, November 3, 1996.

32. Shapley, op cit.

33. Shapley, op cit.

34. Garfield, Bob, "Political Ad Review." *Advertising Age*, October 28, 1996.

35. Victory March—The Inside Story." *Newsweek*, November 18, 1996.

36. Germond, Jack W., and Witcover, Jules, "When Desperate Tactics Won't Work." *National Journal*, October 26, 1996, p. 2309.

37. Orr, op cit.

38. Orr, op cit.

39. Black and Hamburger, "Minnesotans Decidedly Down."

40. Dowd, Anne Reilly, "The Net's Surprising Swing to the Right." *Fortune*, July 10, 1995, p. 113.

41. *Campaign Politics and the Internet*, C-SPAN, August 31, 1995.

42. Faucheaux, Ron, "Campaign Trends '96." *Campaigns & Elections*, July 1996, p. 5.

Index

Proposition 187, 143–144
Public interest, 231–233
Publius, 200
Purdum, Todd, 73–74
Purists, 4–6
Purvis, Martin, 172
Push polls, 277–278

Quayle, Dan, 124, 249
Quinn, Sally, 84

Racism, 57–58, 77, 127–145, 152
  crime issue and, 107–108,
    115–116, 121
  immigration issue and, 110,
    136, 142–145
  ruling-class populism and,
    128–132
  white flight and, 140–142
Radio, 18, 23–27
Rafshoon, Gerald, 54–55, 168
Rage, politics of, 57–59
Rainey, Hal, 102, 105
Rappaport, James, 225
Reader's Digest, 120–121
Reagan, Nancy, 104–105
Reagan, Ronald, 74, 108, 125,
    153, 192, 242, 246, 254,
    257, 261
  antipolitical stance of, 59
  humor of, 224
  Keyes and, 141
  language manipulation by,
    248
  lobbyists and, 183
  racism and, 130–131
  television appearance of,
    87–88, 99–105
Reagan administration, 46, 152,
    235, 247–248, 258
Reese, Matt, 187
Reeves, Rosser, 31, 165–166,
    167

Reform proposals, 229–243
  based on practices of other
    countries, 230–231
  dubious, 242–243
  specific, 231–242
Regan, Edward, 220–221
Reign of Terror, 12–14
Reiner, Rob, 224
Religious issues, 20–21, 33
Religious Right, 100, 157–162
Republican Congressional Com-
    mittee, 30
Republican National Commit-
    tee, 48
Republican Parish Executive
    Committee, 136
Republican Party
  consultants and, 190–191
  language manipulation by,
    246–249
  reemergence of, 256–257
  ruling-class populism and,
    130, 131, 253–255
  suburban vote and, 140–142
  unfair ads and, 223
  Wallace and, 128
Reputation, 186–188
"Revolving Door" (ad), 238
Rhetoric
  classical, 198–199
  of crime, 115–118
  defined, 198
  democratic: *see* Democratic
    rhetoric
Rice, Donna, 74
Richards, Ann, 148, 187, 221–222
Riggs, Frank, 276
Riggs, Marlon, 152
Robb, Chuck, 181, 279
Robertson, Pat, 157, 158, 159, 161
Robinson, Joseph T., 27
Robinson Crusoe (Defoe), 11
Rockefeller, Nelson, 193, 194